The King's 麗 Beast

9

STORY & ART BY

Rei Toma

THE KING'S *Beast*

Characters and Story Thus Far

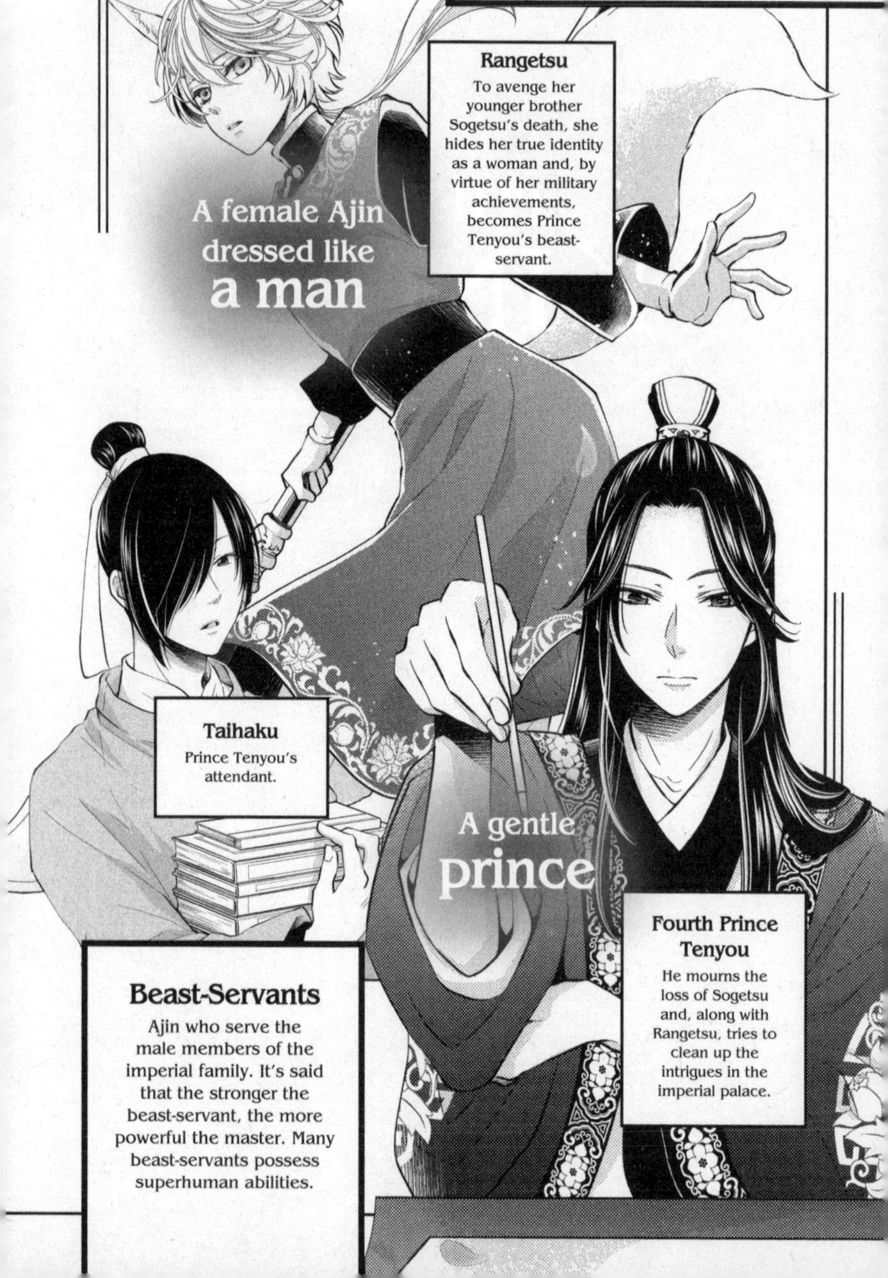
Rangetsu
To avenge her younger brother Sogetsu's death, she hides her true identity as a woman and, by virtue of her military achievements, becomes Prince Tenyou's beast-servant.
A female Ajin dressed like a man
Taihaku
Prince Tenyou's attendant.
A gentle prince
Fourth Prince Tenyou
He mourns the loss of Sogetsu and, along with Rangetsu, tries to clean up the intrigues in the imperial palace.
Beast-Servants
Ajin who serve the male members of the imperial family. It's said that the stronger the beast-servant, the more powerful the master. Many beast-servants possess superhuman abilities.

The Imperial Family and Their Beast-Servants

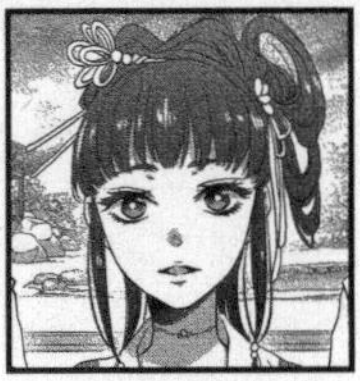

Ririn

A bubbly, jovial imperial princess.

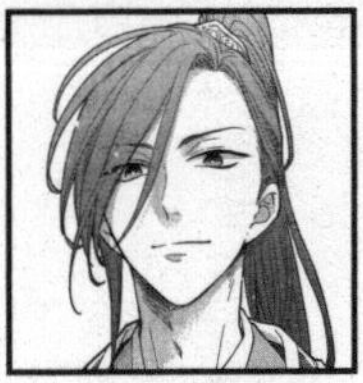

Kougai

The third prince. Two-faced and ambitious.

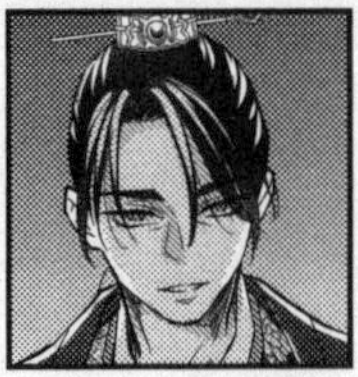

The Emperor

Father of Tenyou, Ririn, and the other princes. He seeks immortality.

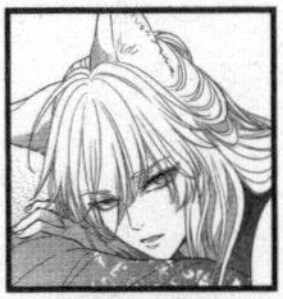

Sogetsu

Rangetsu's twin brother.

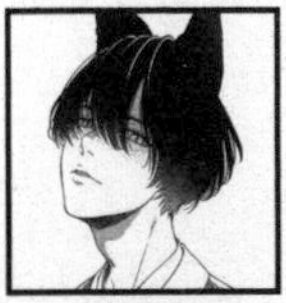

Boku

Kougai's beast servant.

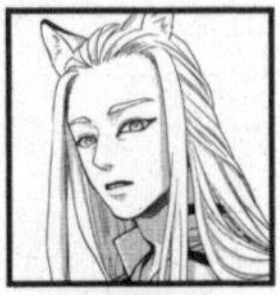

Kyoko

The emperor's beast-servant.

The Assassination of Sogetsu

Rangetsu's twin was brought to the imperial palace to serve Prince Tenyou as his beast-servant, but he was brutally killed soon after.

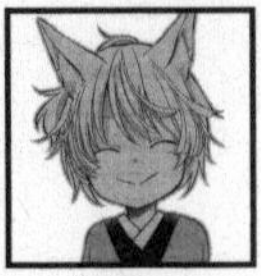

Young Sogetsu

In a world where humans rule the half-beast Ajin, Rangetsu disguises herself as a man to become Fourth Prince Tenyou's beast-servant. Although initially believing the prince to be responsible for her brother's death, Rangetsu soon sees his true nature and vows to help him rule with virtue. When she tells him of her secret, their relationship elevates into something beyond that of beast-servant and master.

Following rumors of a mysterious concubine, Rangetsu infiltrates the inner palace and discovers her brother is still alive. But her happiness is short-lived—Kyoko, the emperor's beast-servant, attacks her, and Prince Tenyou is wounded in the ensuing struggle. Will she save her brother or her prince?!

THE KING'S *Beast*

9

CONTENTS

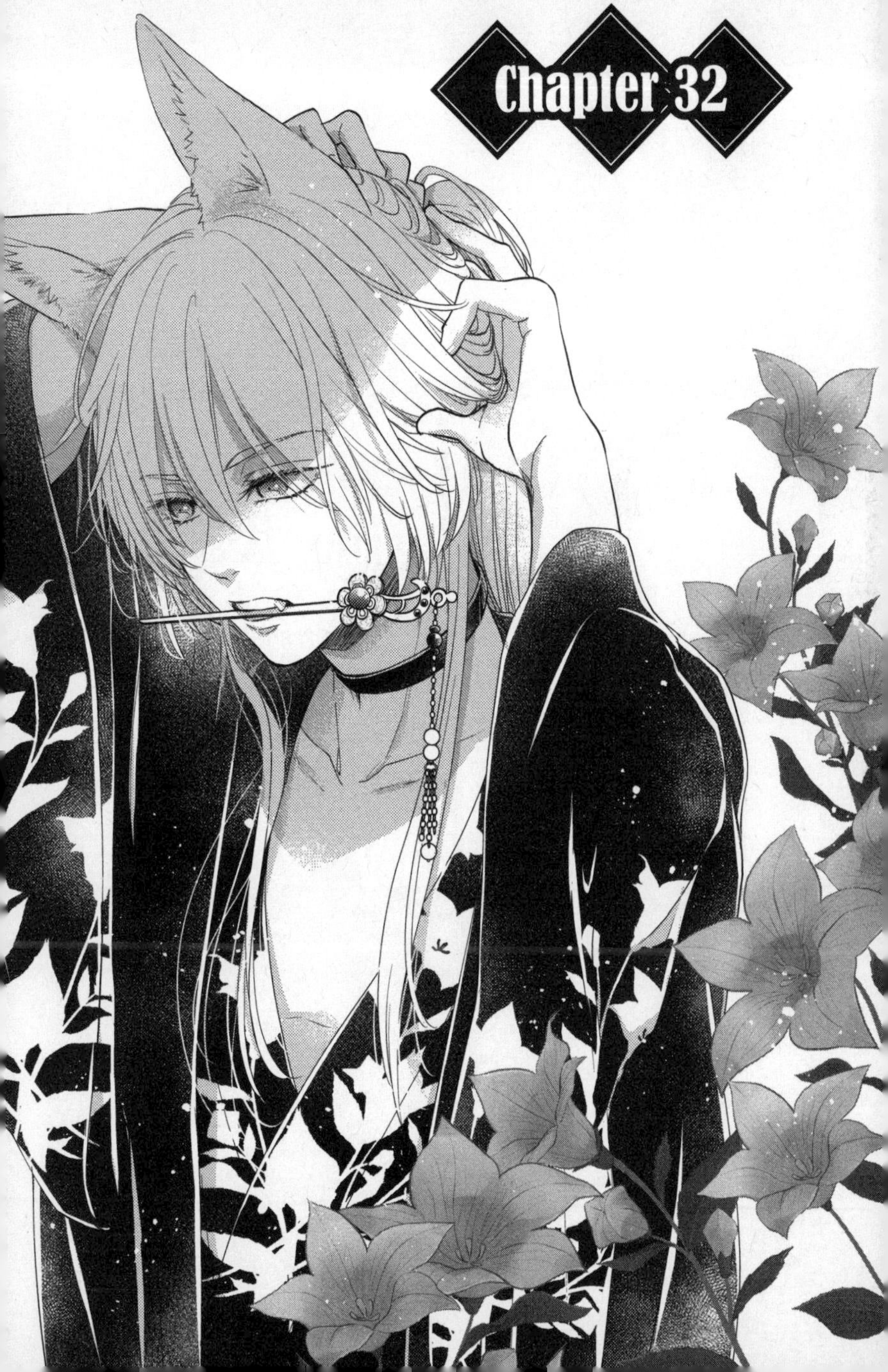
Chapter 32

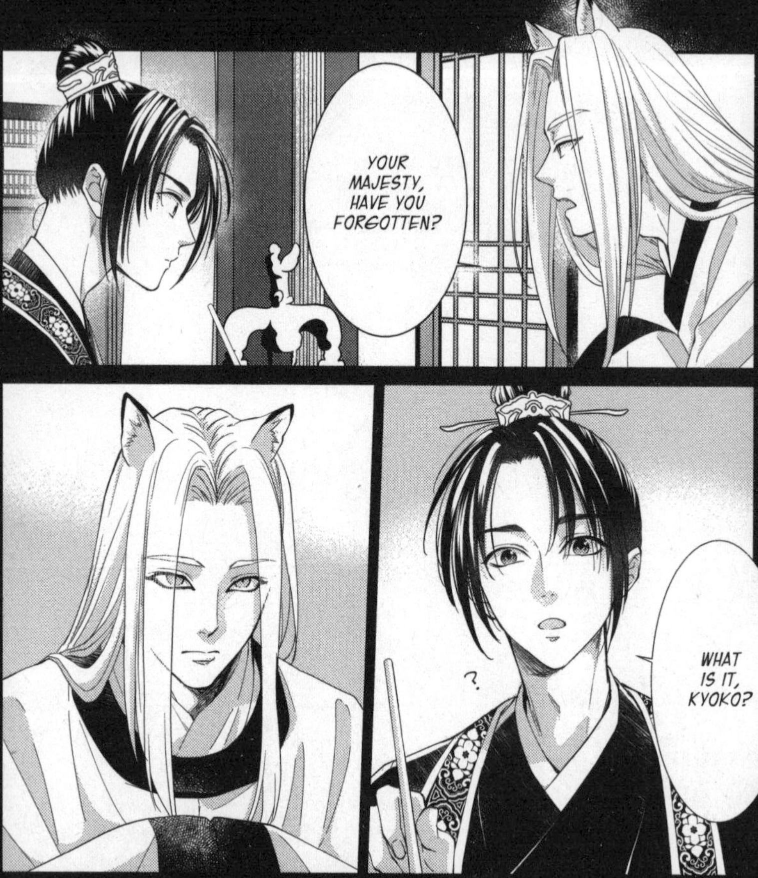
YOUR MAJESTY, HAVE YOU FORGOTTEN?
WHAT IS IT, KYOKO?
?

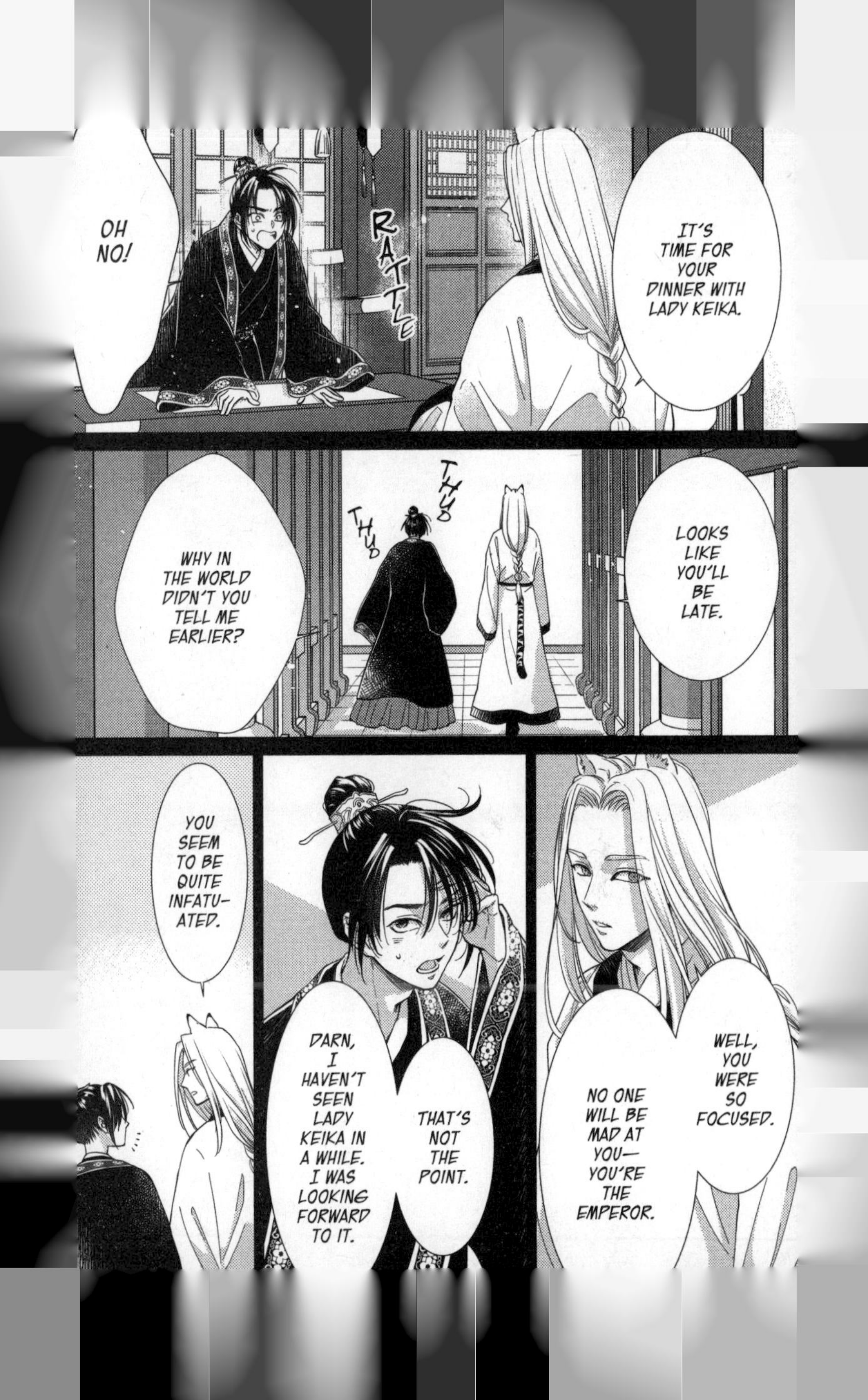
IT'S TIME FOR YOUR DINNER WITH LADY KEIKA.
RATTLE
OH NO!
LOOKS LIKE YOU'LL BE LATE.
THUD
THUD
WHY IN THE WORLD DIDN'T YOU TELL ME EARLIER?
WELL, YOU WERE SO FOCUSED.
NO ONE WILL BE MAD AT YOU— YOU'RE THE EMPEROR.
THAT'S NOT THE POINT.
DARN, I HAVEN'T SEEN LADY KEIKA IN A WHILE. I WAS LOOKING FORWARD TO IT.
YOU SEEM TO BE QUITE INFATU-ATED.

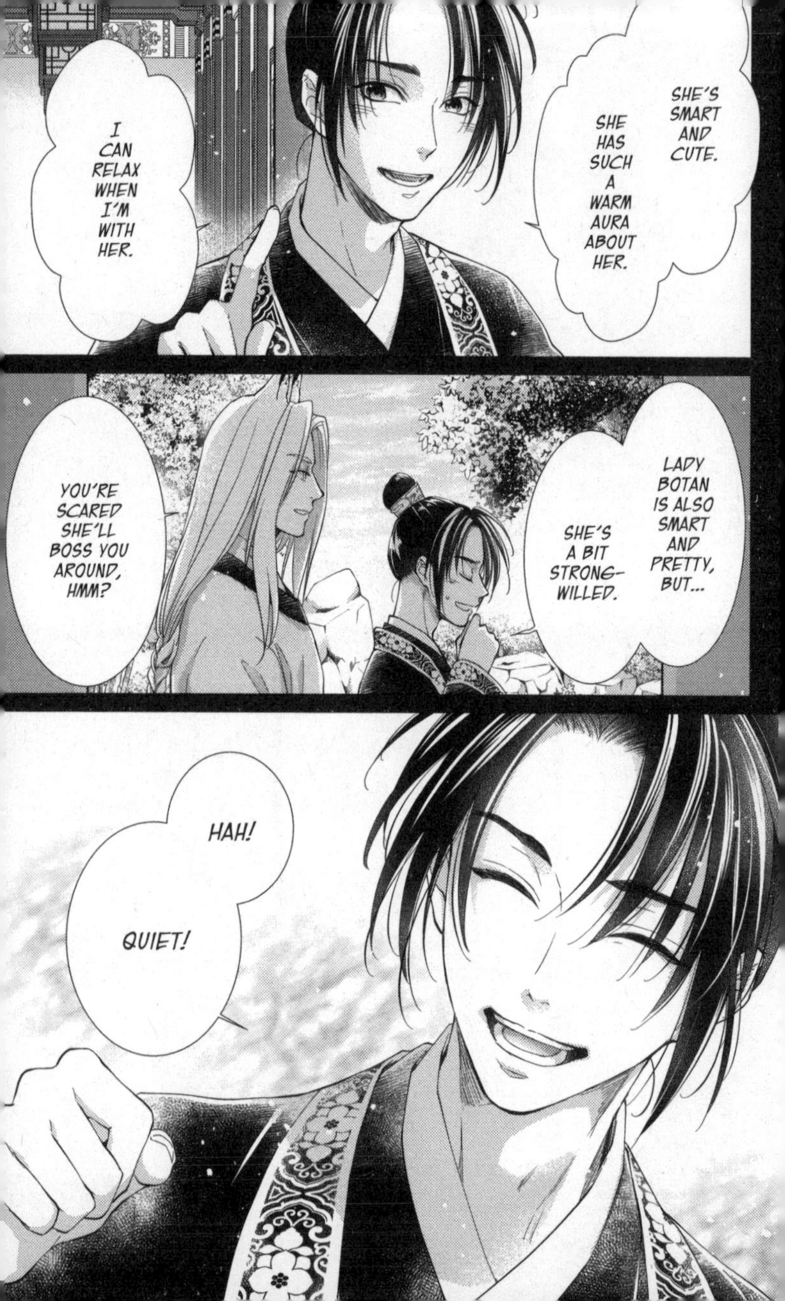
SHE'S SMART AND CUTE.
SHE HAS SUCH A WARM AURA ABOUT HER.
I CAN RELAX WHEN I'M WITH HER.
LADY BOTAN IS ALSO SMART AND PRETTY, BUT...
SHE'S A BIT STRONG-WILLED.
YOU'RE SCARED SHE'LL BOSS YOU AROUND, HMM?
HAH!
QUIET!

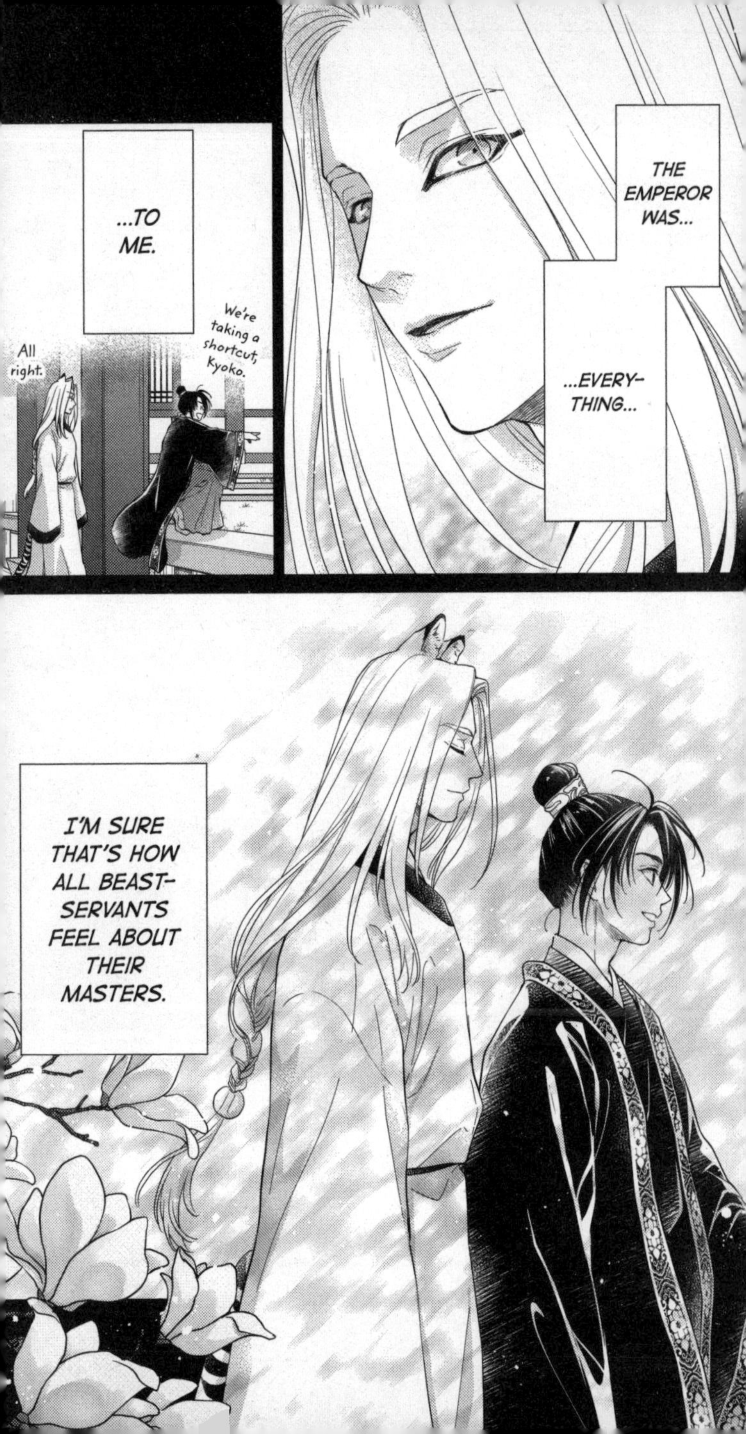

THE EMPEROR WAS...
...EVERY-THING...
...TO ME.
We're taking a shortcut, Kyoko.
All right.
I'M SURE THAT'S HOW ALL BEAST-SERVANTS FEEL ABOUT THEIR MASTERS.

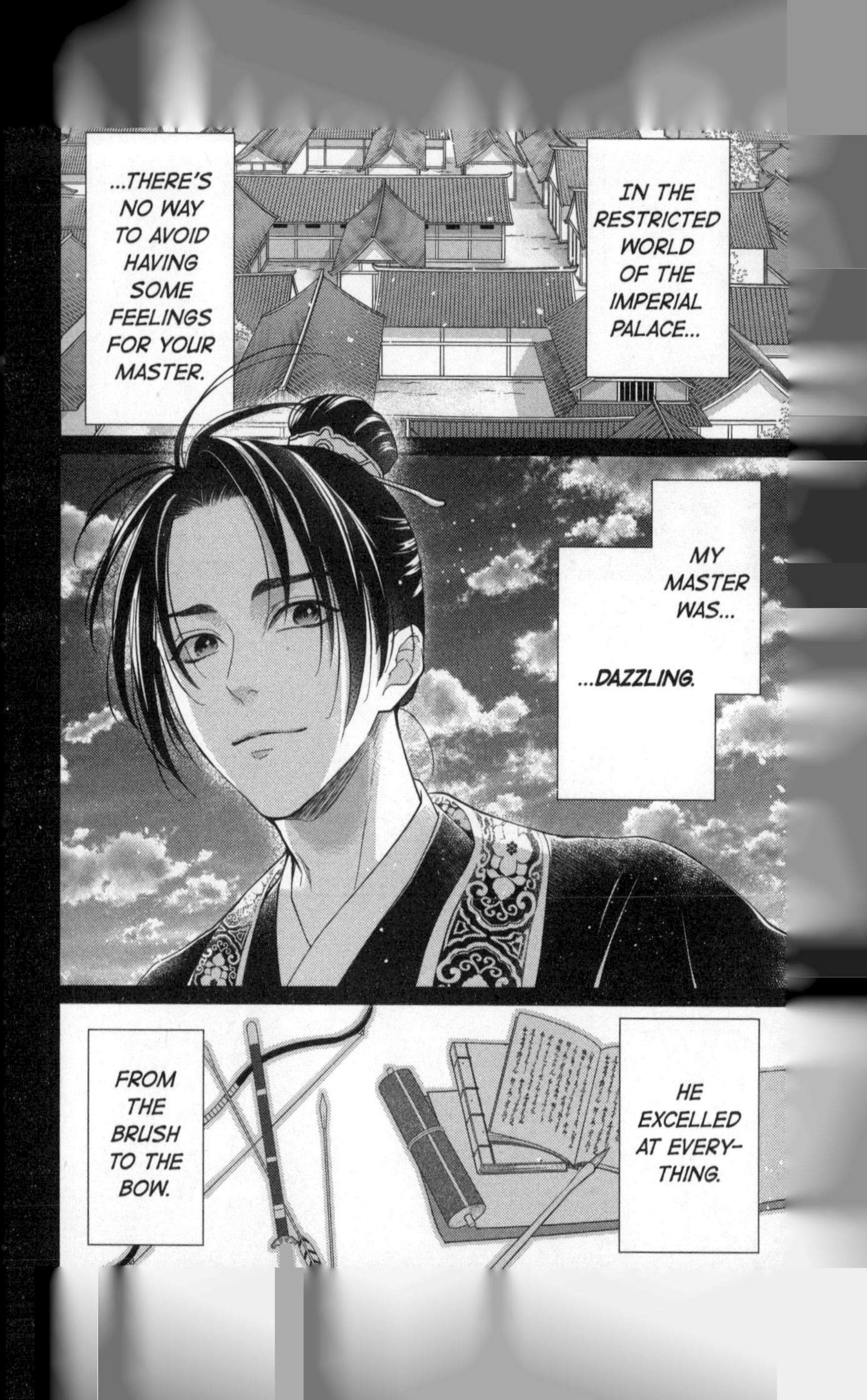
IN THE RESTRICTED WORLD OF THE IMPERIAL PALACE...
...THERE'S NO WAY TO AVOID HAVING SOME FEELINGS FOR YOUR MASTER.
MY MASTER WAS...
...DAZZLING.
HE EXCELLED AT EVERY-THING.
FROM THE BRUSH TO THE BOW.

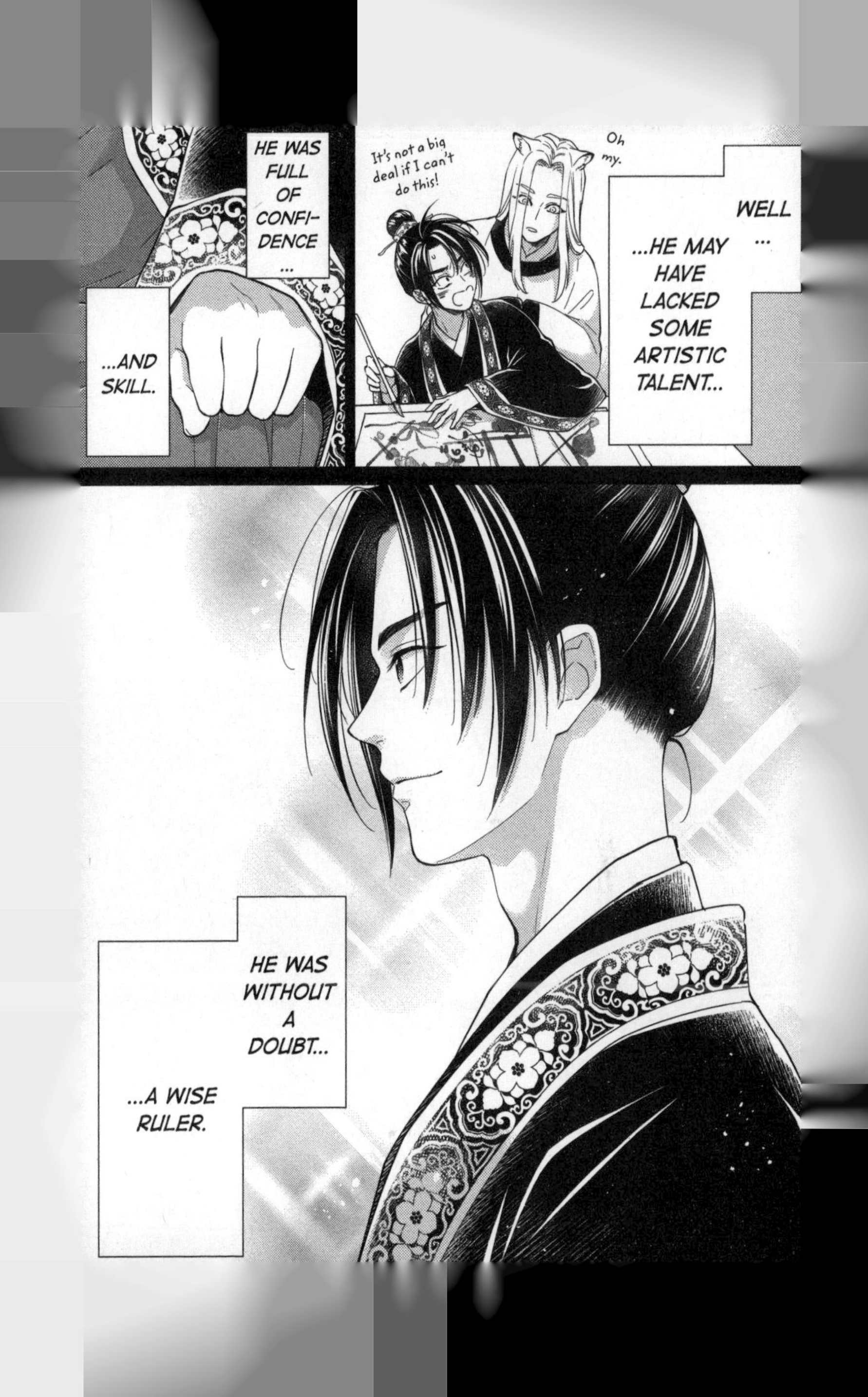
WELL ...
...HE MAY HAVE LACKED SOME ARTISTIC TALENT...
Oh my.
It's not a big deal if I can't do this!
HE WAS FULL OF CONFI-DENCE ...
...AND SKILL.
HE WAS WITHOUT A DOUBT...
...A WISE RULER.

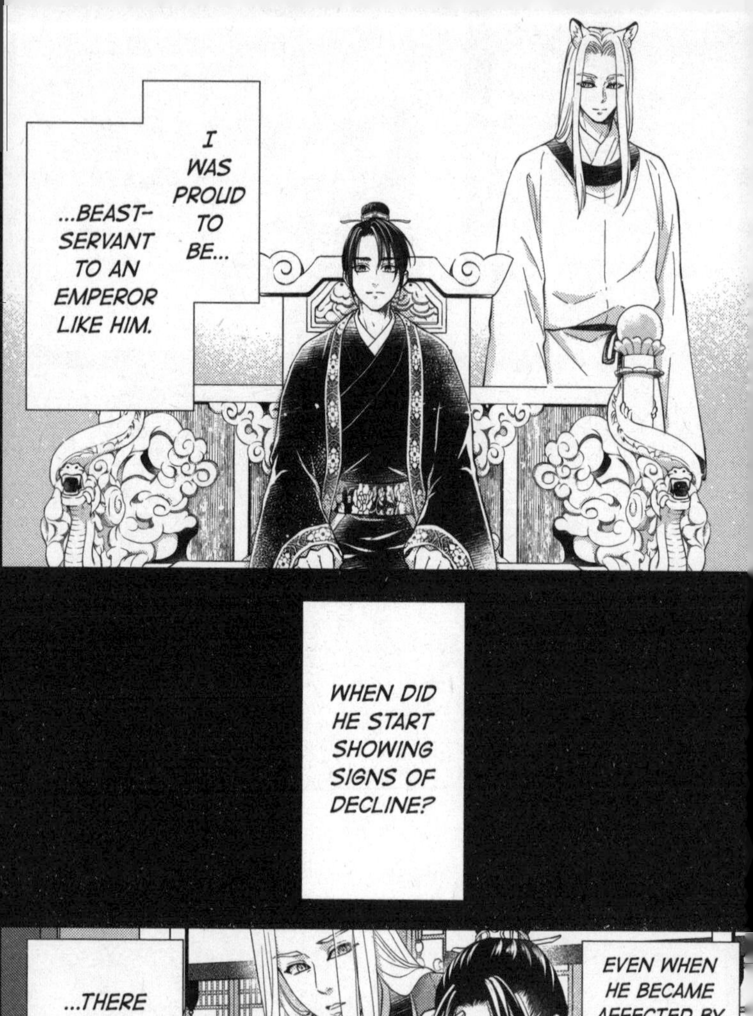
I WAS PROUD TO BE...
...BEAST-SERVANT TO AN EMPEROR LIKE HIM.
WHEN DID HE START SHOWING SIGNS OF DECLINE?
EVEN WHEN HE BECAME AFFECTED BY ILLNESS AND STARTED TO FEEL UNWELL...
...THERE WAS NO CLEAR DETERIORATION.

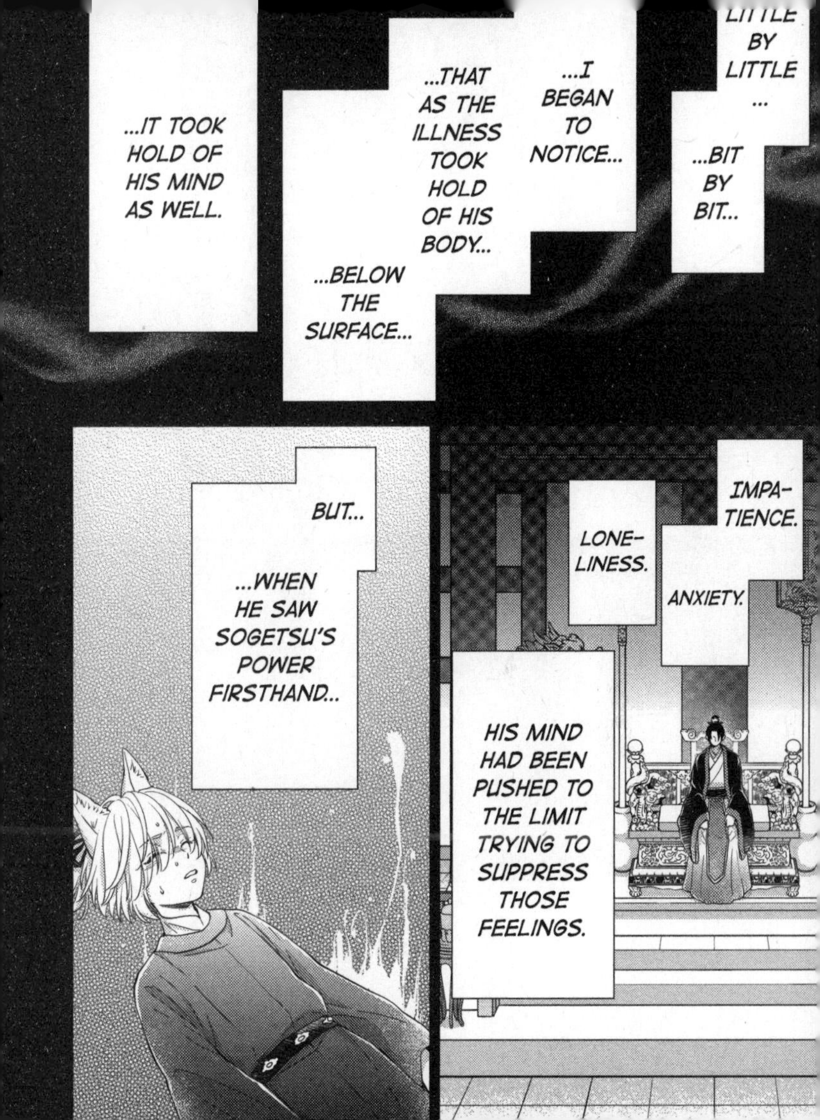
LITTLE BY LITTLE ...
...BIT BY BIT...
...I BEGAN TO NOTICE...
...THAT AS THE ILLNESS TOOK HOLD OF HIS BODY...
...BELOW THE SURFACE...
...IT TOOK HOLD OF HIS MIND AS WELL.
IMPA-TIENCE.
ANXIETY.
LONE-LINESS.
HIS MIND HAD BEEN PUSHED TO THE LIMIT TRYING TO SUPPRESS THOSE FEELINGS.
BUT...
...WHEN HE SAW SOGETSU'S POWER FIRSTHAND...

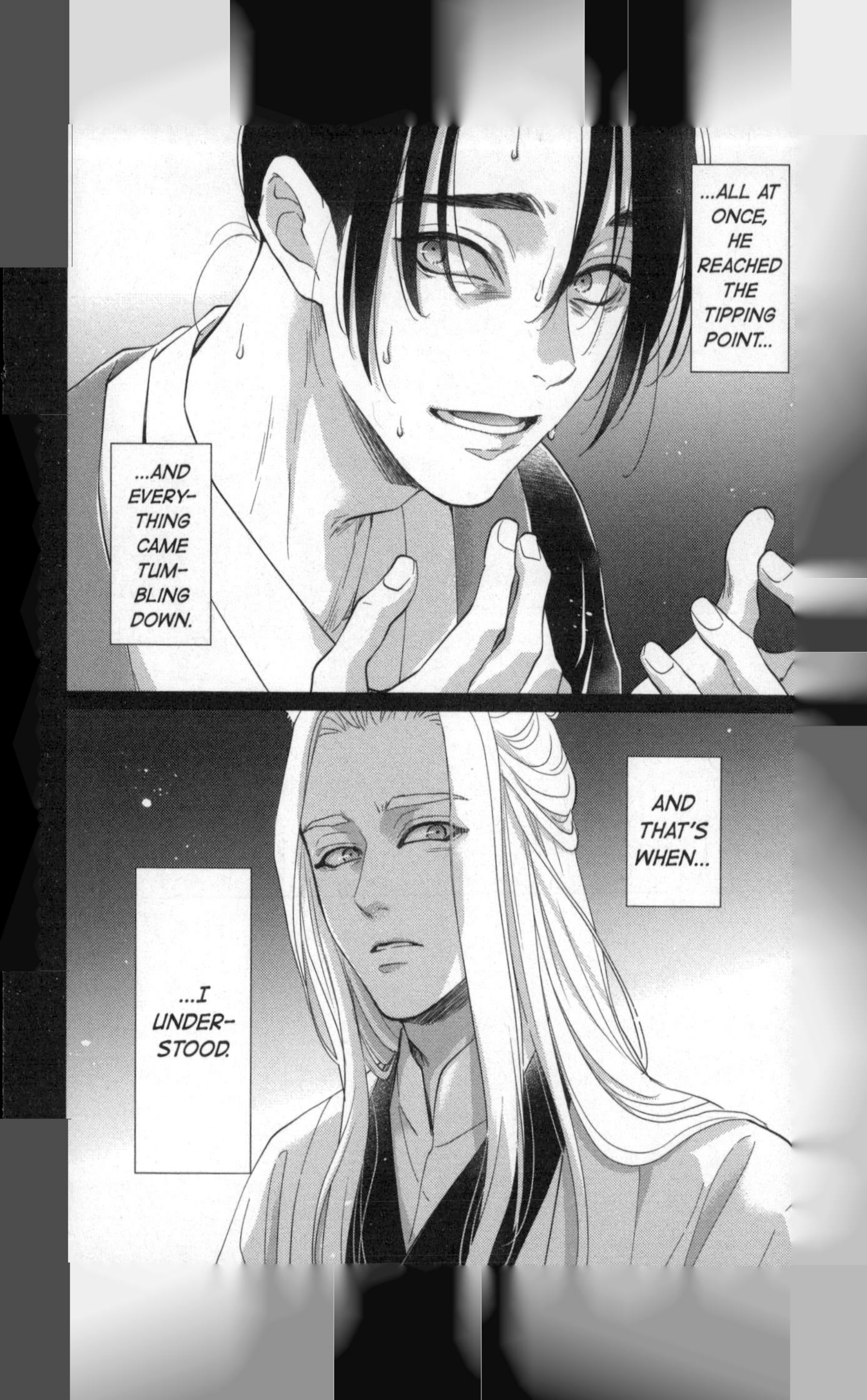
...ALL AT ONCE, HE REACHED THE TIPPING POINT...
...AND EVERYTHING CAME TUMBLING DOWN.
AND THAT'S WHEN...
...I UNDERSTOOD.

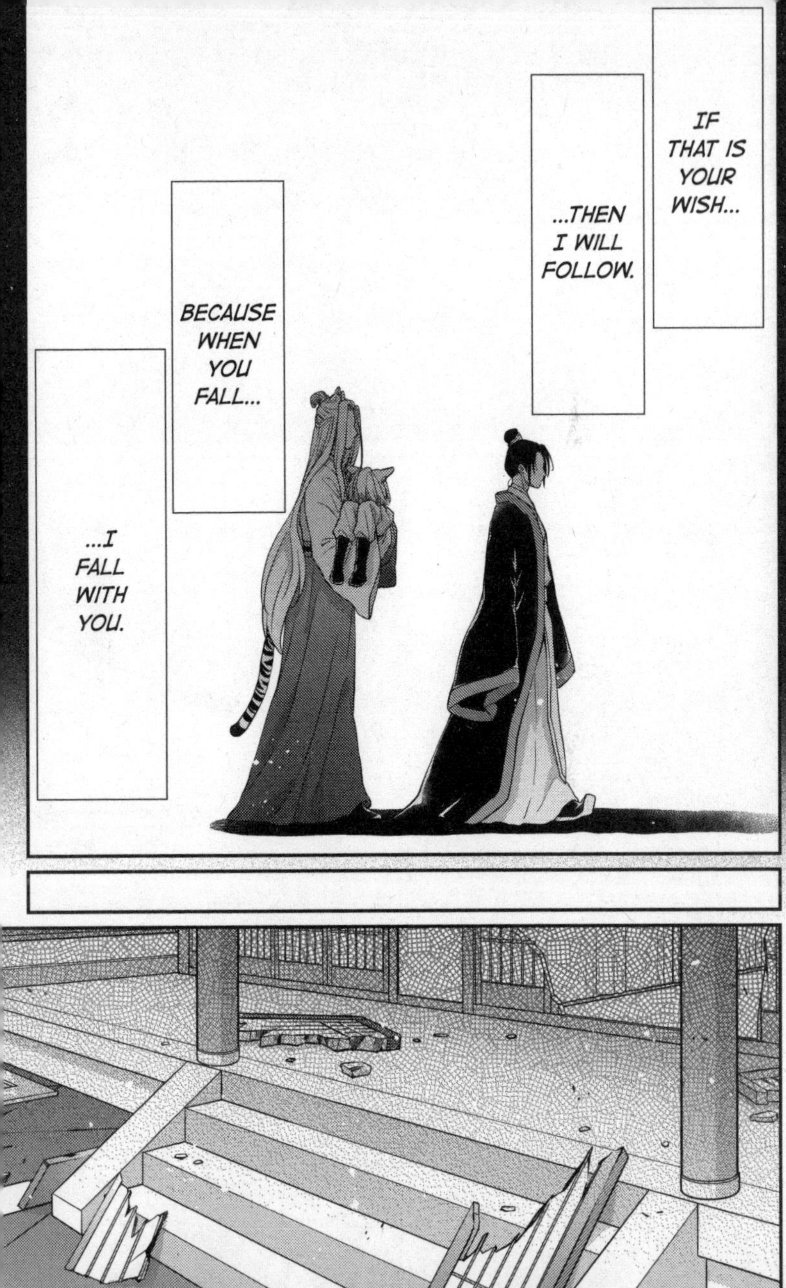
IF THAT IS YOUR WISH...
...THEN I WILL FOLLOW.
BECAUSE WHEN YOU FALL...
...I FALL WITH YOU.

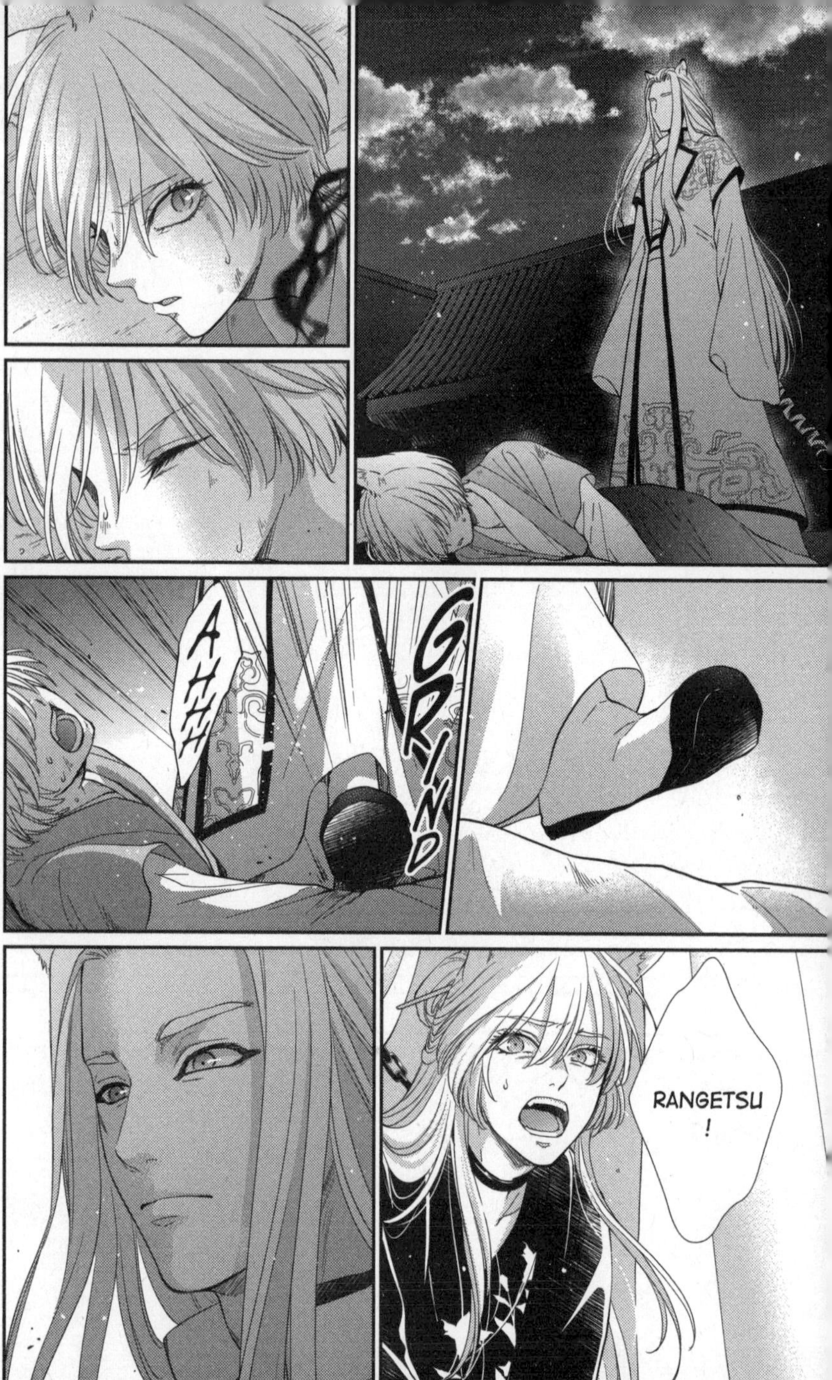
GRIND
AHH
RANGETSU!

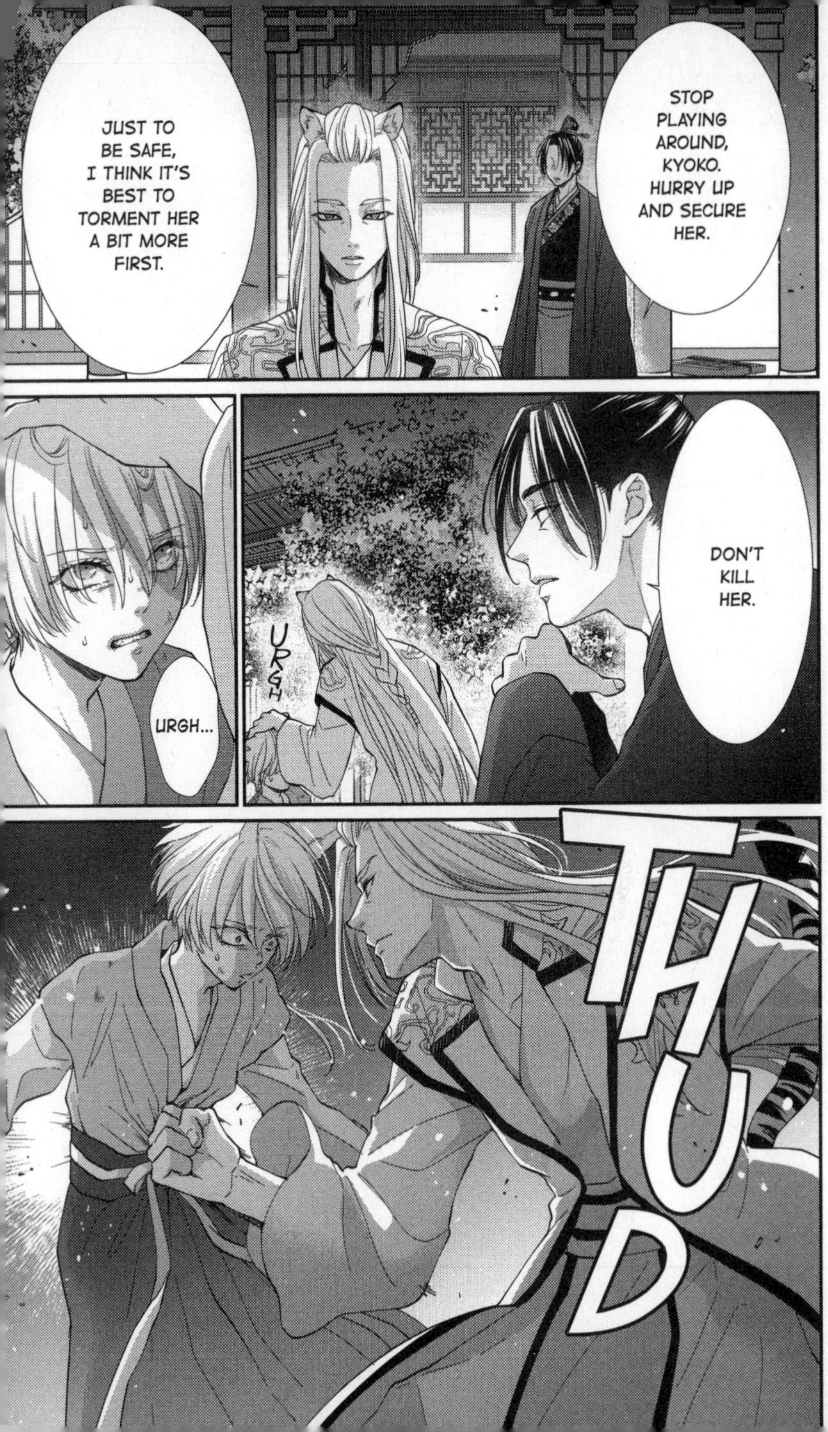
STOP PLAYING AROUND, KYOKO. HURRY UP AND SECURE HER.
JUST TO BE SAFE, I THINK IT'S BEST TO TORMENT HER A BIT MORE FIRST.
DON'T KILL HER.
URGH
URGH...
THUD

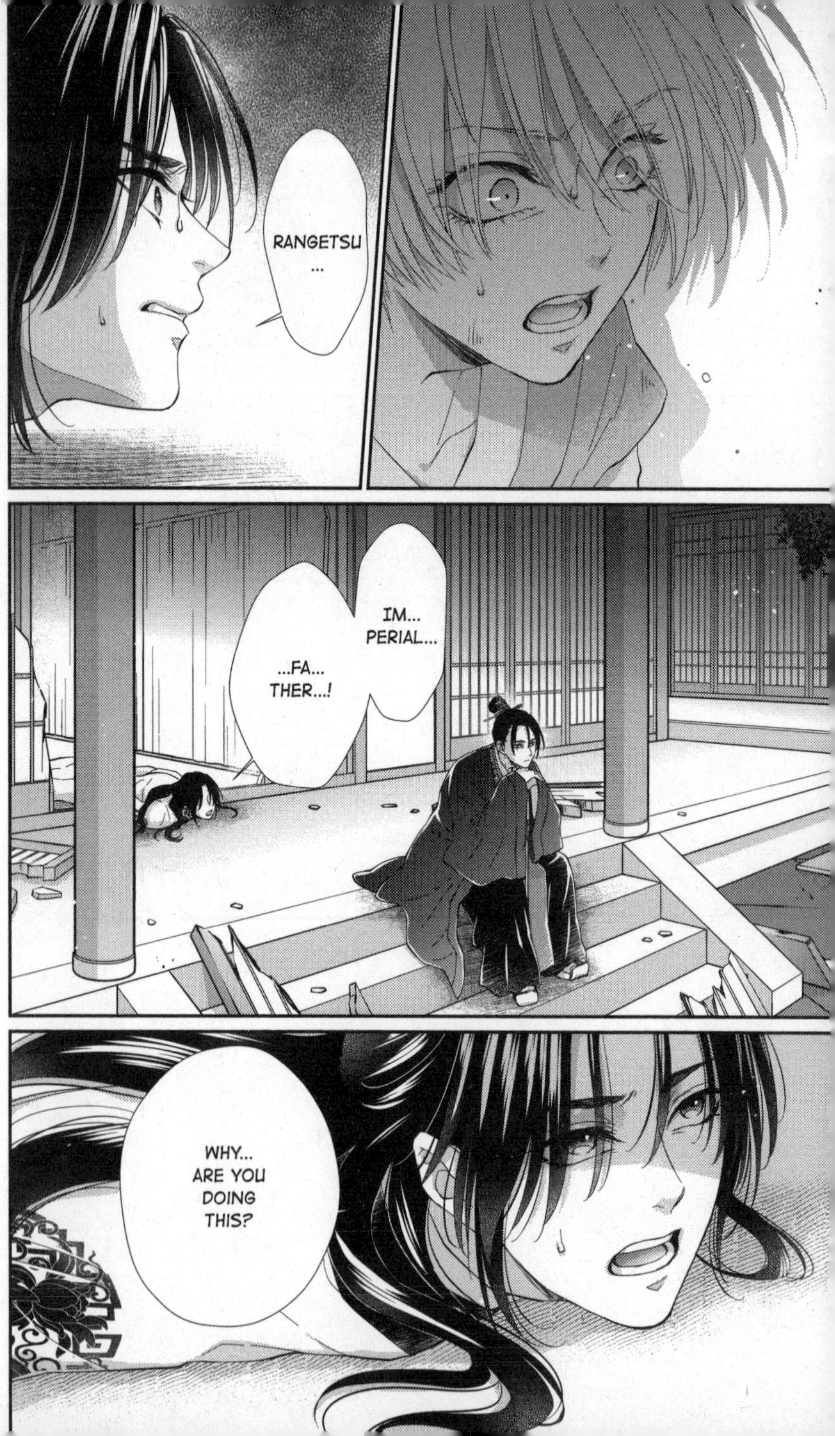
RANGETSU
...
IM... PERIAL...
...FA... THER...!
WHY... ARE YOU DOING THIS?

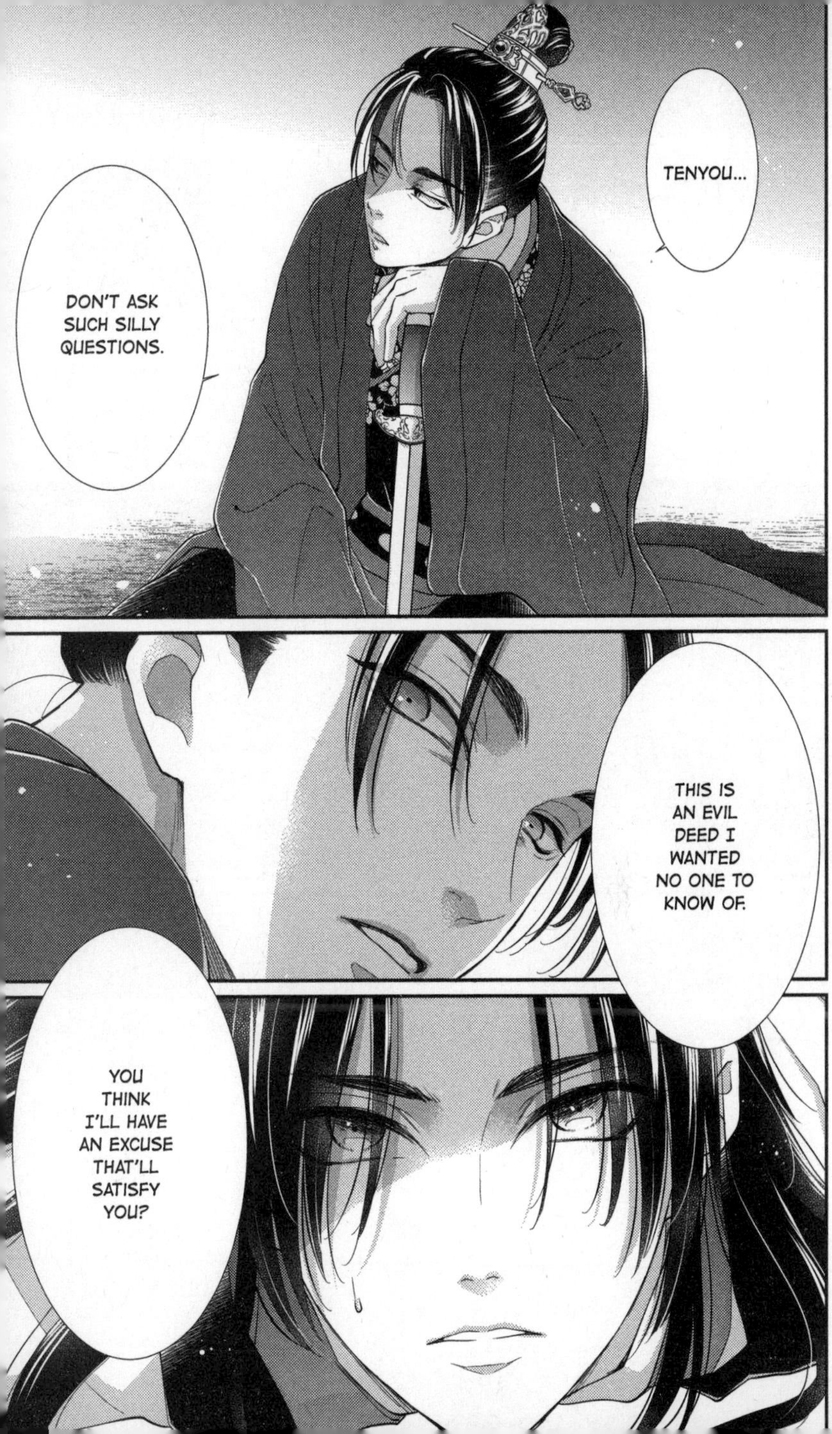
TENYOU...
DON'T ASK SUCH SILLY QUESTIONS.
THIS IS AN EVIL DEED I WANTED NO ONE TO KNOW OF.
YOU THINK I'LL HAVE AN EXCUSE THAT'LL SATISFY YOU?

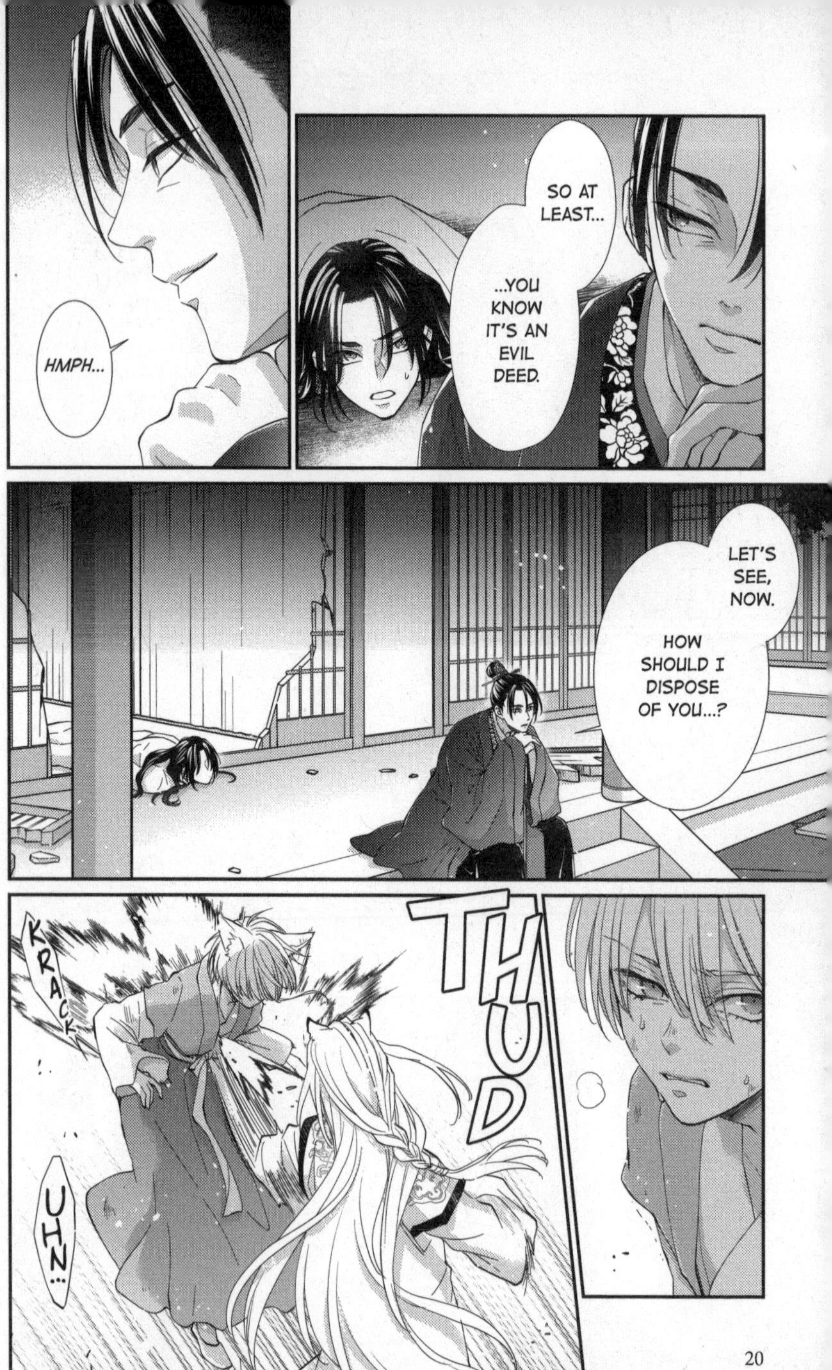
SO AT LEAST...
...YOU KNOW IT'S AN EVIL DEED.
HMPH...
LET'S SEE, NOW.
HOW SHOULD I DISPOSE OF YOU...?
THUD
KRACK
UHN...

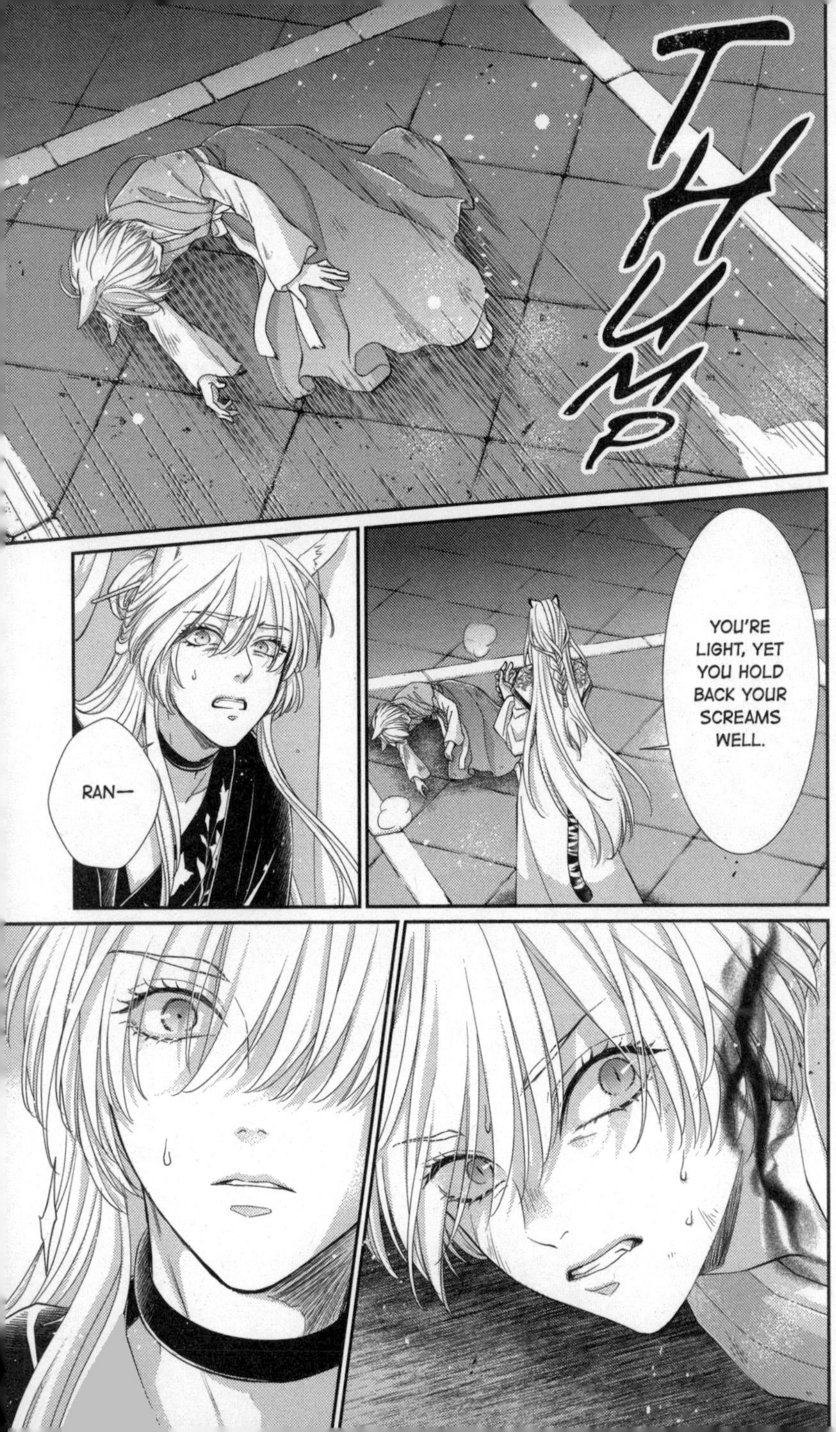
THUMP
YOU'RE LIGHT, YET YOU HOLD BACK YOUR SCREAMS WELL.
RAN—

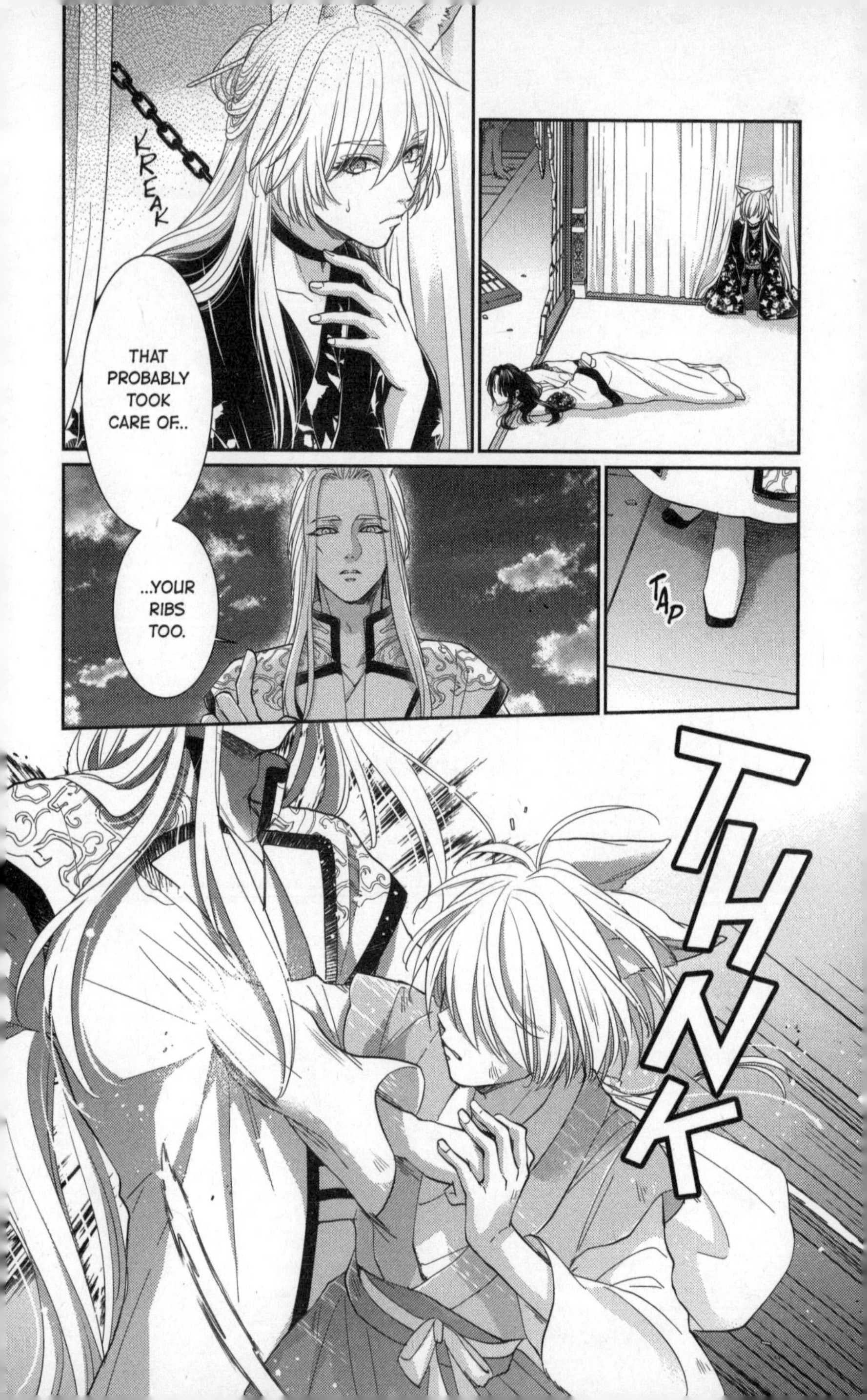
KREAK
THAT PROBABLY TOOK CARE OF...
TAP
...YOUR RIBS TOO.
THNK

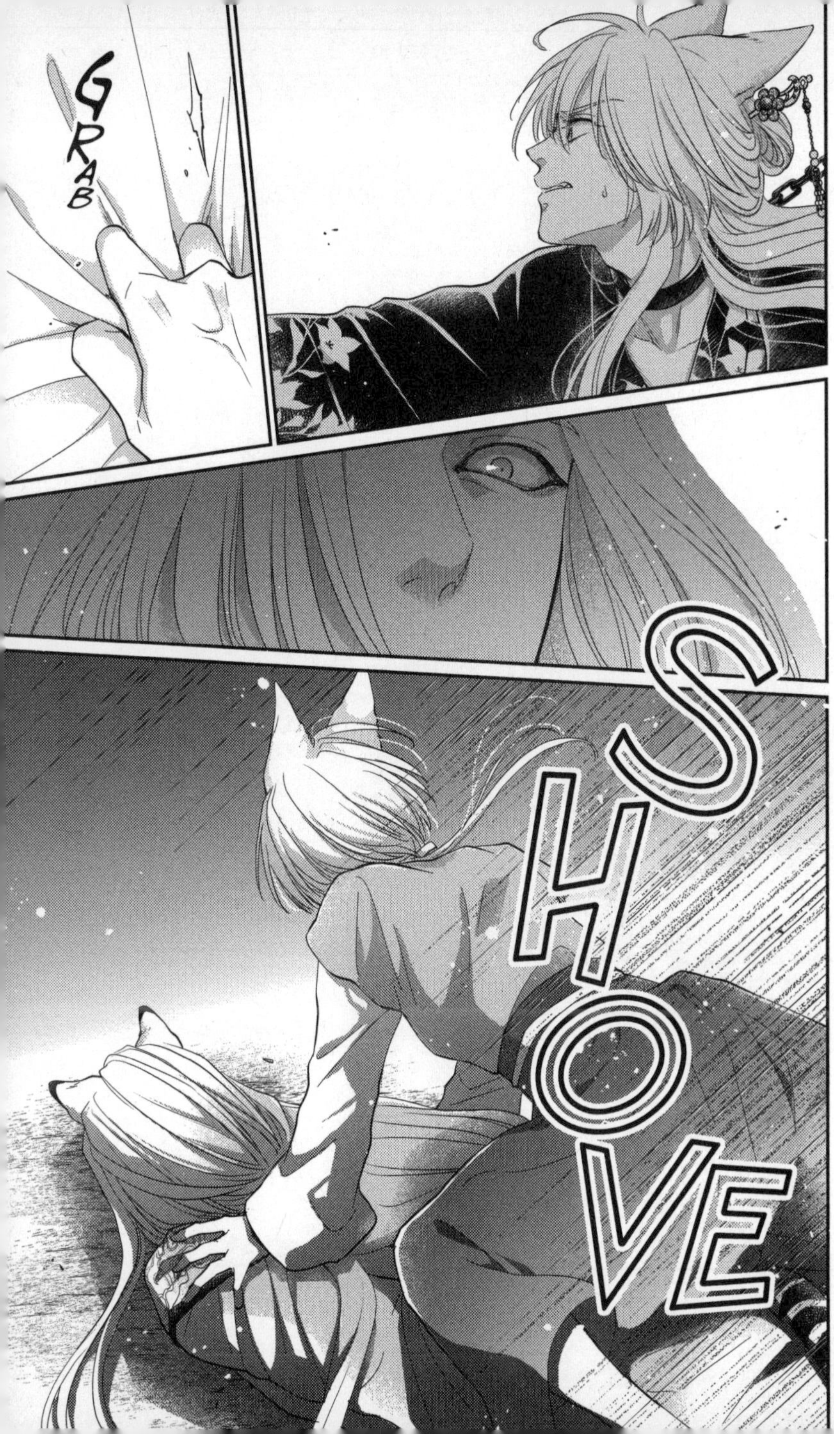
GRAB
SHOVE

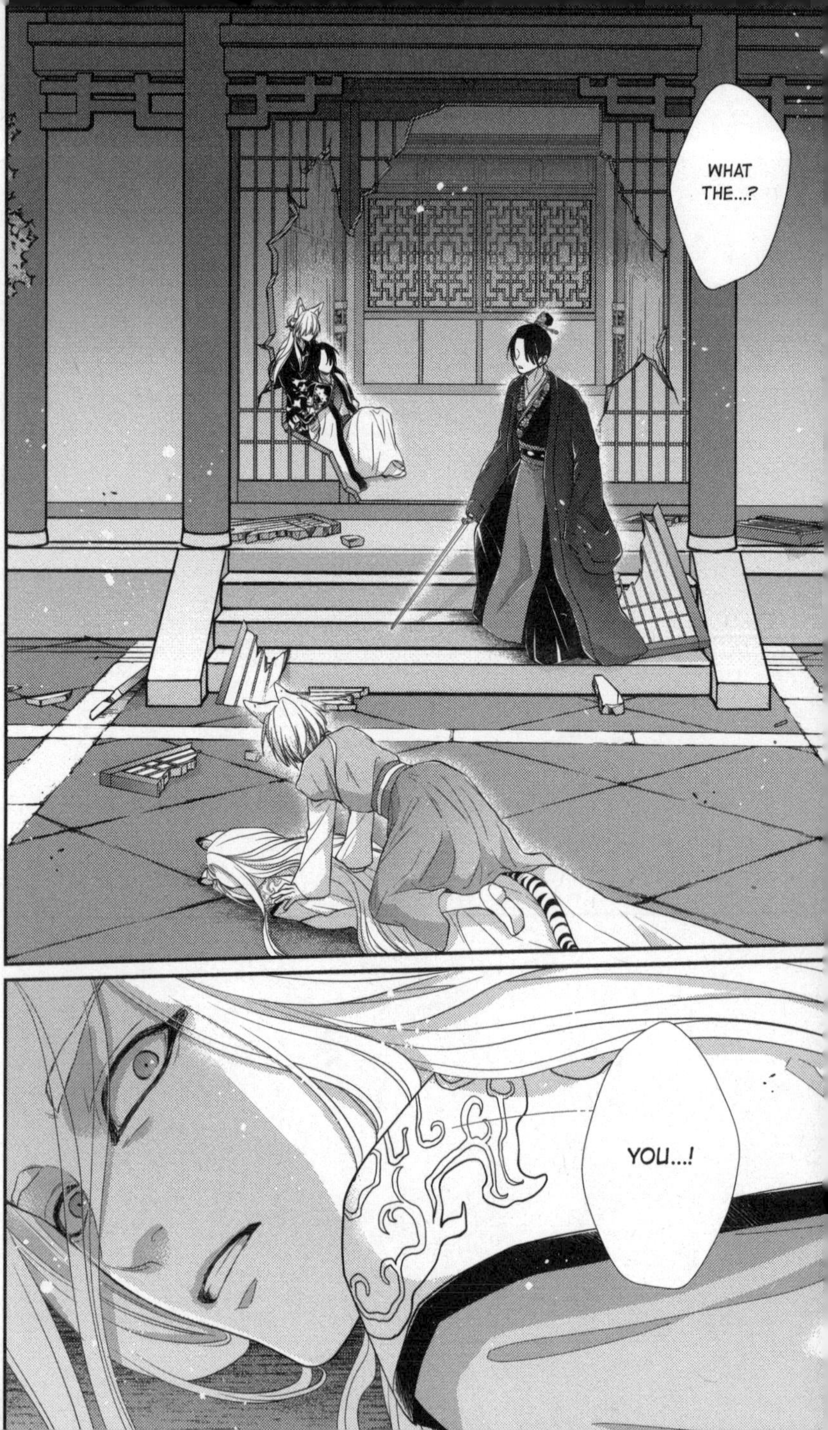
WHAT THE...?
YOU...!

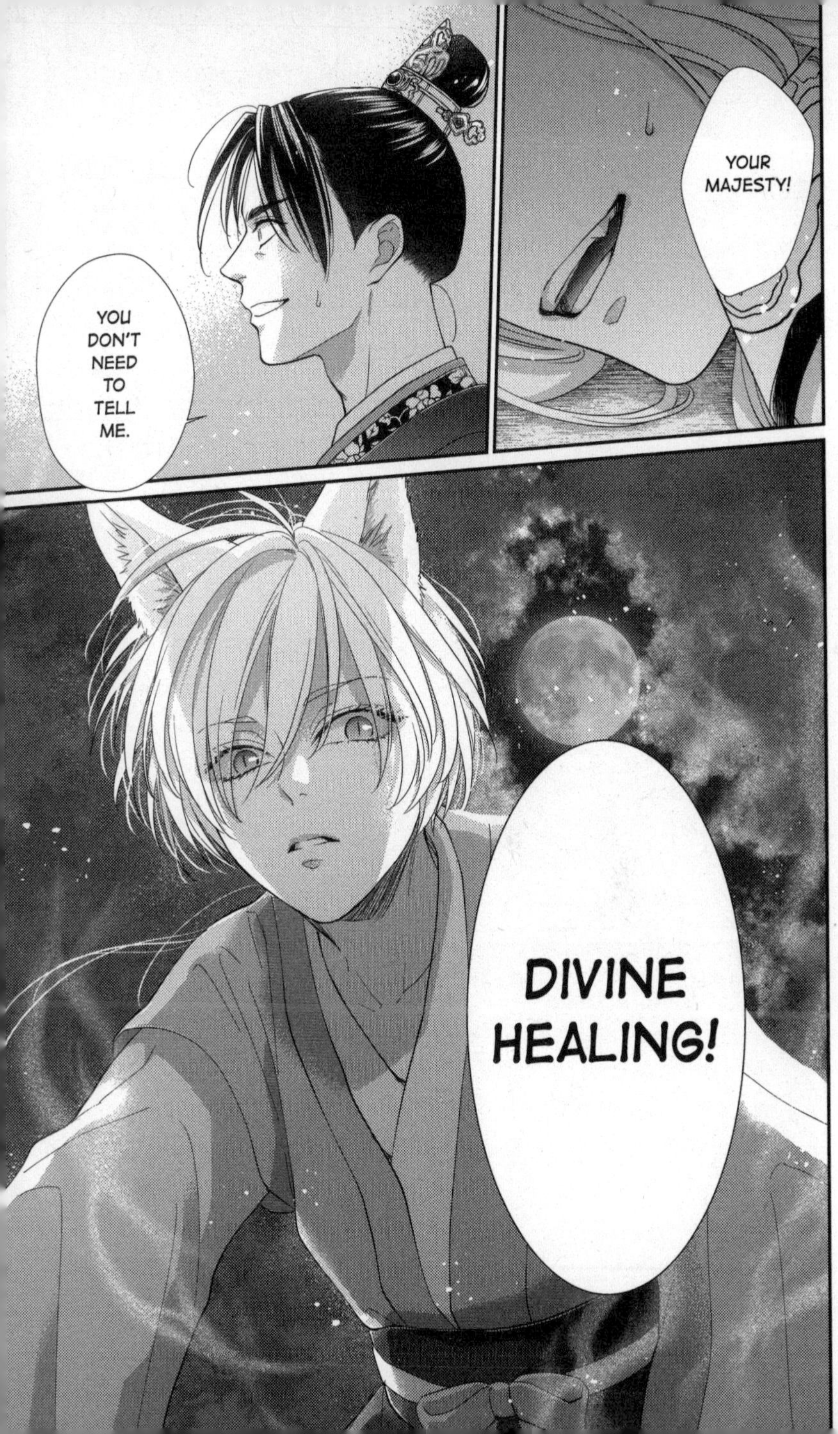
YOUR MAJESTY!
YOU DON'T NEED TO TELL ME.
DIVINE HEALING!

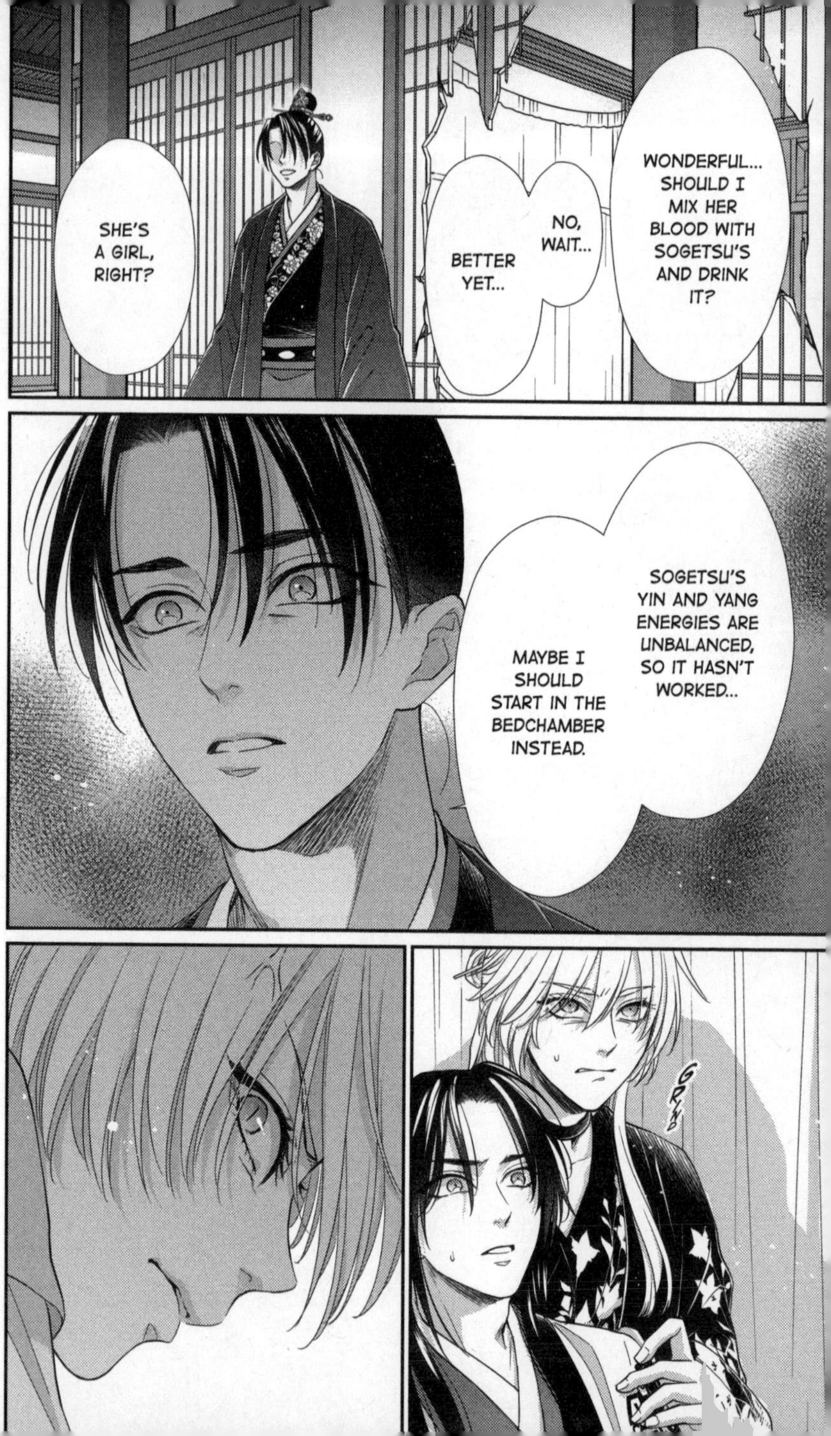
WONDERFUL... SHOULD I MIX HER BLOOD WITH SOGETSU'S AND DRINK IT?
NO, WAIT...
BETTER YET...
SHE'S A GIRL, RIGHT?
SOGETSU'S YIN AND YANG ENERGIES ARE UNBALANCED, SO IT HASN'T WORKED...
MAYBE I SHOULD START IN THE BEDCHAMBER INSTEAD.
GRIND

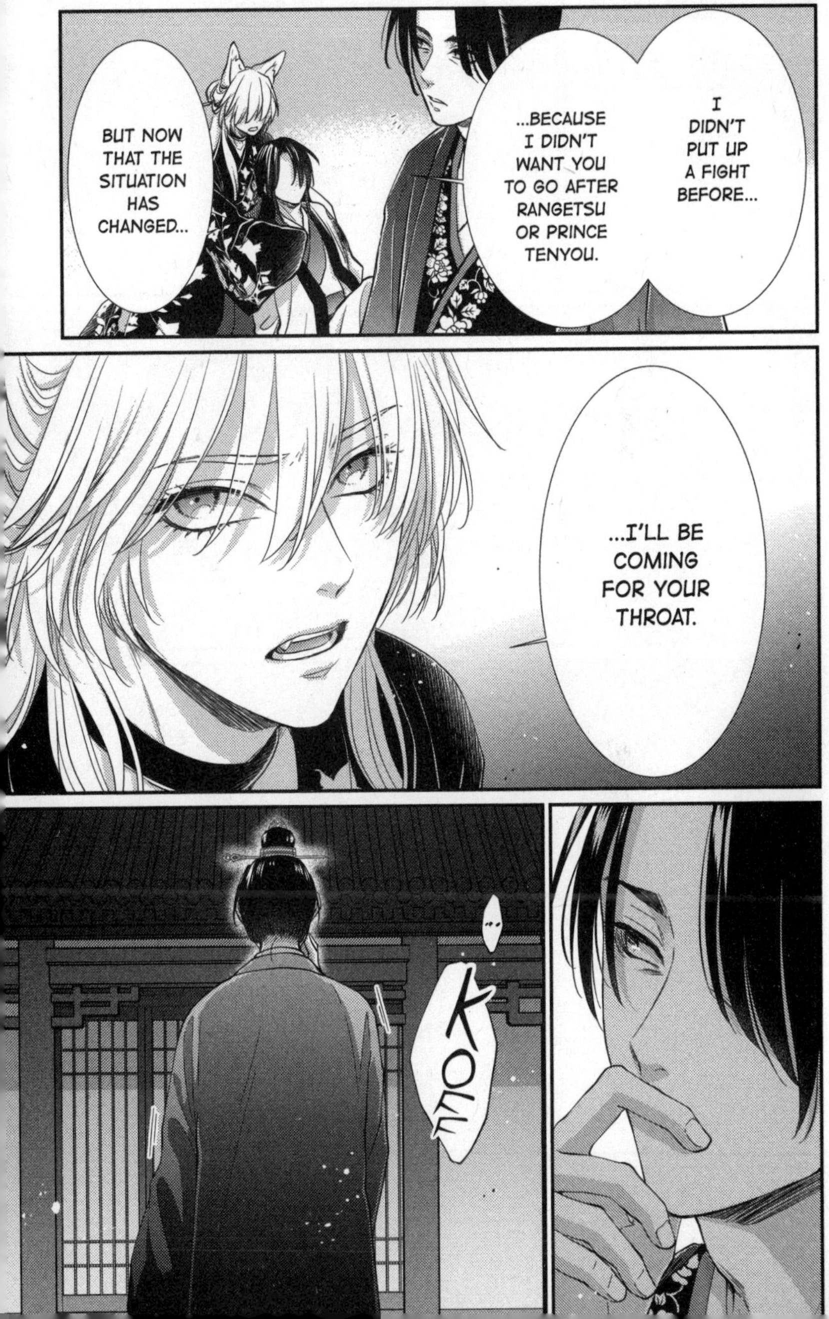
I DIDN'T PUT UP A FIGHT BEFORE...
...BECAUSE I DIDN'T WANT YOU TO GO AFTER RANGETSU OR PRINCE TENYOU.
BUT NOW THAT THE SITUATION HAS CHANGED...
...I'LL BE COMING FOR YOUR THROAT.
...
KOFF

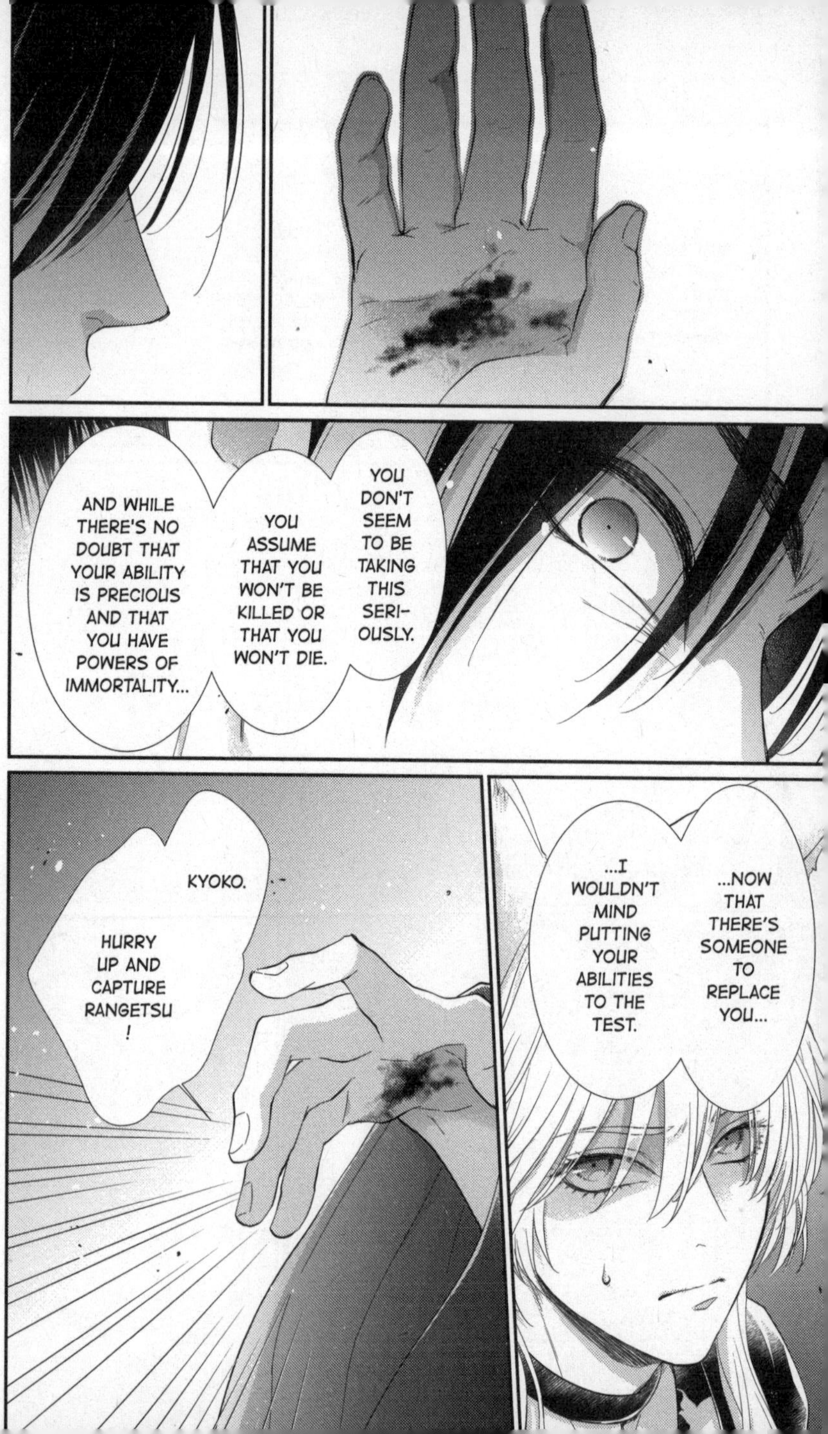
YOU DON'T SEEM TO BE TAKING THIS SERI-OUSLY.
YOU ASSUME THAT YOU WON'T BE KILLED OR THAT YOU WON'T DIE.
AND WHILE THERE'S NO DOUBT THAT YOUR ABILITY IS PRECIOUS AND THAT YOU HAVE POWERS OF IMMORTALITY...
...NOW THAT THERE'S SOMEONE TO REPLACE YOU...
...I WOULDN'T MIND PUTTING YOUR ABILITIES TO THE TEST.
KYOKO.
HURRY UP AND CAPTURE RANGETSU!

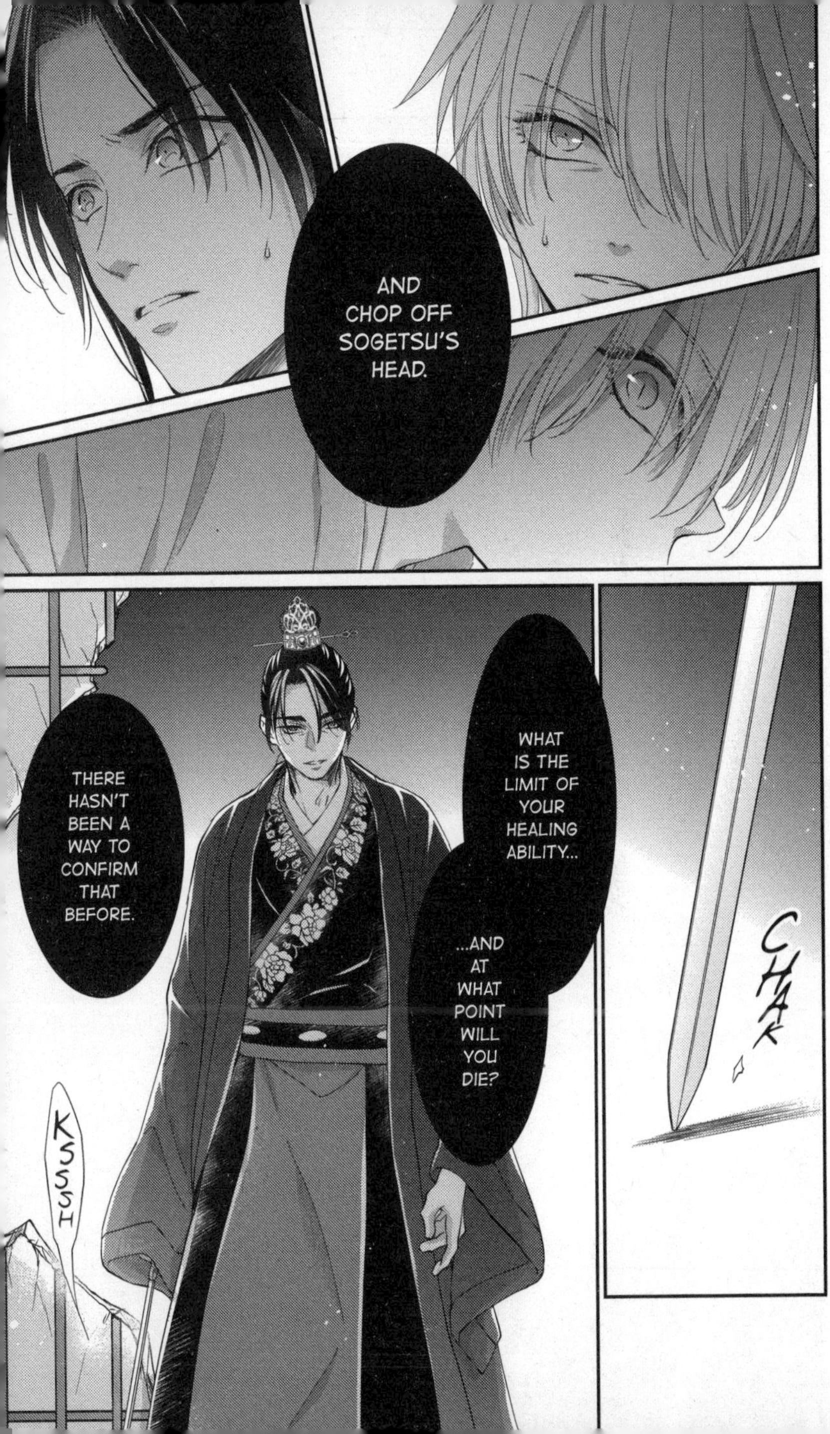
AND CHOP OFF SOGETSU'S HEAD.
CHAK
WHAT IS THE LIMIT OF YOUR HEALING ABILITY...
...AND AT WHAT POINT WILL YOU DIE?
THERE HASN'T BEEN A WAY TO CONFIRM THAT BEFORE.
KSSSH

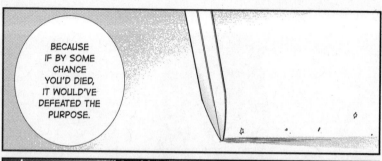

BECAUSE IF BY SOME CHANCE YOU'D DIED, IT WOULD'VE DEFEATED THE PURPOSE.

HOWEVER...

AH...

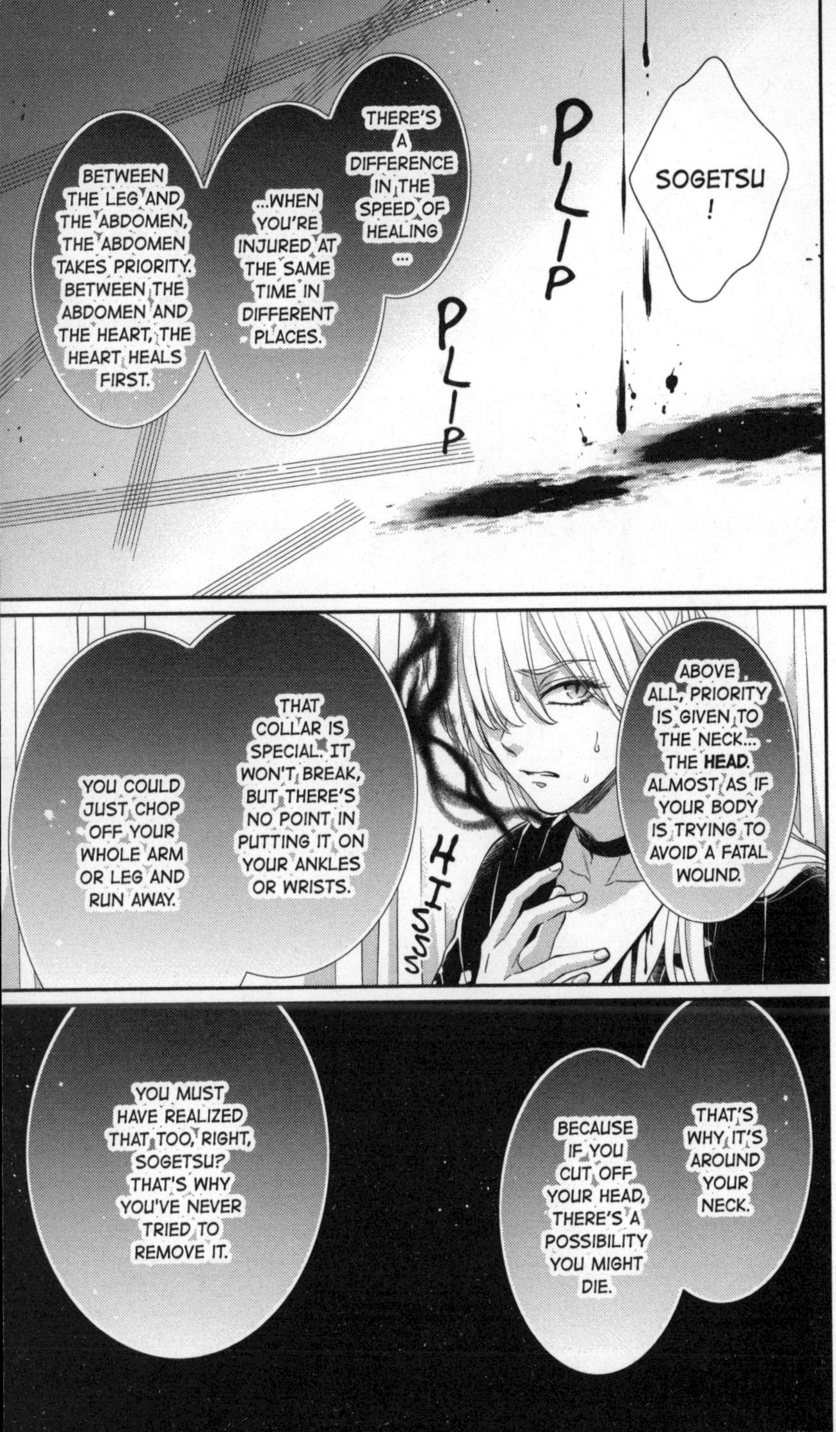
SOGETSU!
PLIP
PLIP
THERE'S A DIFFERENCE IN THE SPEED OF HEALING...
...WHEN YOU'RE INJURED AT THE SAME TIME IN DIFFERENT PLACES.
BETWEEN THE LEG AND THE ABDOMEN, THE ABDOMEN TAKES PRIORITY. BETWEEN THE ABDOMEN AND THE HEART, THE HEART HEALS FIRST.
ABOVE ALL, PRIORITY IS GIVEN TO THE NECK... THE **HEAD**. ALMOST AS IF YOUR BODY IS TRYING TO AVOID A FATAL WOUND.
HISS
THAT COLLAR IS SPECIAL. IT WON'T BREAK, BUT THERE'S NO POINT IN PUTTING IT ON YOUR ANKLES OR WRISTS.
YOU COULD JUST CHOP OFF YOUR WHOLE ARM OR LEG AND RUN AWAY.
THAT'S WHY IT'S AROUND YOUR NECK.
BECAUSE IF YOU CUT OFF YOUR HEAD, THERE'S A POSSIBILITY YOU MIGHT DIE.
YOU MUST HAVE REALIZED THAT TOO, RIGHT, SOGETSU? THAT'S WHY YOU'VE NEVER TRIED TO REMOVE IT.

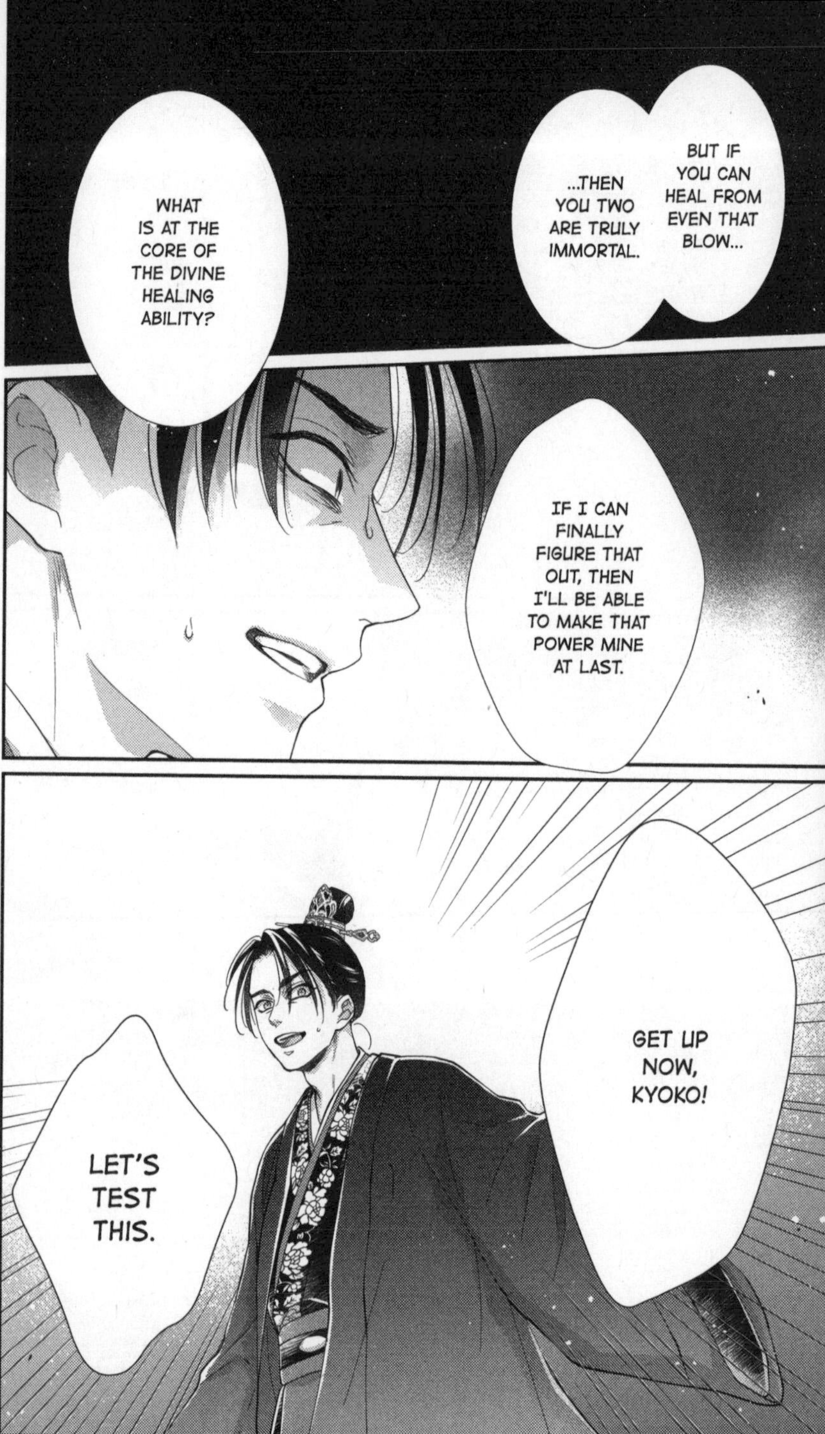
BUT IF YOU CAN HEAL FROM EVEN THAT BLOW...
...THEN YOU TWO ARE TRULY IMMORTAL.
WHAT IS AT THE CORE OF THE DIVINE HEALING ABILITY?
IF I CAN FINALLY FIGURE THAT OUT, THEN I'LL BE ABLE TO MAKE THAT POWER MINE AT LAST.
GET UP NOW, KYOKO!
LET'S TEST THIS.

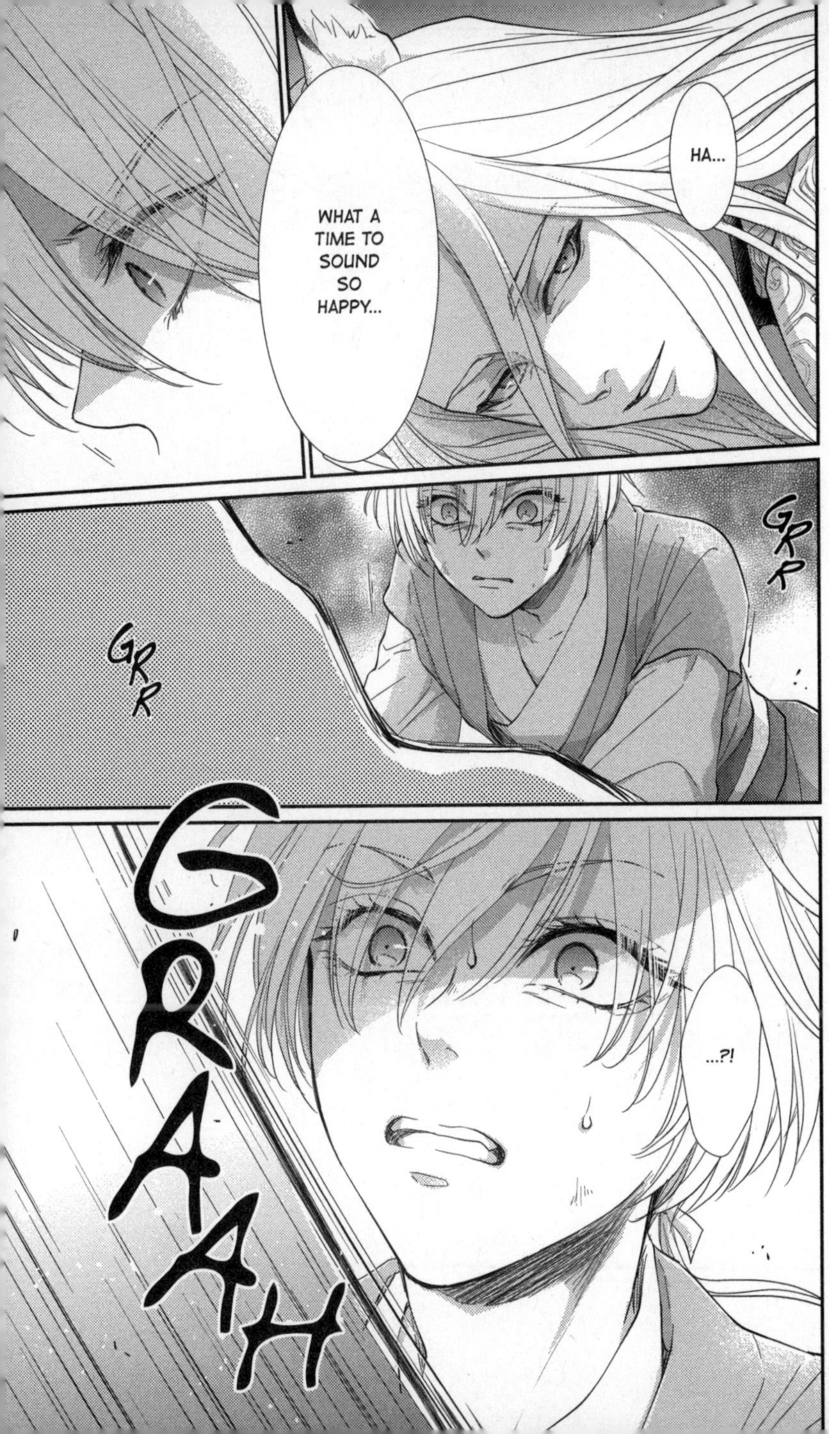

HA...
WHAT A TIME TO SOUND SO HAPPY...
GRR
GRR
...?!
GRAAH

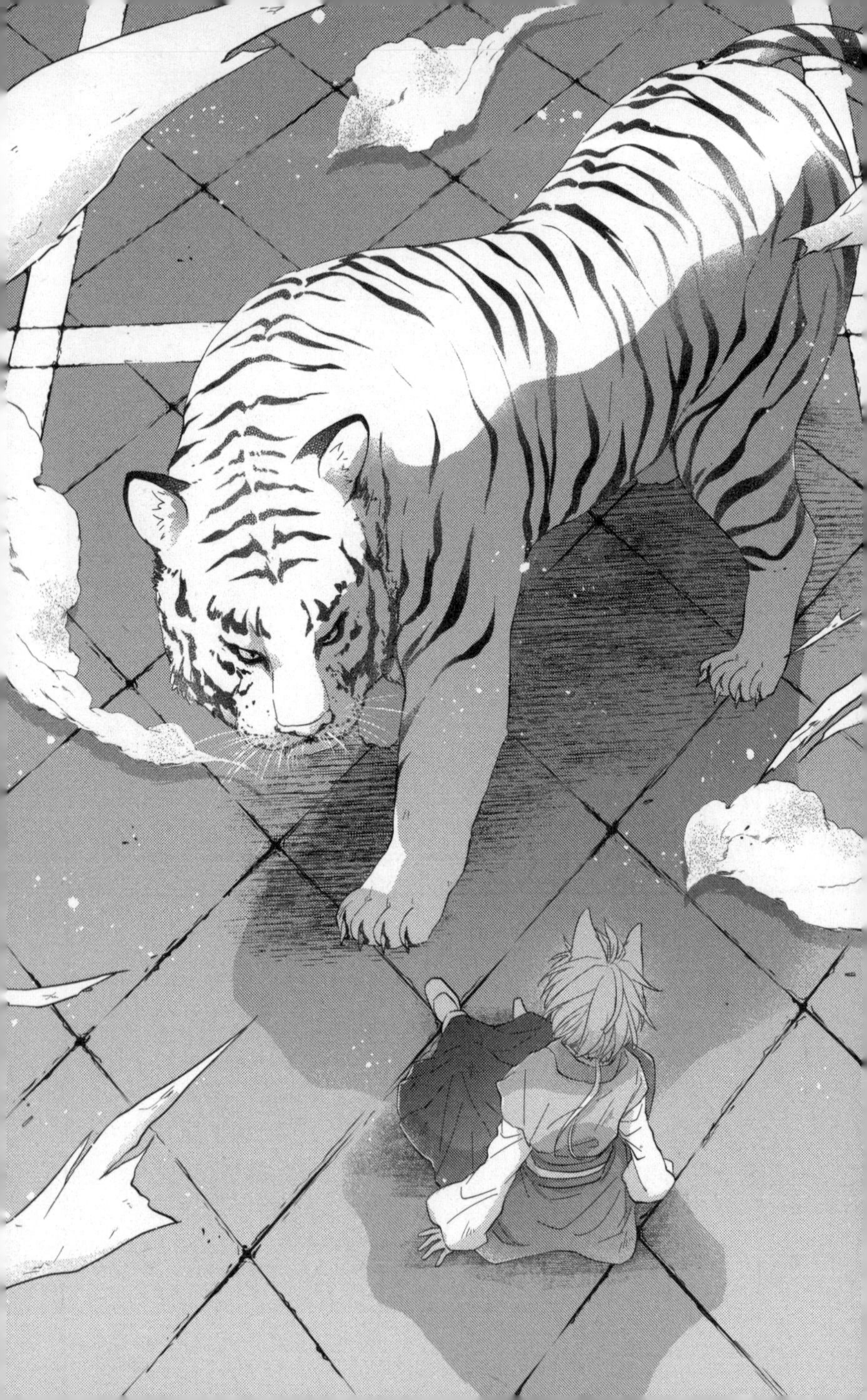

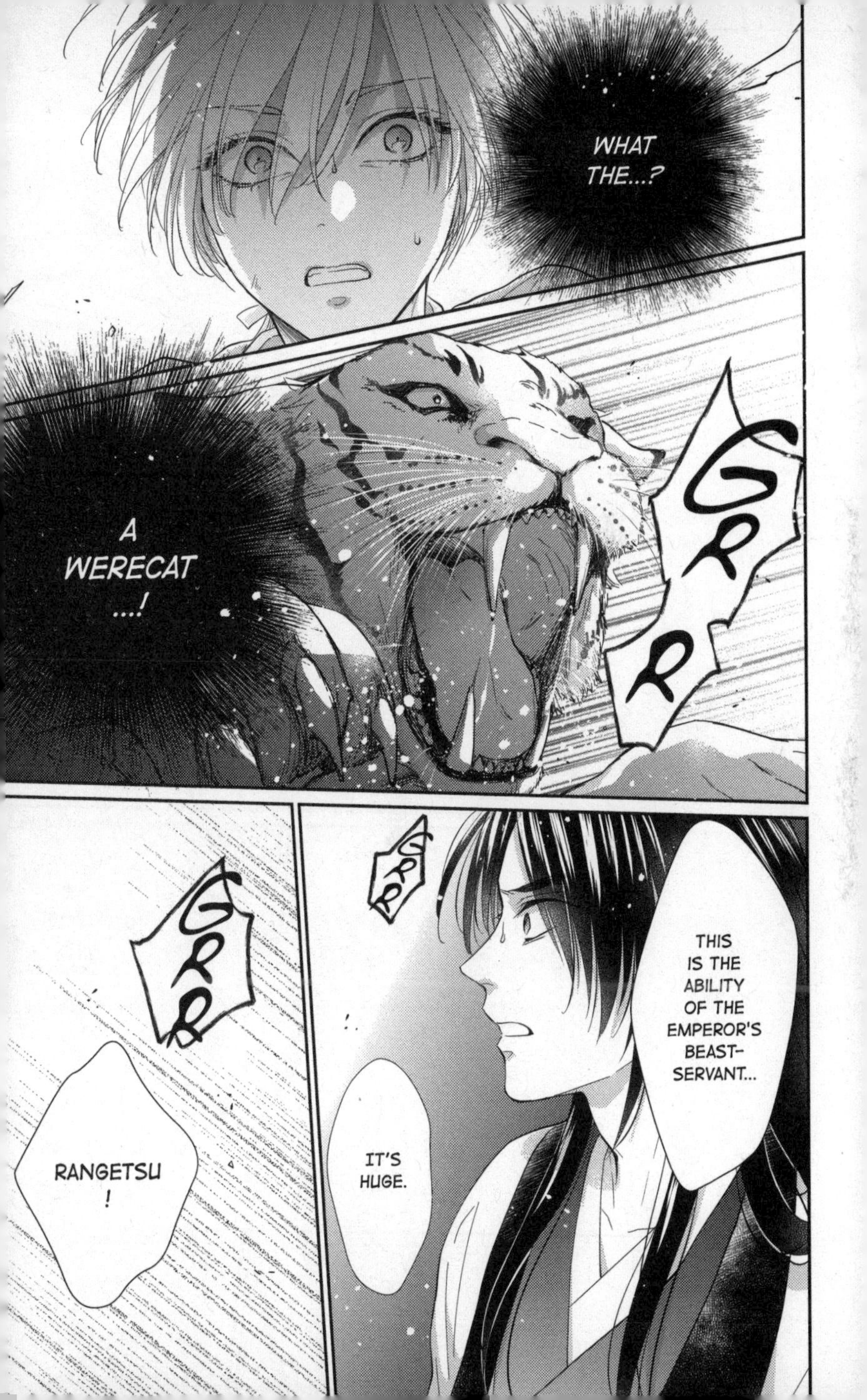
WHAT THE...?
GRR
A WERECAT ...!
THIS IS THE ABILITY OF THE EMPEROR'S BEAST-SERVANT...
GRR
IT'S HUGE.
GRR
RANGETSU !

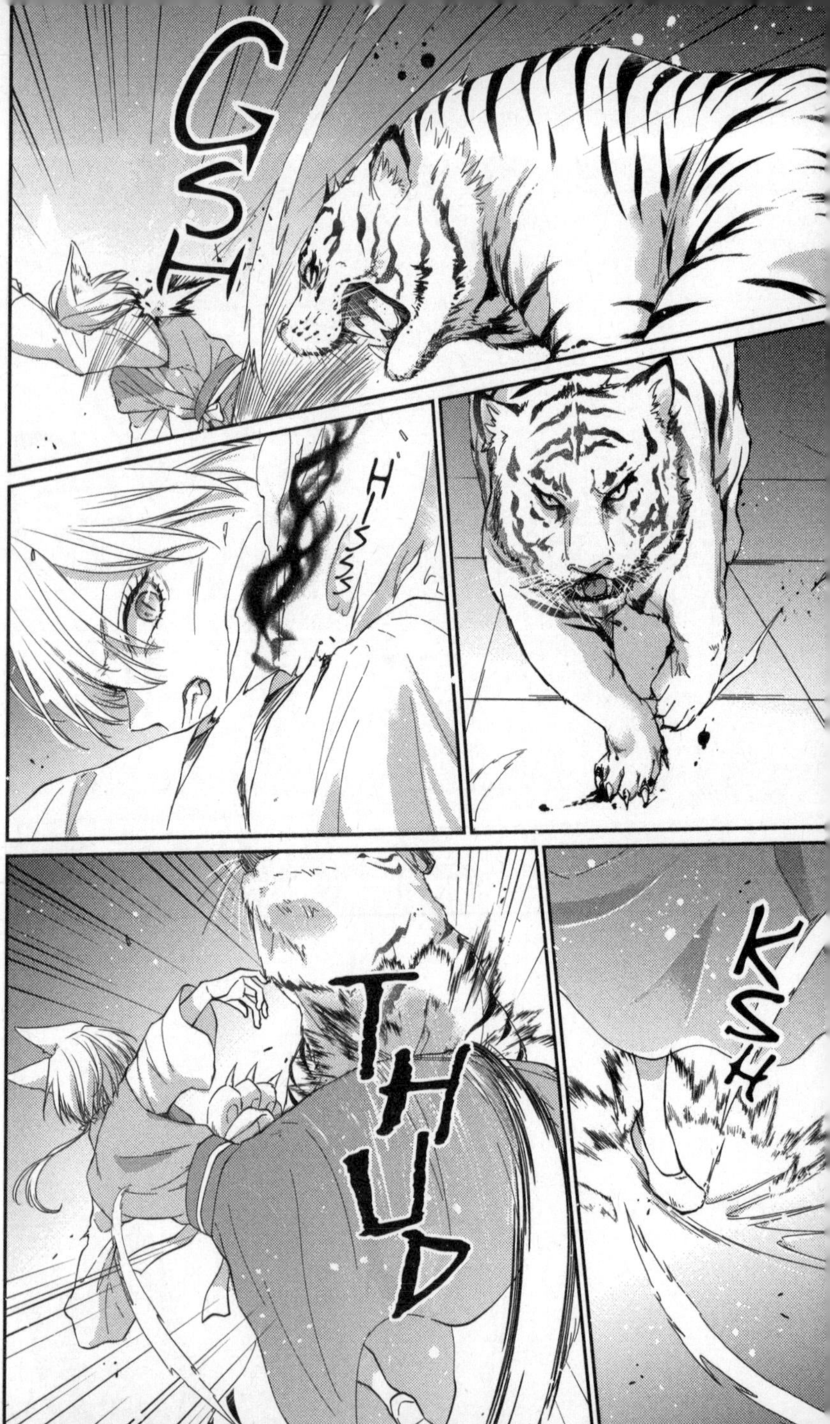
GSH
HISSS
KSH
THUD

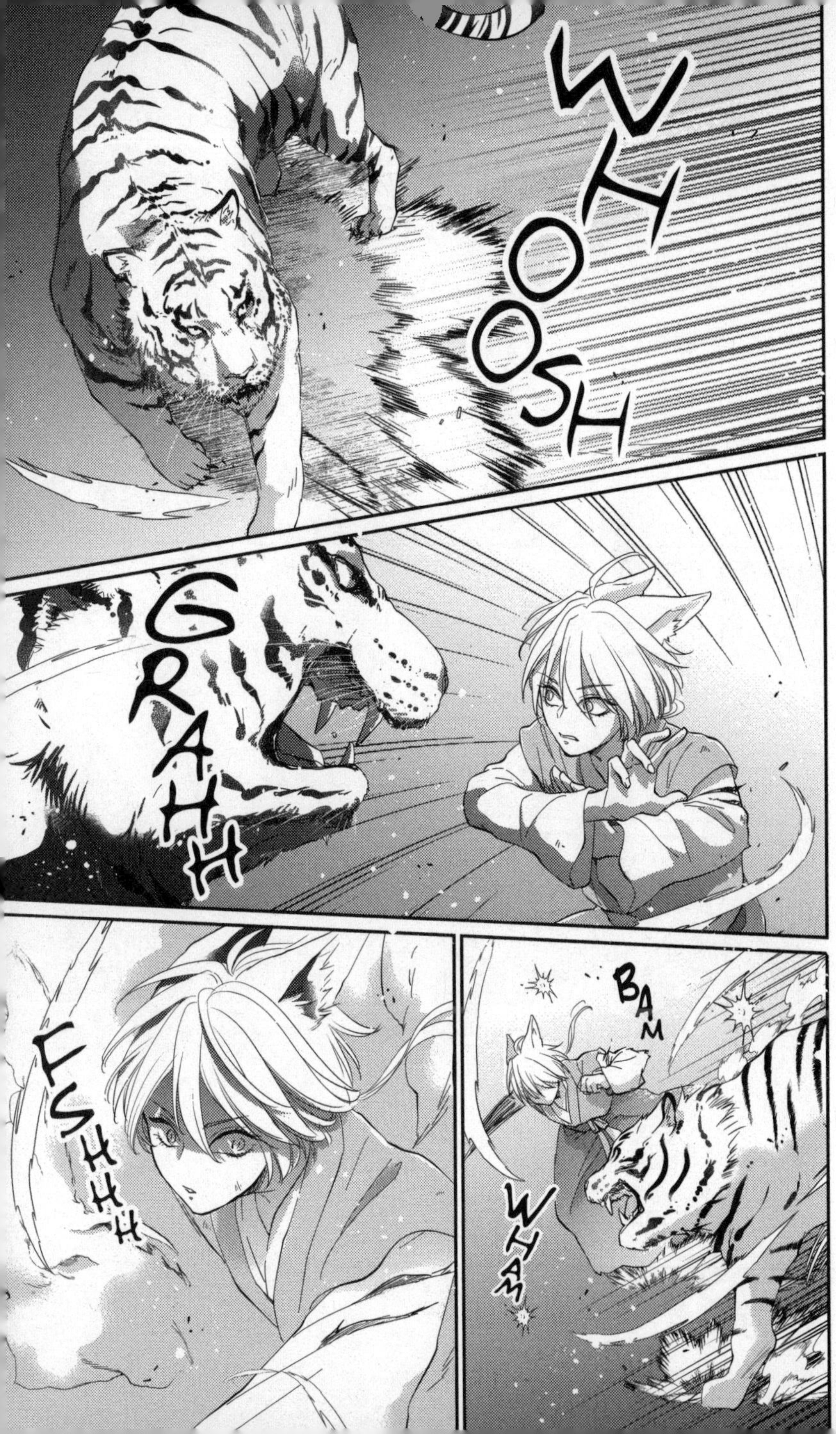
WHOOSH
GRAHH
BAM
WHAM
FSHHH

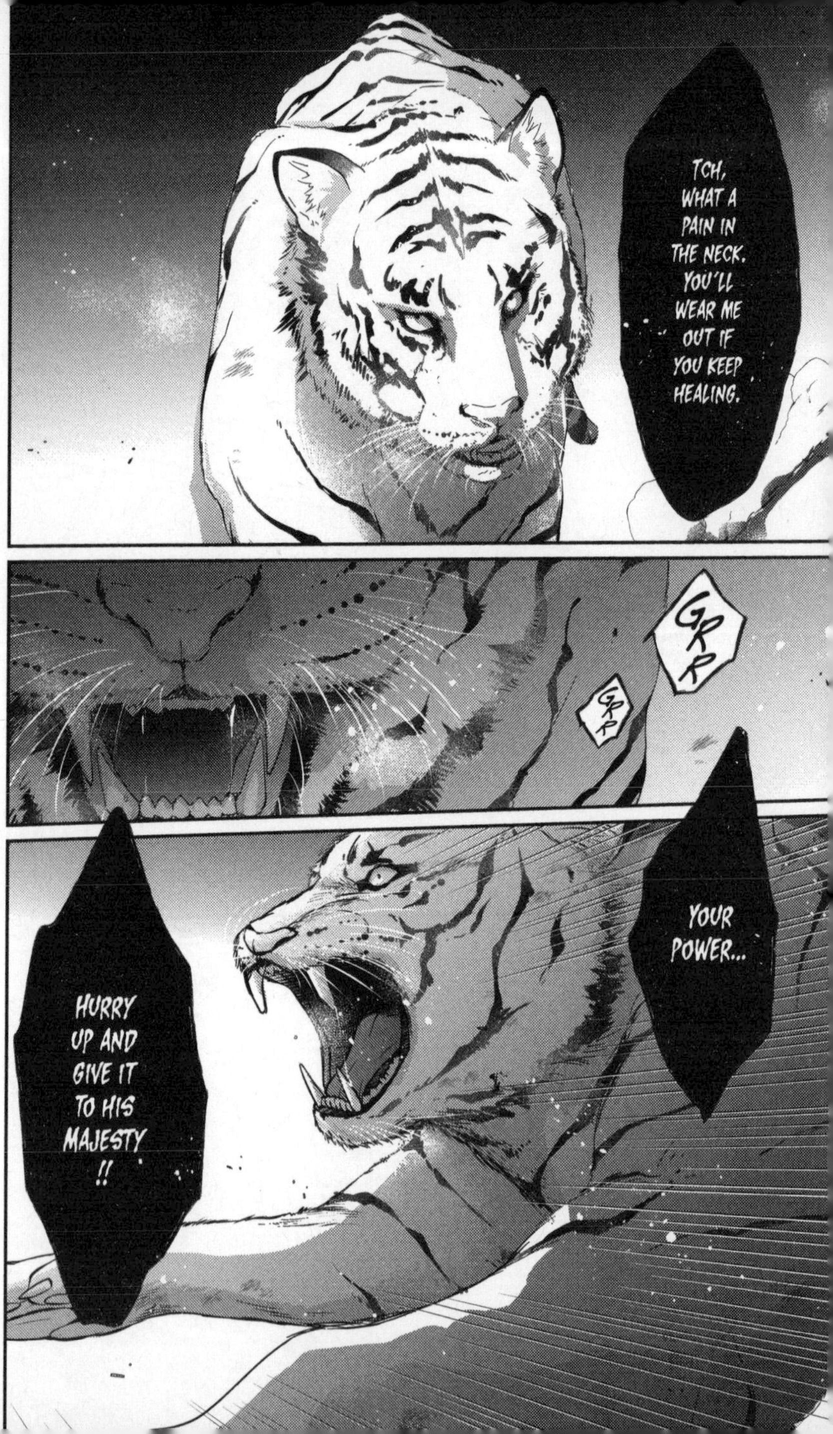
TCH, WHAT A PAIN IN THE NECK. YOU'LL WEAR ME OUT IF YOU KEEP HEALING.
GRR
GRR
YOUR POWER...
HURRY UP AND GIVE IT TO HIS MAJESTY!!

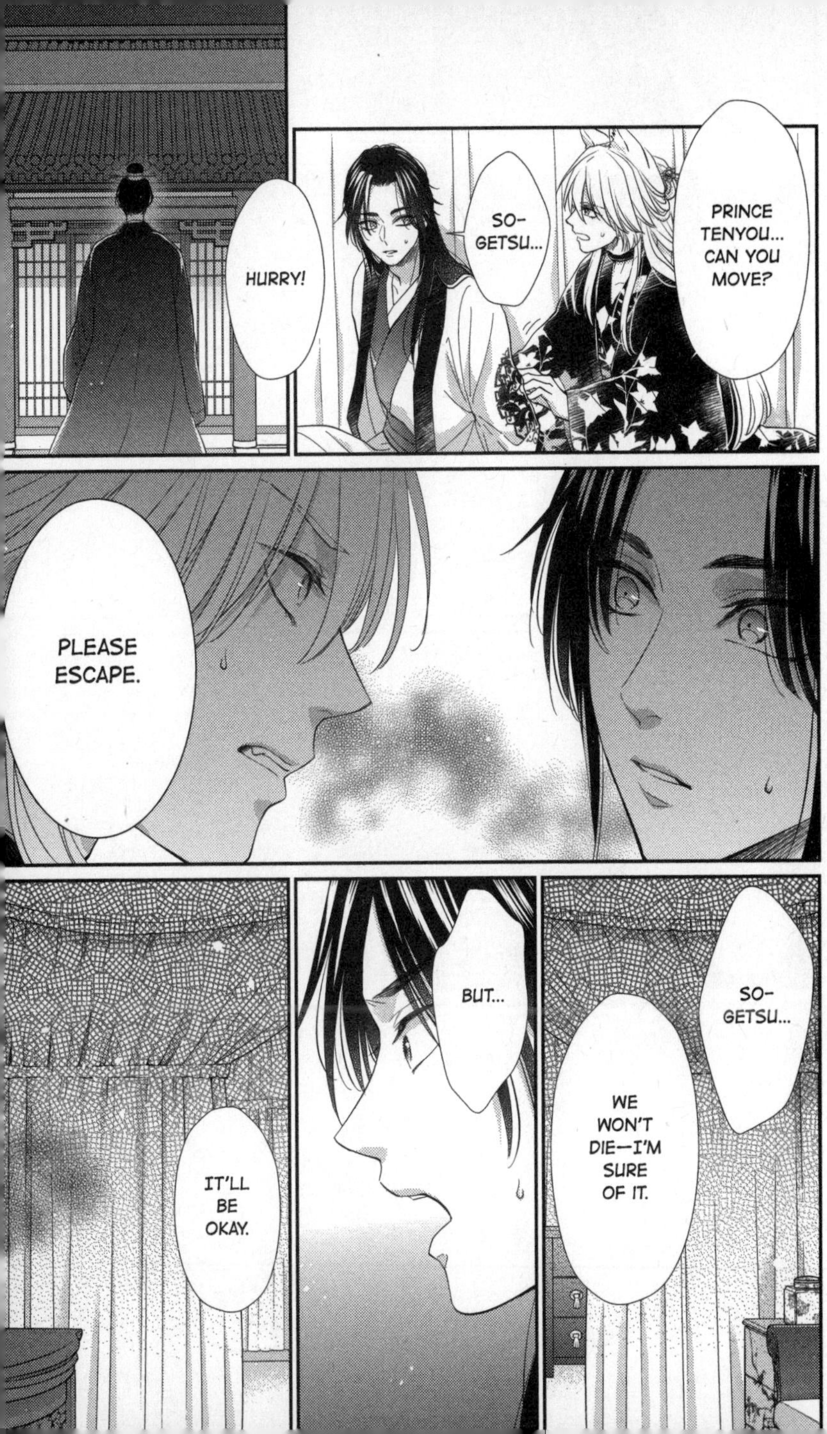
PRINCE TENYOU... CAN YOU MOVE?
SO-GETSU...
HURRY!
PLEASE ESCAPE.
SO-GETSU...
WE WON'T DIE—I'M SURE OF IT.
BUT...
IT'LL BE OKAY.

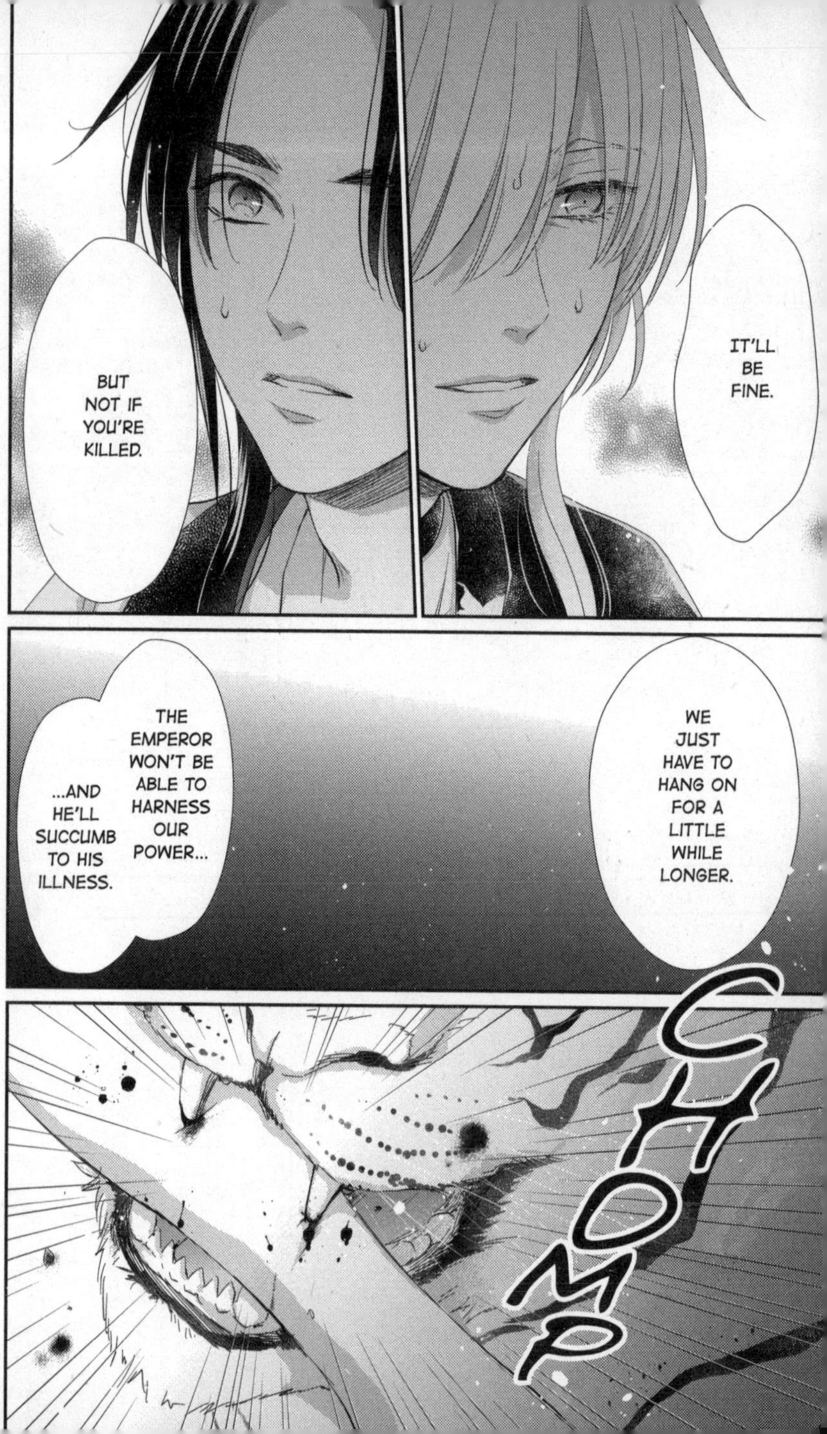
IT'LL BE FINE.
BUT NOT IF YOU'RE KILLED.
WE JUST HAVE TO HANG ON FOR A LITTLE WHILE LONGER.
THE EMPEROR WON'T BE ABLE TO HARNESS OUR POWER...
...AND HE'LL SUCCUMB TO HIS ILLNESS.
CHOMP

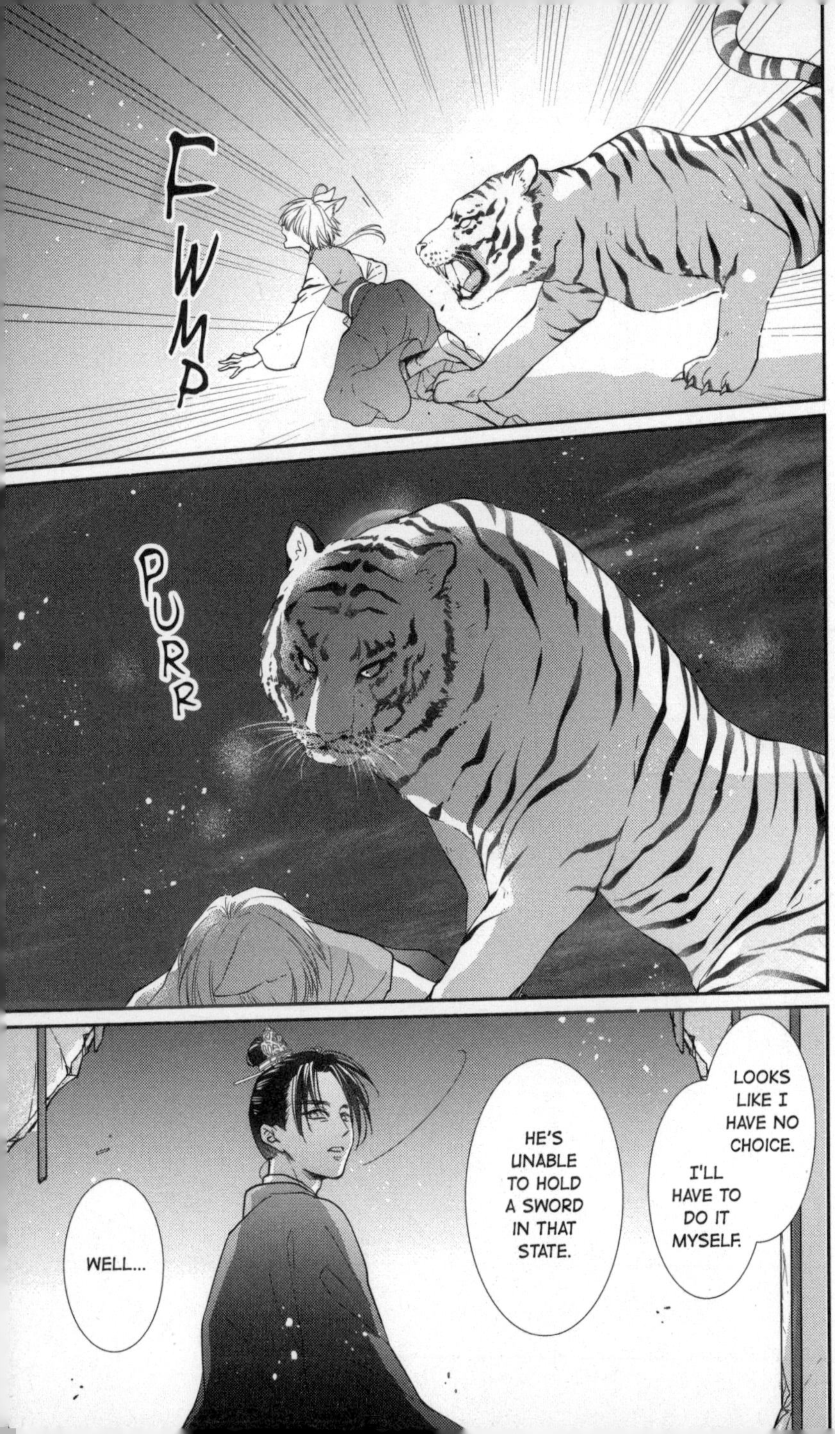
FWMP
PURR
LOOKS LIKE I HAVE NO CHOICE. I'LL HAVE TO DO IT MYSELF.
HE'S UNABLE TO HOLD A SWORD IN THAT STATE.
WELL...

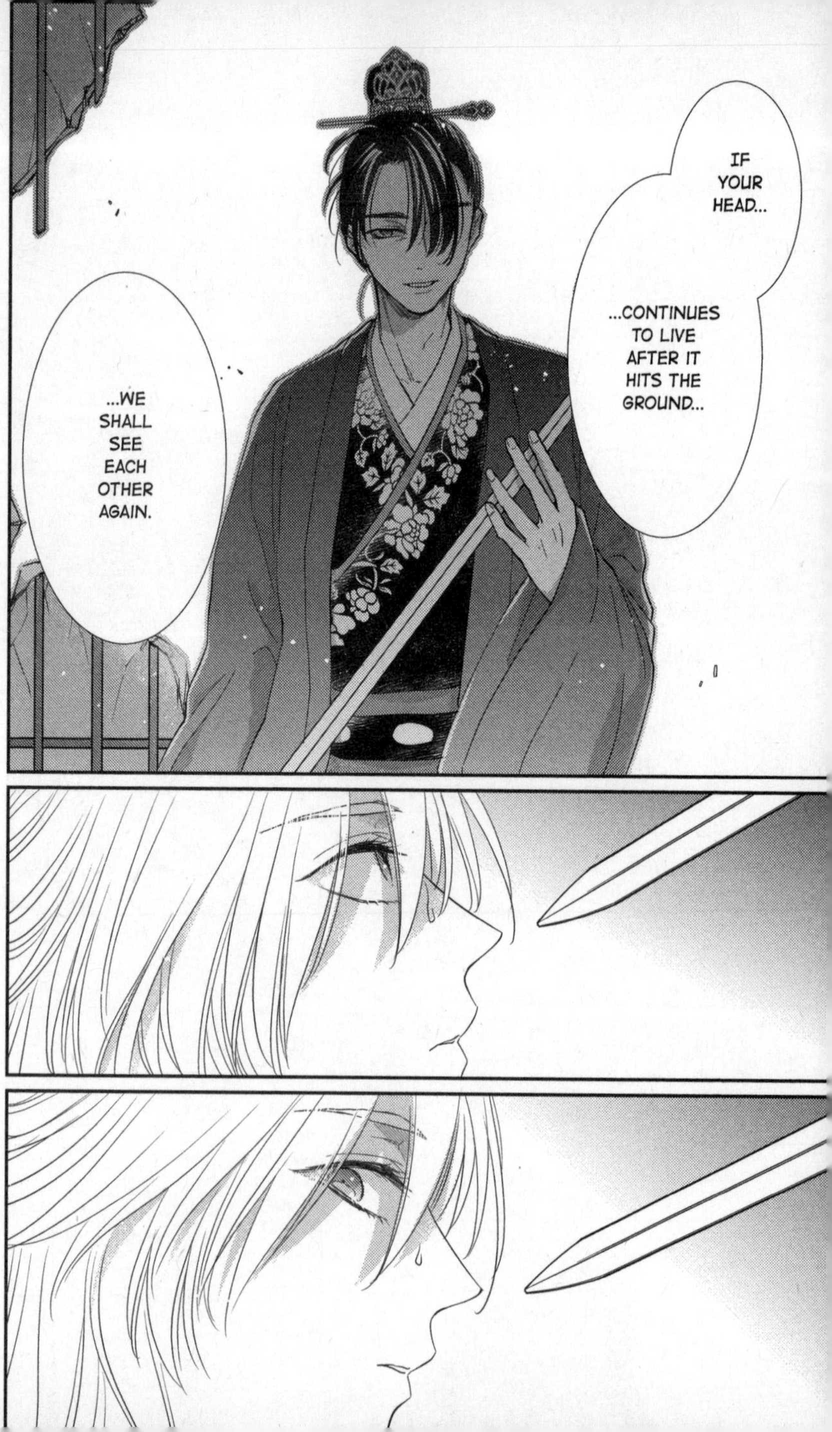
IF YOUR HEAD...
...CONTINUES TO LIVE AFTER IT HITS THE GROUND...
...WE SHALL SEE EACH OTHER AGAIN.

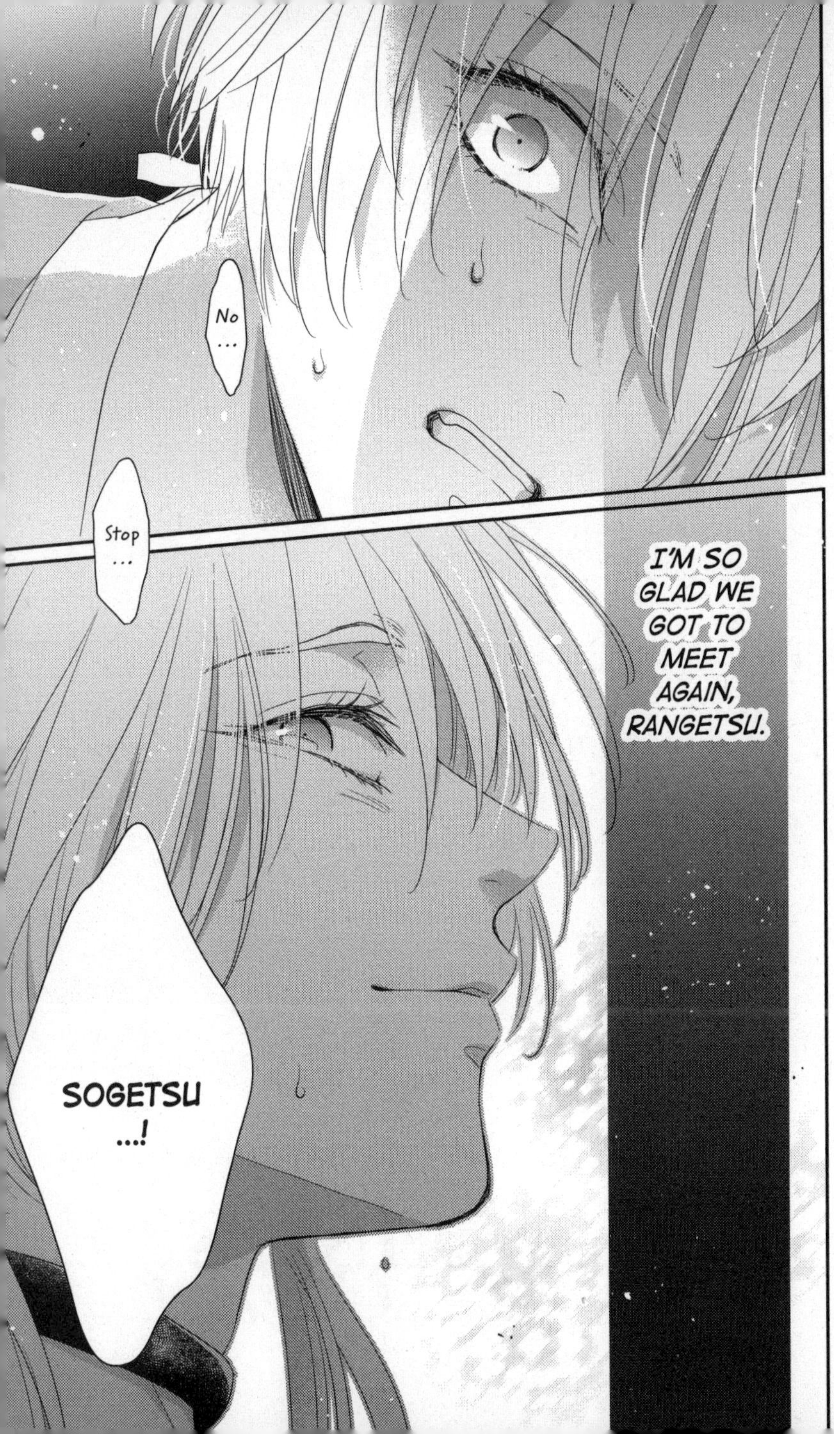
No ...
Stop ...
I'M SO GLAD WE GOT TO MEET AGAIN, RANGETSU.
SOGETSU ...!

THE
KING'S
Beast

Chapter 33

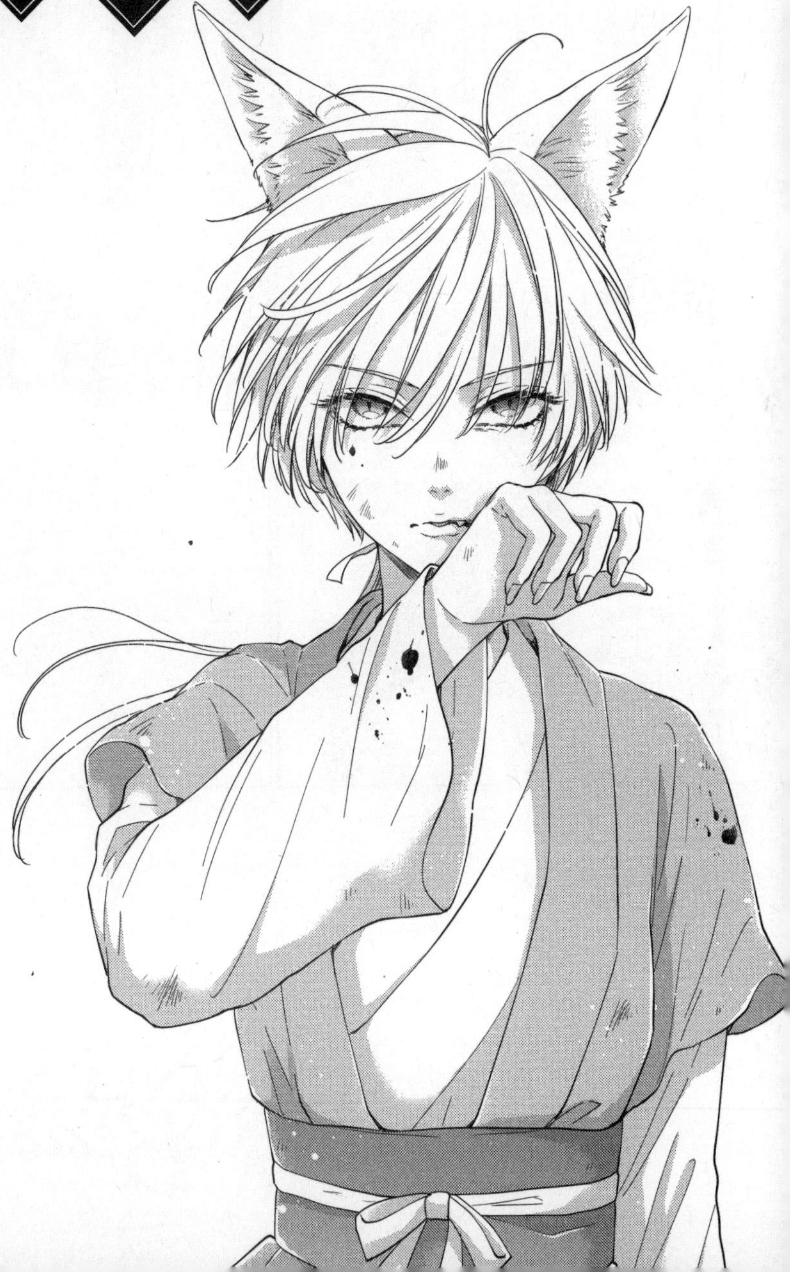

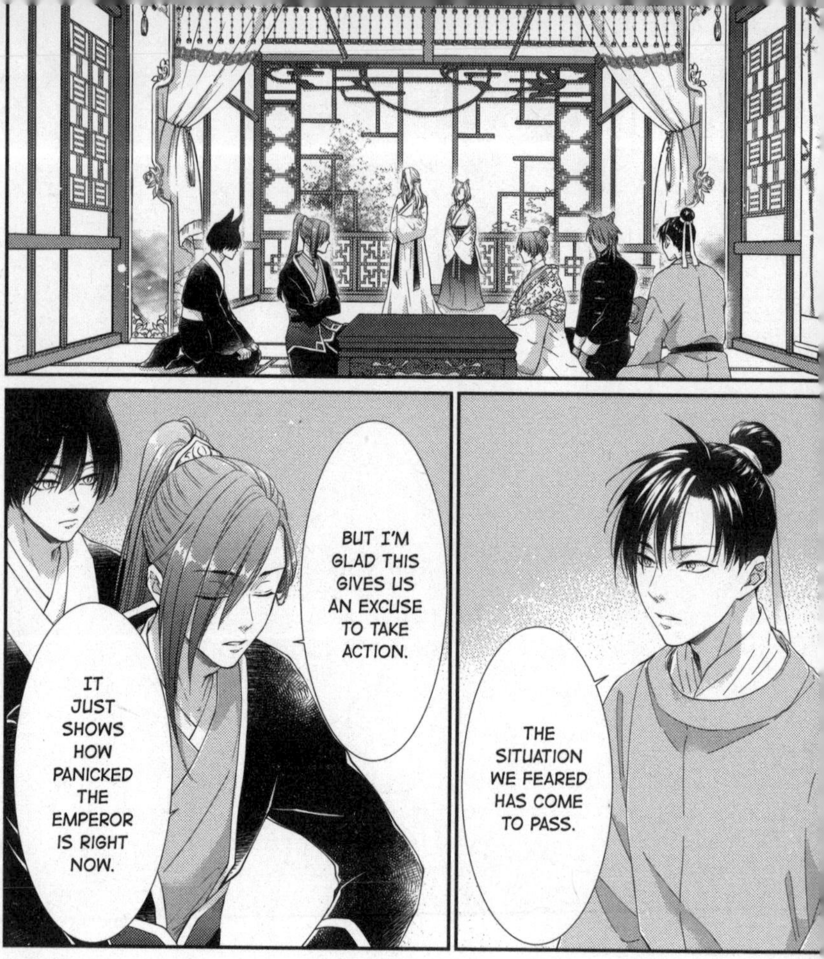
THE SITUATION WE FEARED HAS COME TO PASS.
BUT I'M GLAD THIS GIVES US AN EXCUSE TO TAKE ACTION.
IT JUST SHOWS HOW PANICKED THE EMPEROR IS RIGHT NOW.

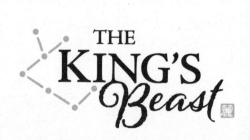

THE KING'S Beast

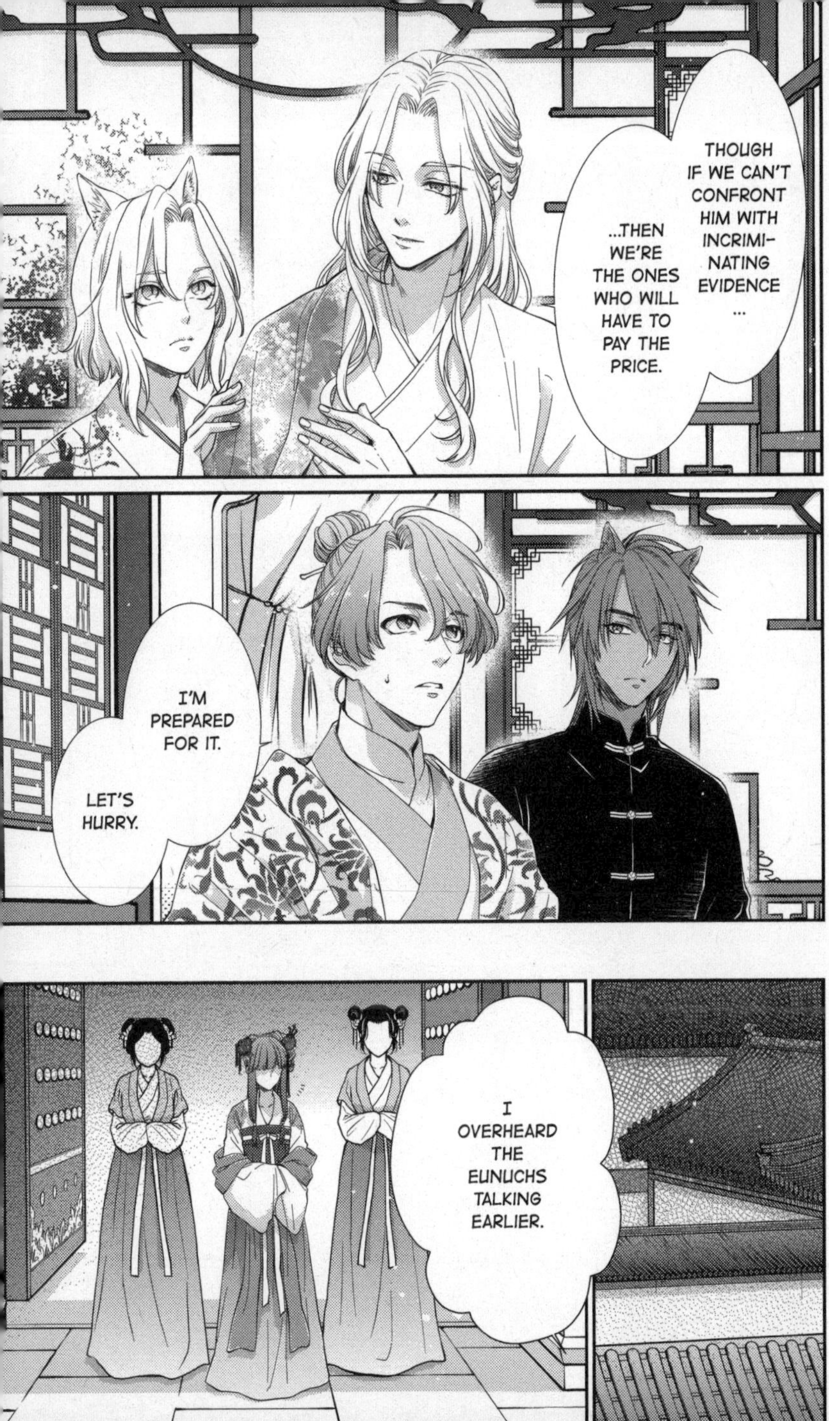
THOUGH IF WE CAN'T CONFRONT HIM WITH INCRIMI-NATING EVIDENCE...
...THEN WE'RE THE ONES WHO WILL HAVE TO PAY THE PRICE.
I'M PREPARED FOR IT.
LET'S HURRY.
I OVERHEARD THE EUNUCHS TALKING EARLIER.

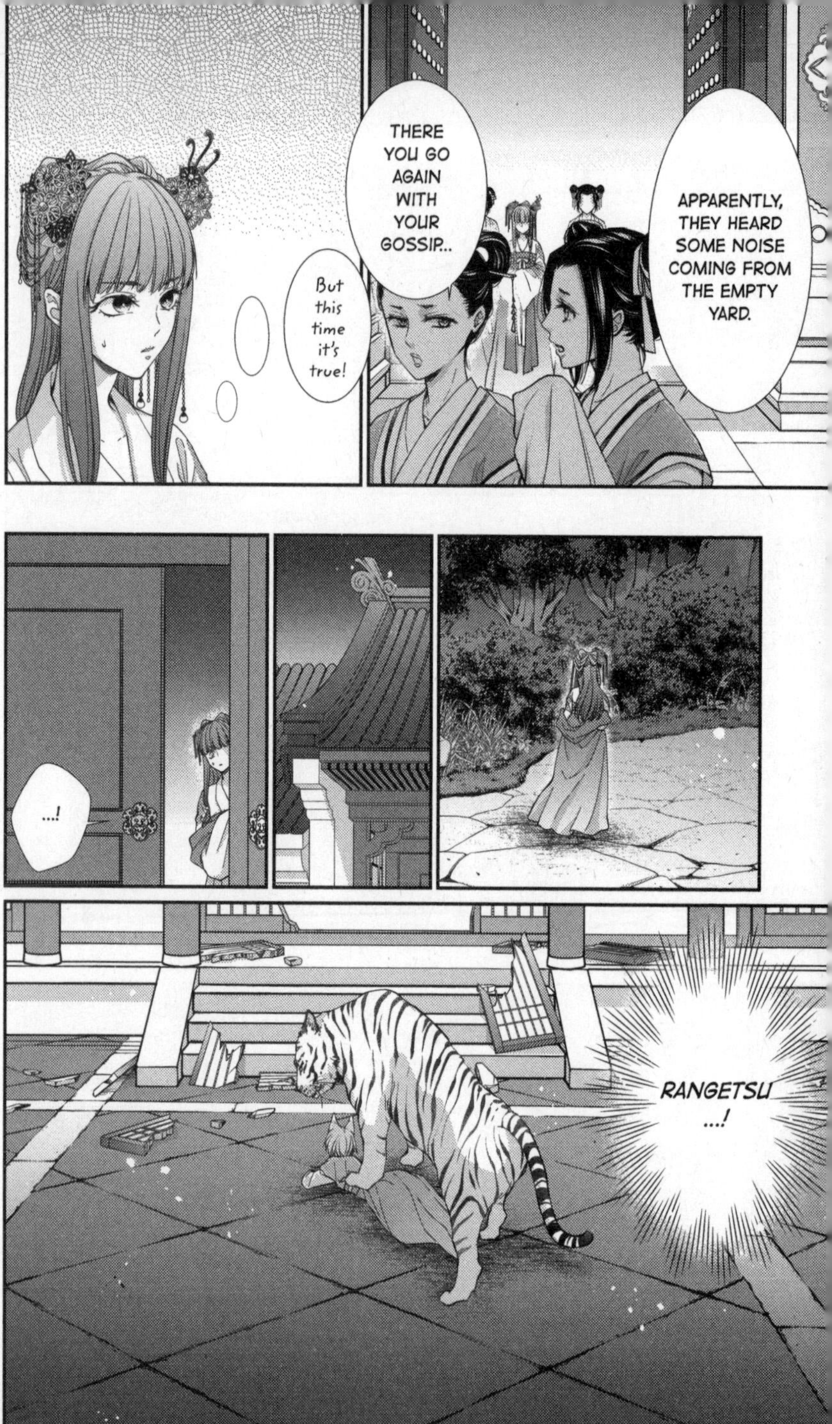
APPARENTLY, THEY HEARD SOME NOISE COMING FROM THE EMPTY YARD.
THERE YOU GO AGAIN WITH YOUR GOSSIP...
But this time it's true!
...!
RANGETSU ...!

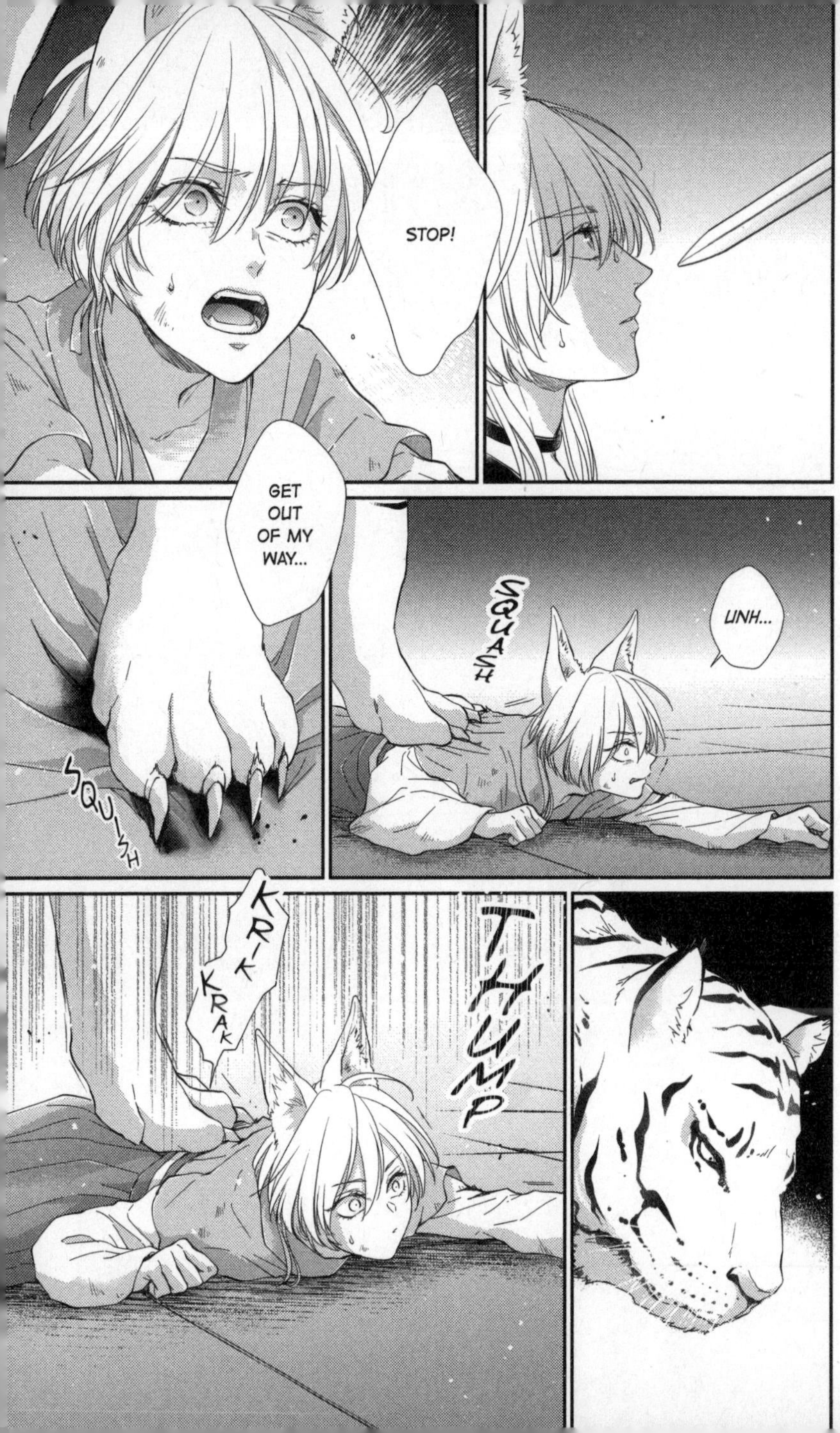
STOP!
GET OUT OF MY WAY...
UNH...
SQUASH
SQUISH
THUMP
KRIK
KRAK

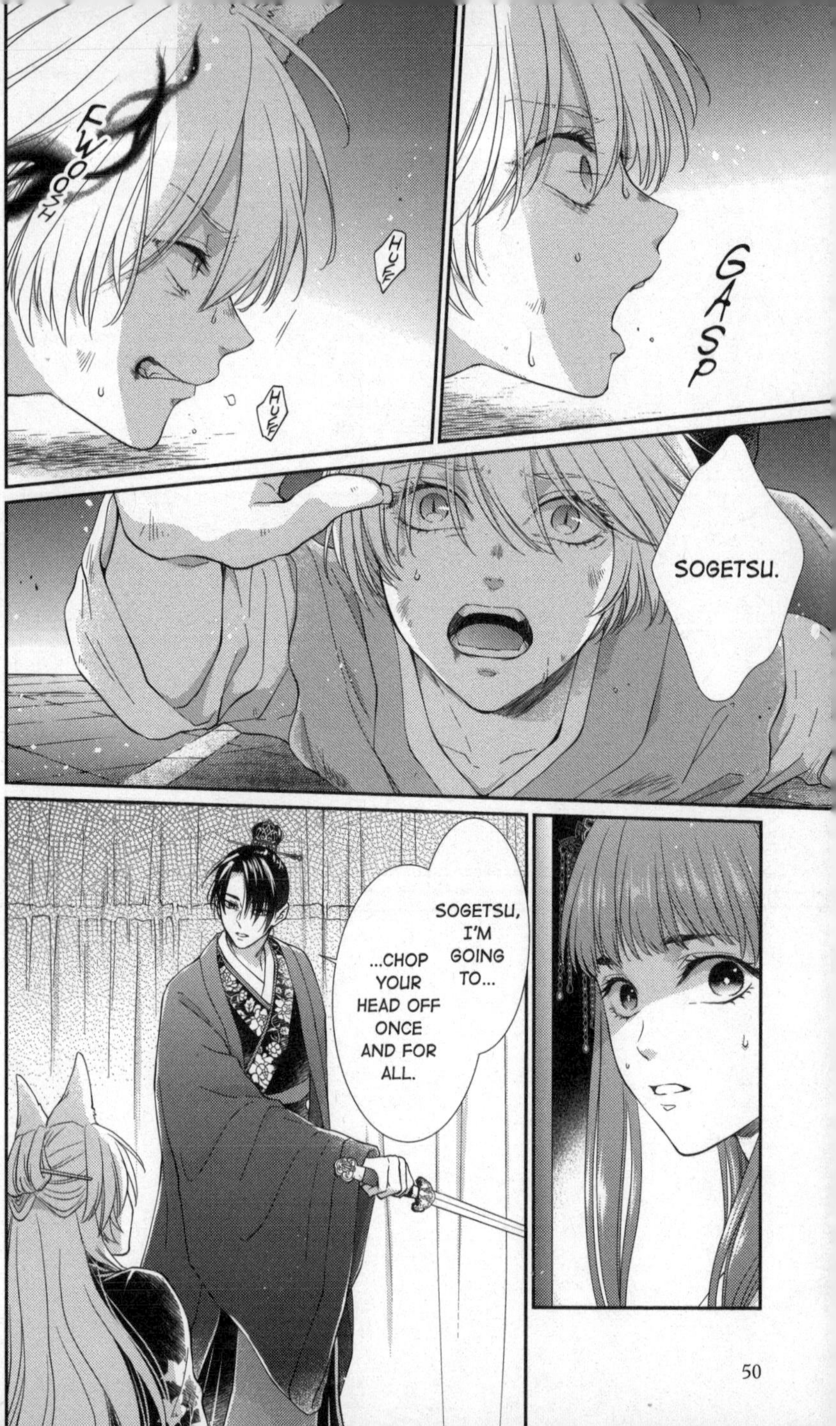
GASP
KWOOSH
HUF
HUF
SOGETSU.
SOGETSU, I'M GOING TO...
...CHOP YOUR HEAD OFF ONCE AND FOR ALL.

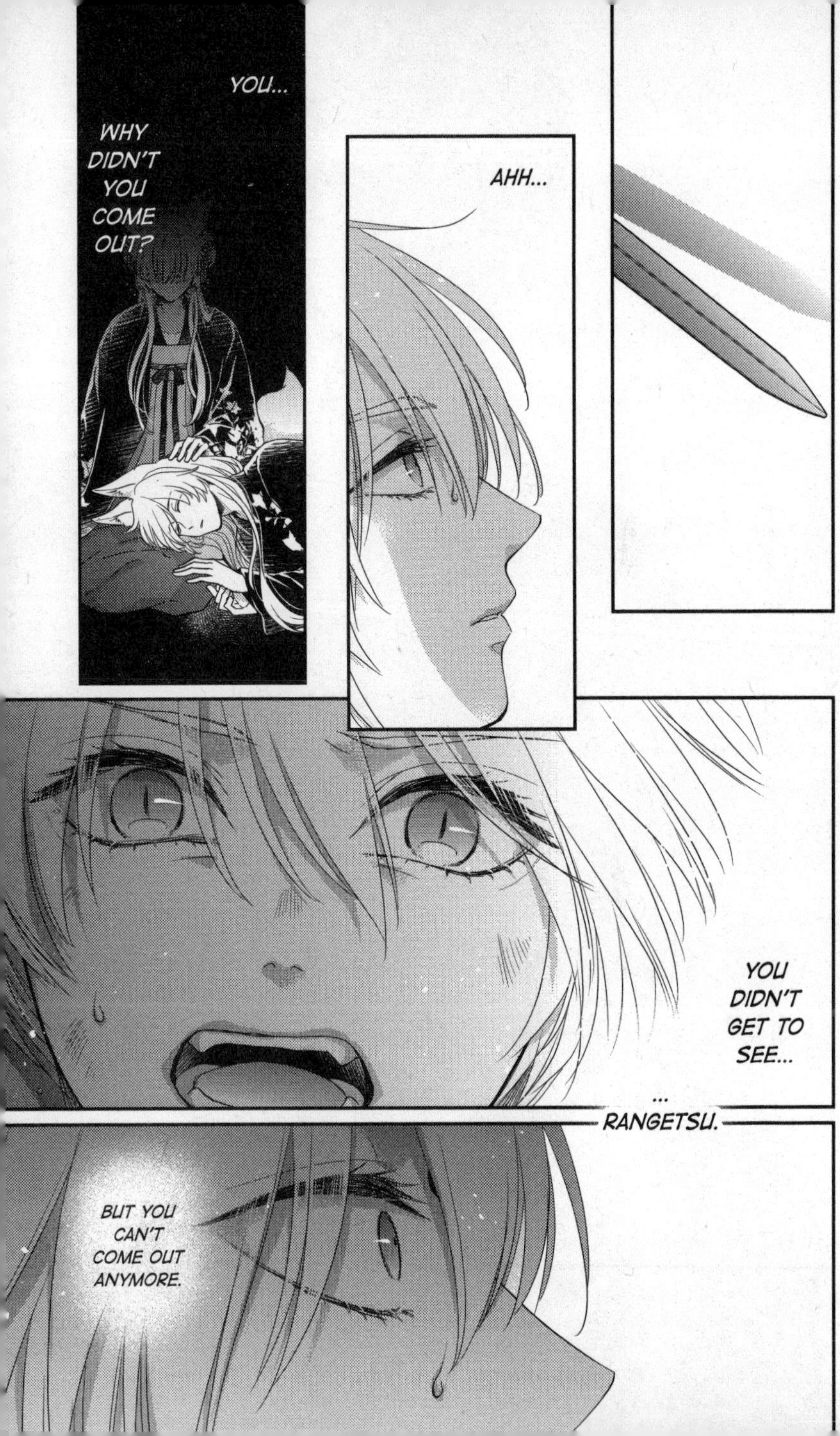
AHH...
YOU...
WHY DIDN'T YOU COME OUT?
YOU DIDN'T GET TO SEE...
...RANGETSU.
BUT YOU CAN'T COME OUT ANYMORE.

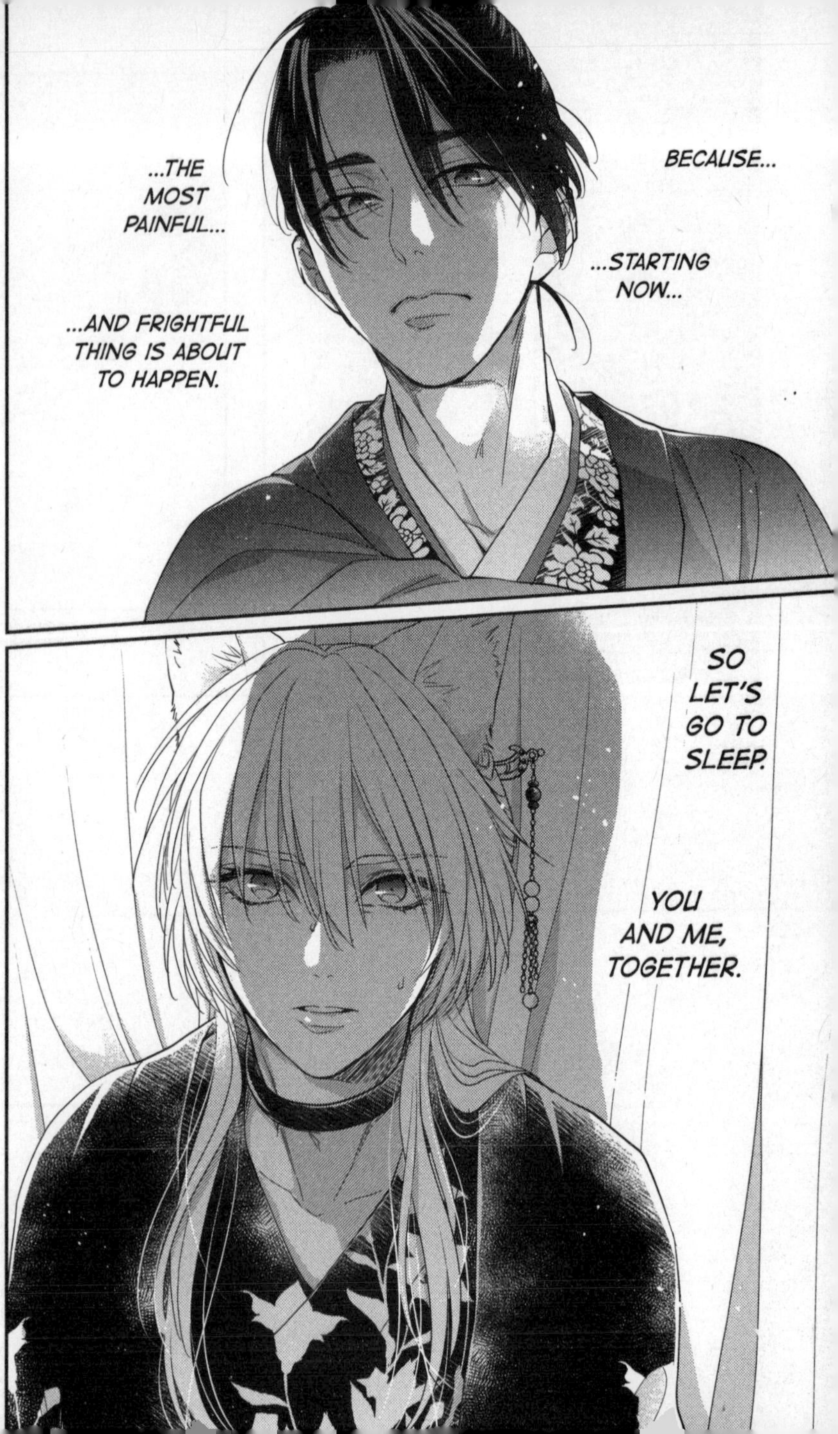
BECAUSE...
...STARTING NOW...
...THE MOST PAINFUL...
...AND FRIGHTFUL THING IS ABOUT TO HAPPEN.
SO LET'S GO TO SLEEP.
YOU AND ME, TOGETHER.

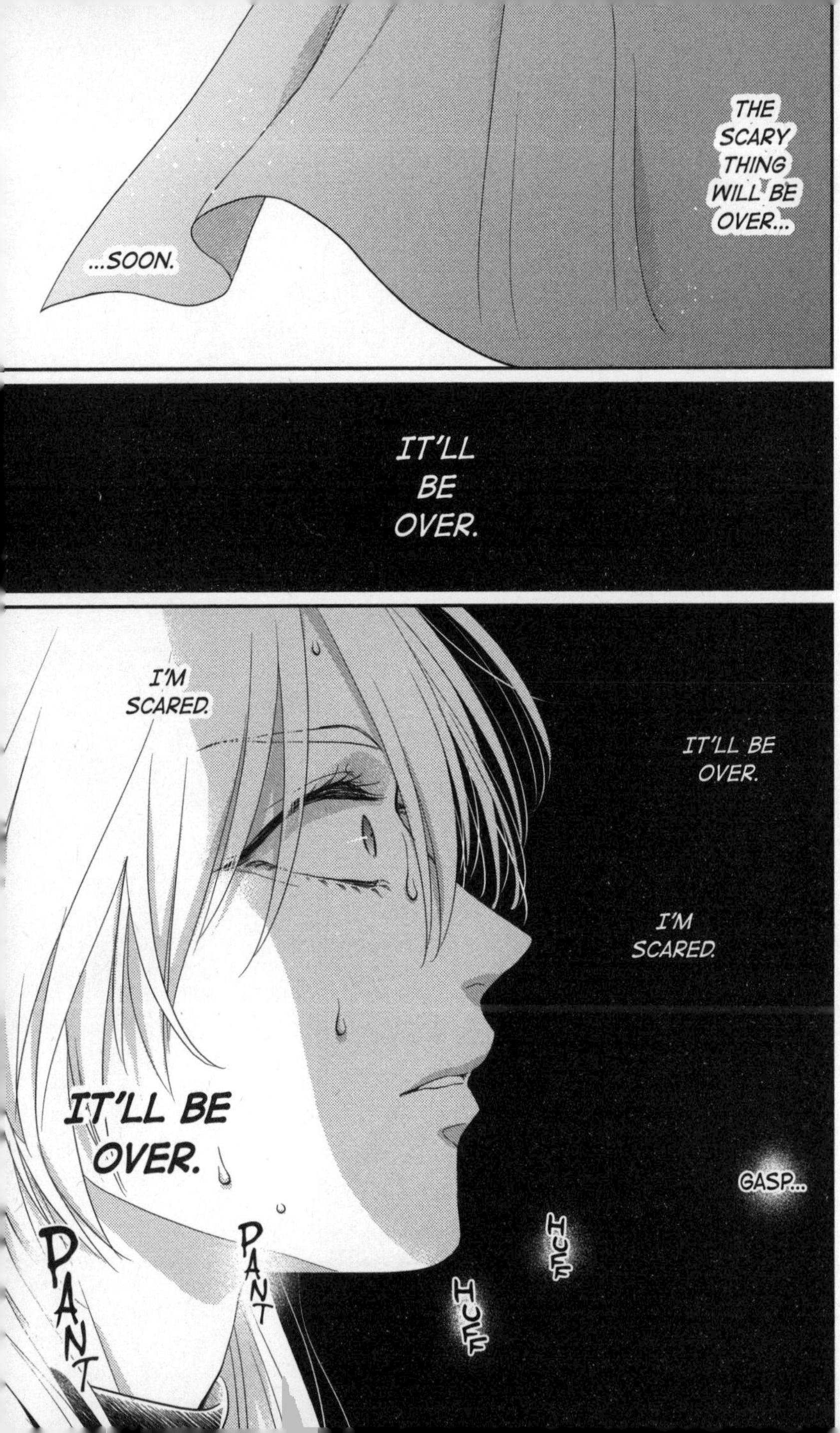
THE SCARY THING WILL BE OVER...
...SOON.
IT'LL BE OVER.
I'M SCARED.
IT'LL BE OVER.
I'M SCARED.
IT'LL BE OVER.
GASP...
HUFF
HUFF
PANT
PANT

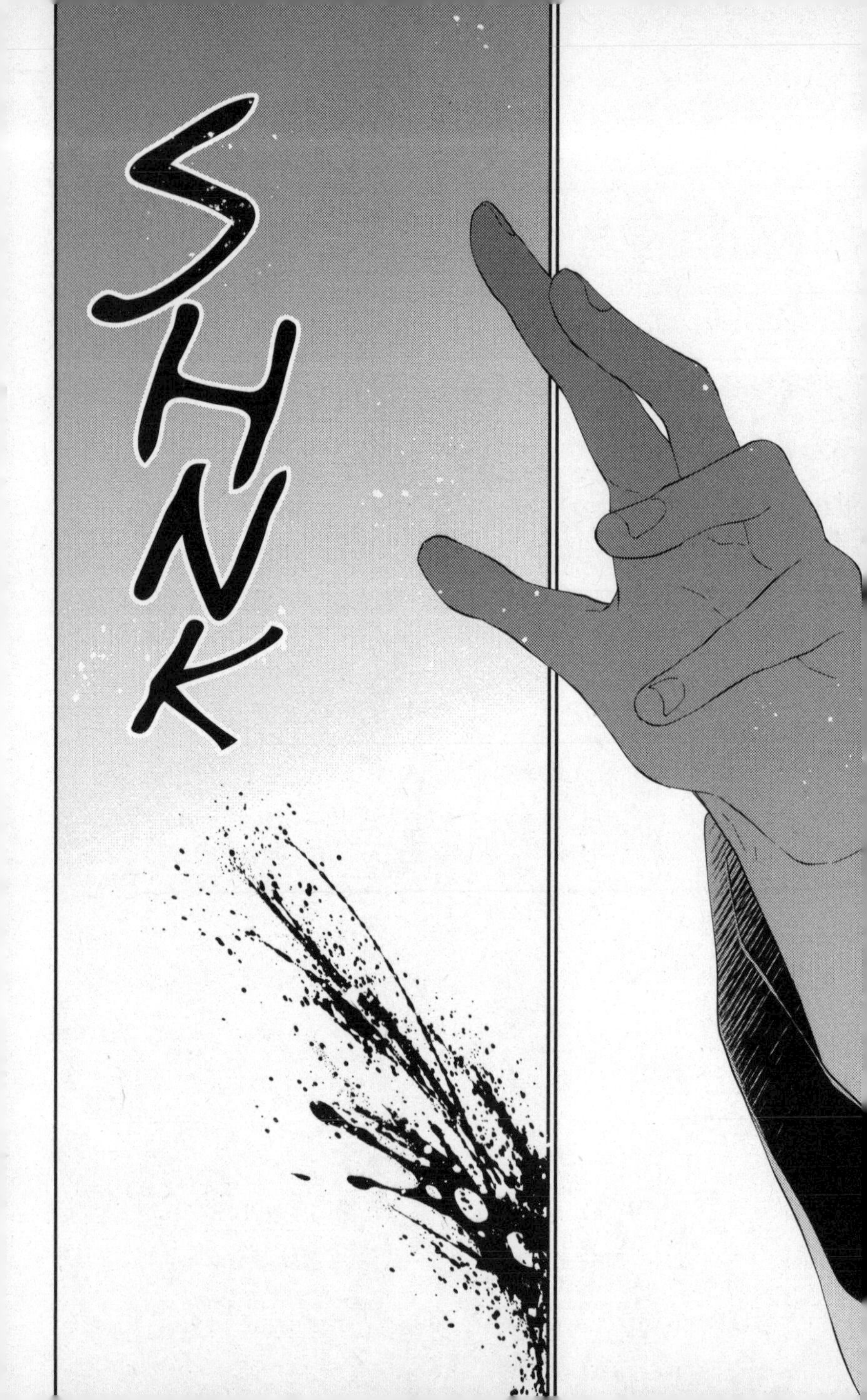
SHNK

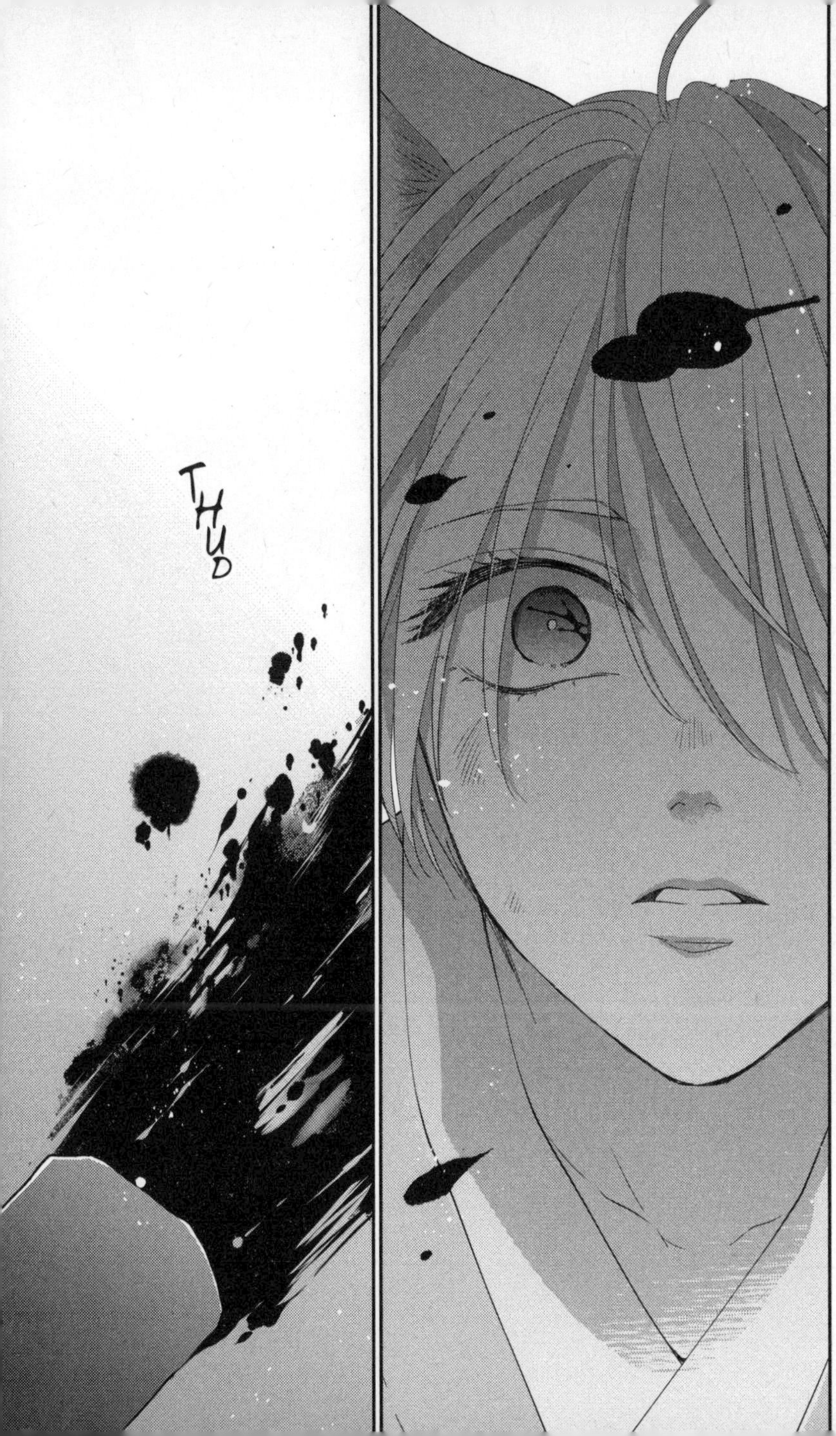
THUD

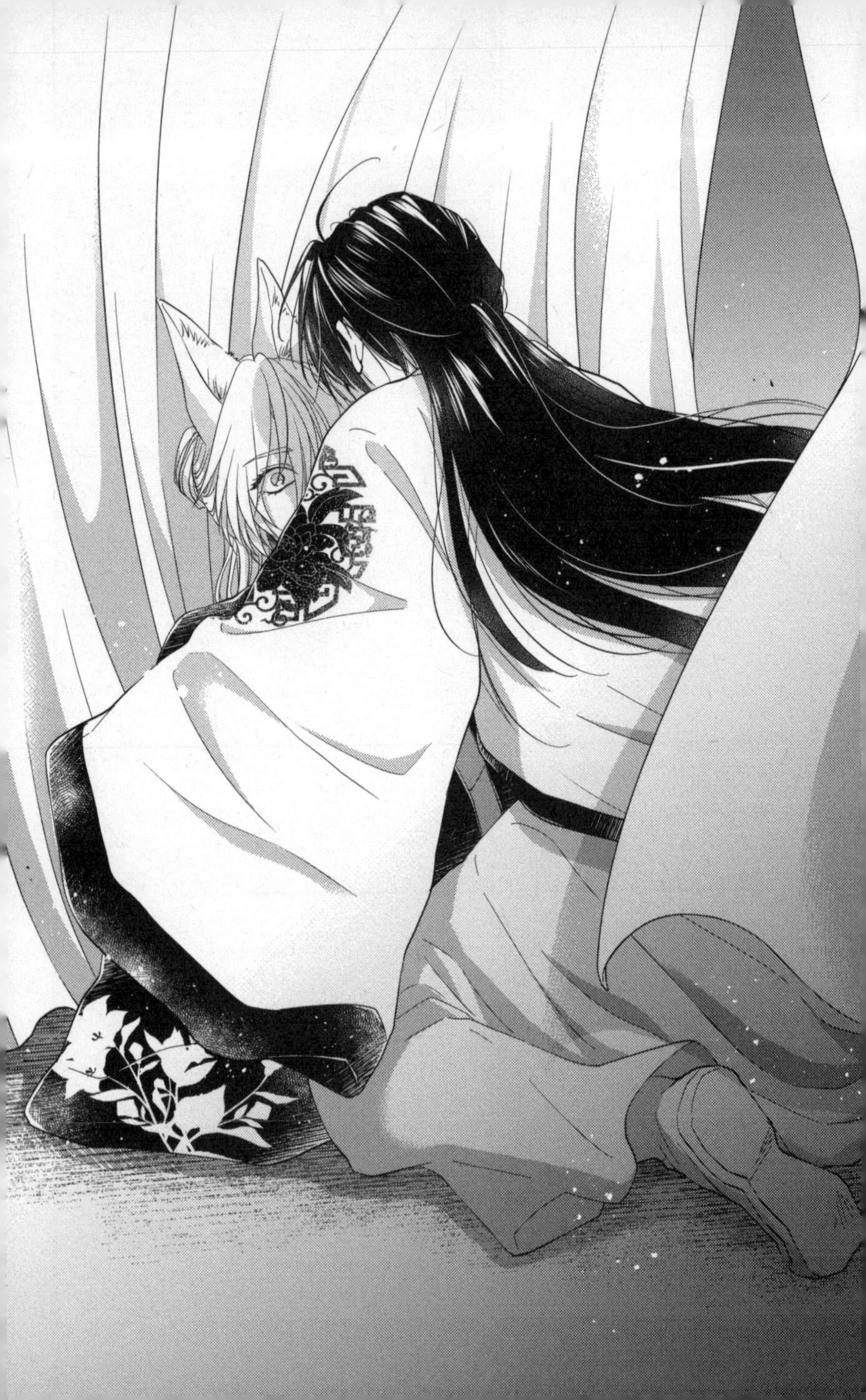

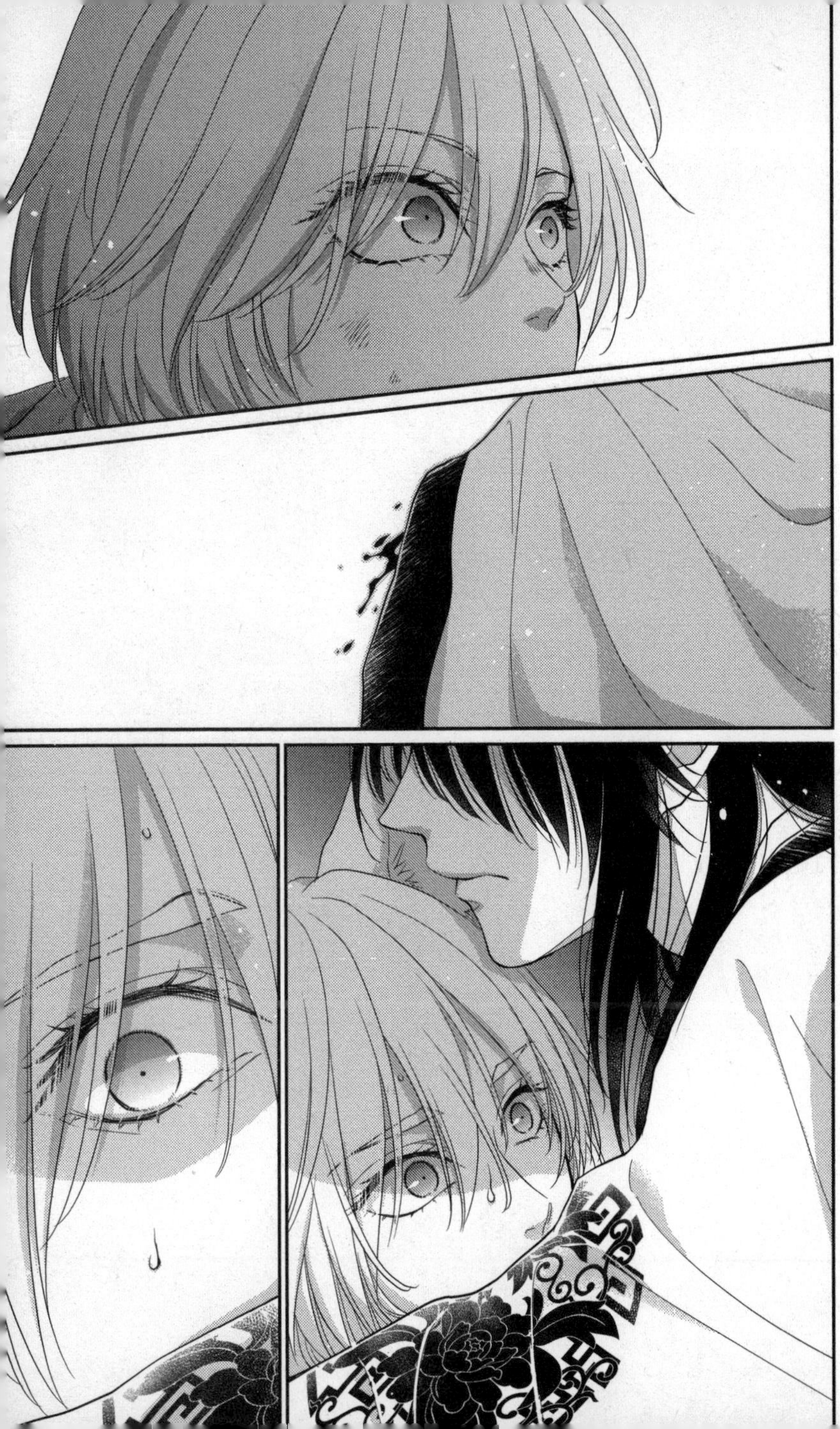

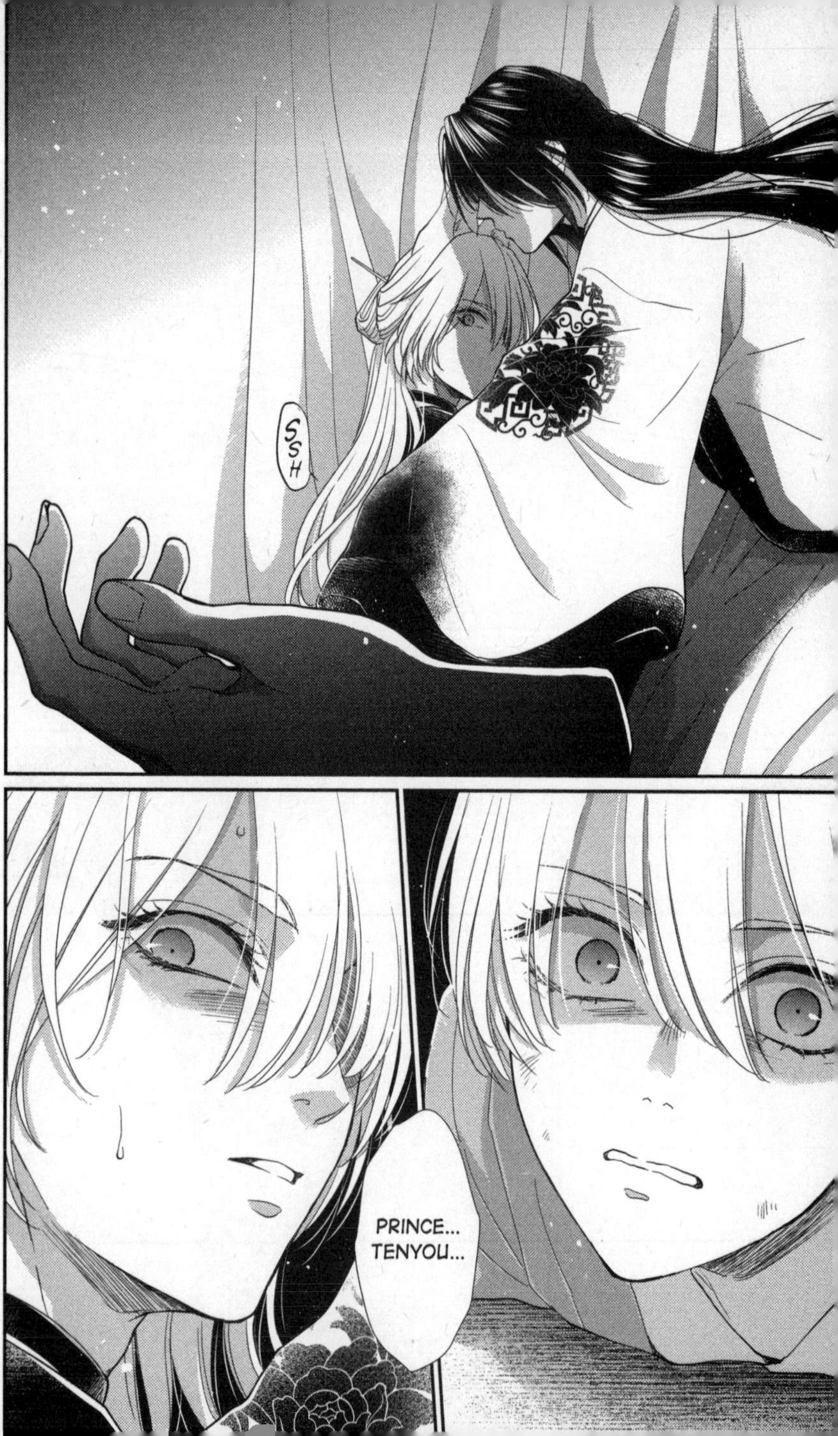
SSH
PRINCE... TENYOU...

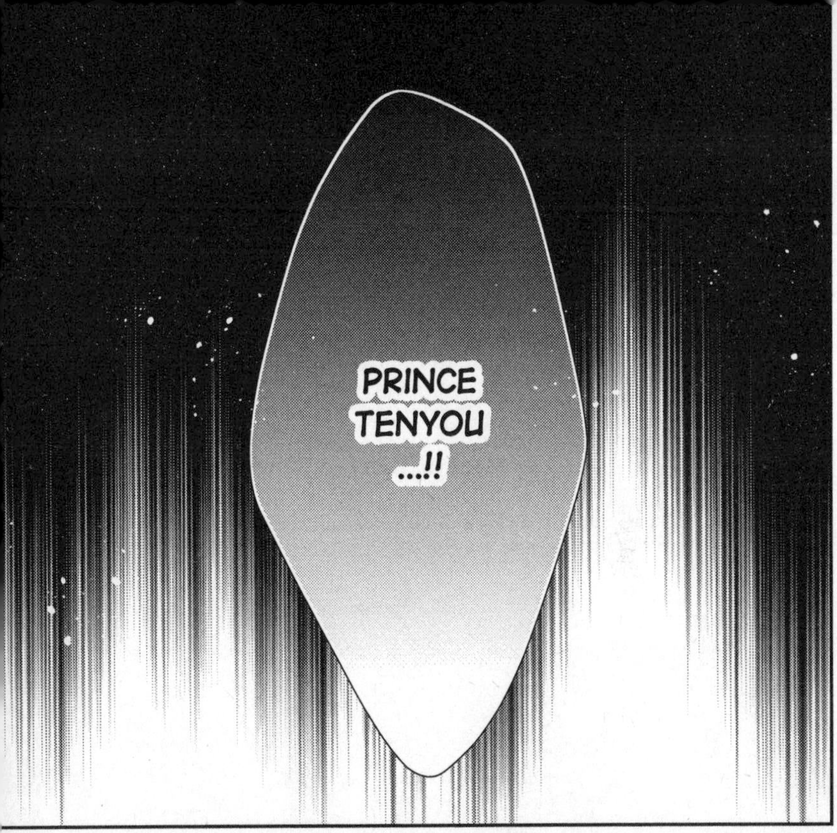
PRINCE TENYOU ...!!
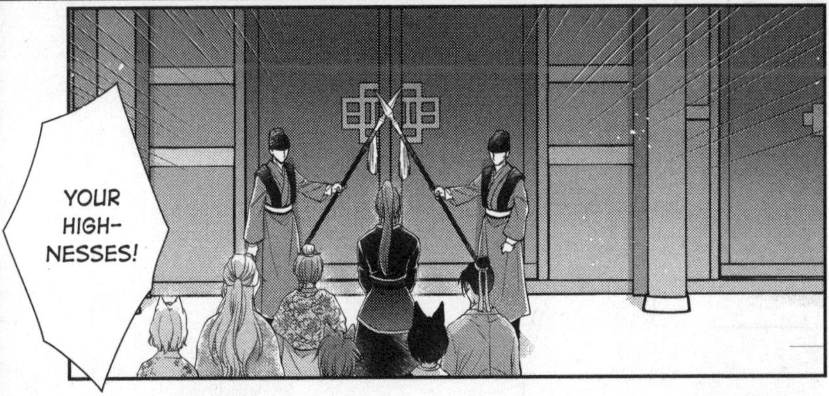
YOUR HIGH-NESSES!

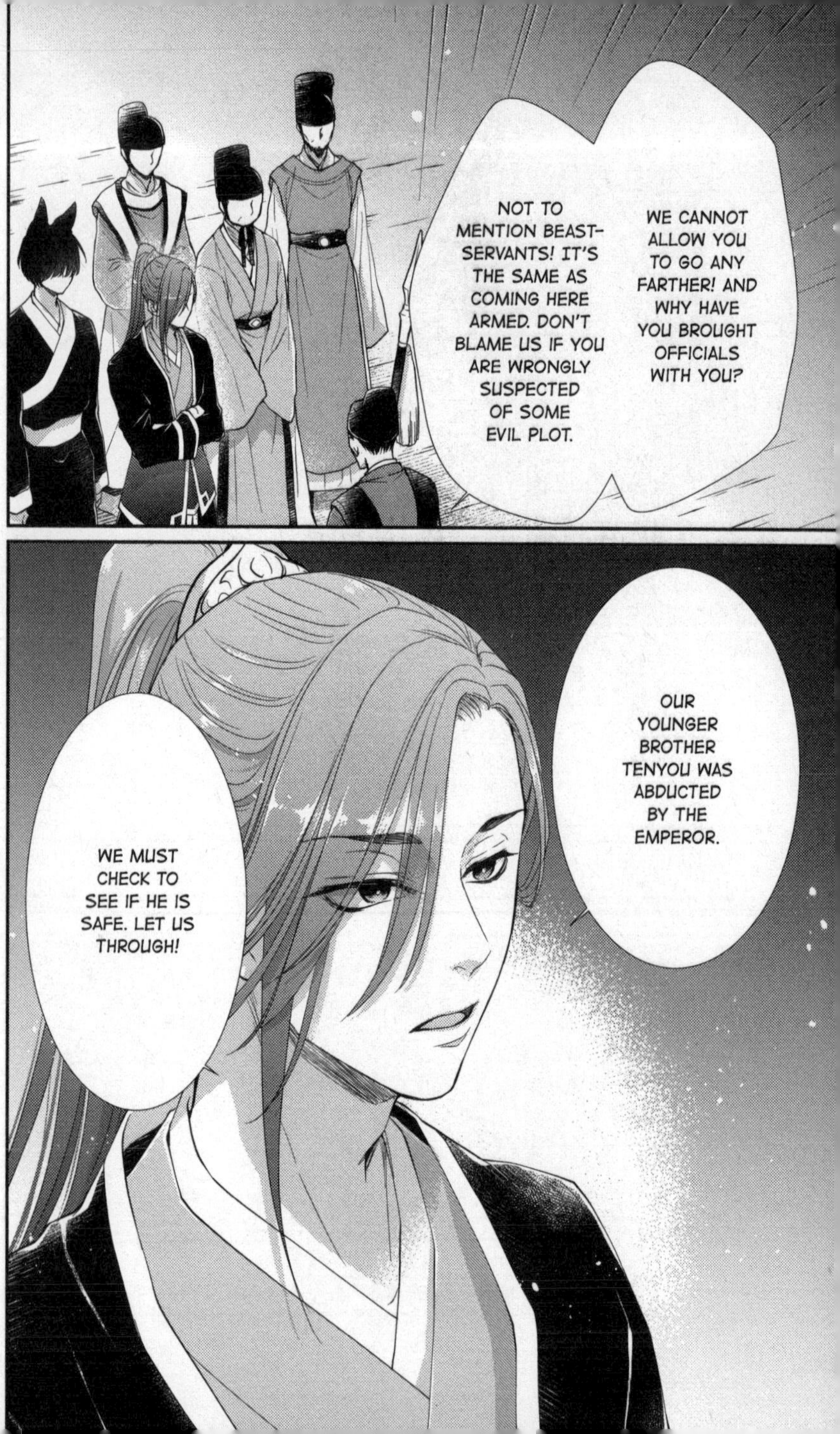
WE CANNOT ALLOW YOU TO GO ANY FARTHER! AND WHY HAVE YOU BROUGHT OFFICIALS WITH YOU?
NOT TO MENTION BEAST-SERVANTS! IT'S THE SAME AS COMING HERE ARMED. DON'T BLAME US IF YOU ARE WRONGLY SUSPECTED OF SOME EVIL PLOT.
OUR YOUNGER BROTHER TENYOU WAS ABDUCTED BY THE EMPEROR.
WE MUST CHECK TO SEE IF HE IS SAFE. LET US THROUGH!

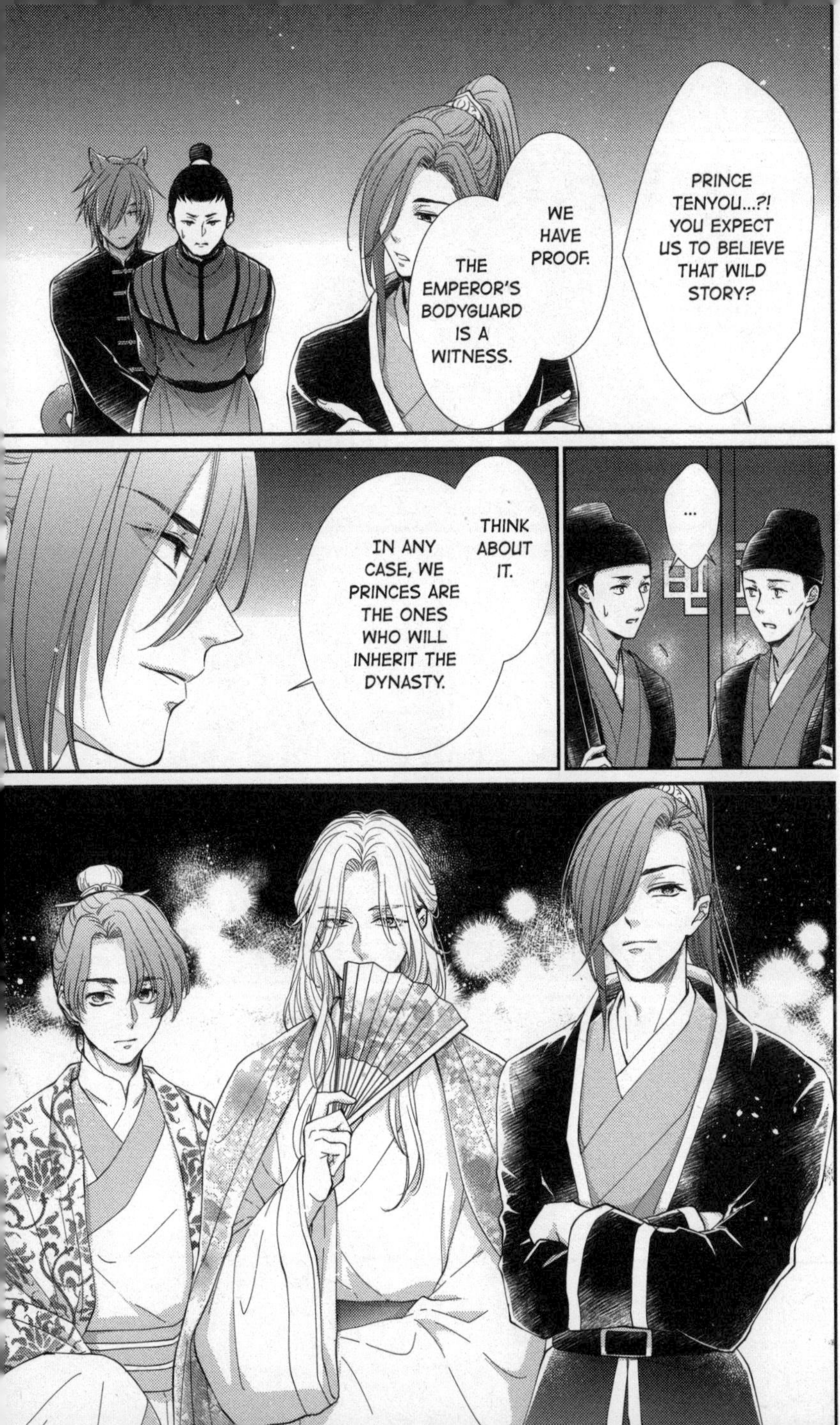
PRINCE TENYOU...?! YOU EXPECT US TO BELIEVE THAT WILD STORY?
WE HAVE PROOF.
THE EMPEROR'S BODYGUARD IS A WITNESS.
...
THINK ABOUT IT.
IN ANY CASE, WE PRINCES ARE THE ONES WHO WILL INHERIT THE DYNASTY.

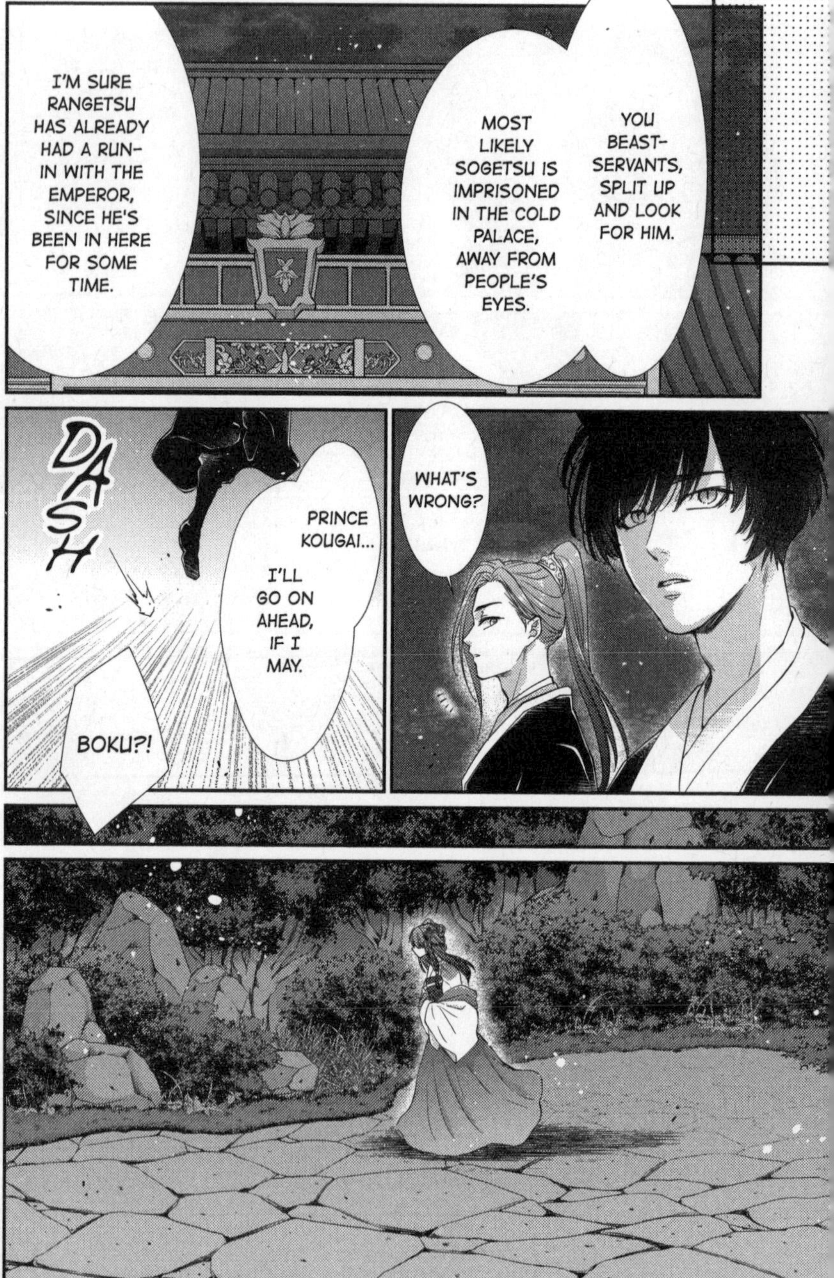
YOU BEAST-SERVANTS, SPLIT UP AND LOOK FOR HIM.
MOST LIKELY SOGETSU IS IMPRISONED IN THE COLD PALACE, AWAY FROM PEOPLE'S EYES.
I'M SURE RANGETSU HAS ALREADY HAD A RUN-IN WITH THE EMPEROR, SINCE HE'S BEEN IN HERE FOR SOME TIME.
WHAT'S WRONG?
PRINCE KOUGAI...
I'LL GO ON AHEAD, IF I MAY.
DASH
BOKU?!

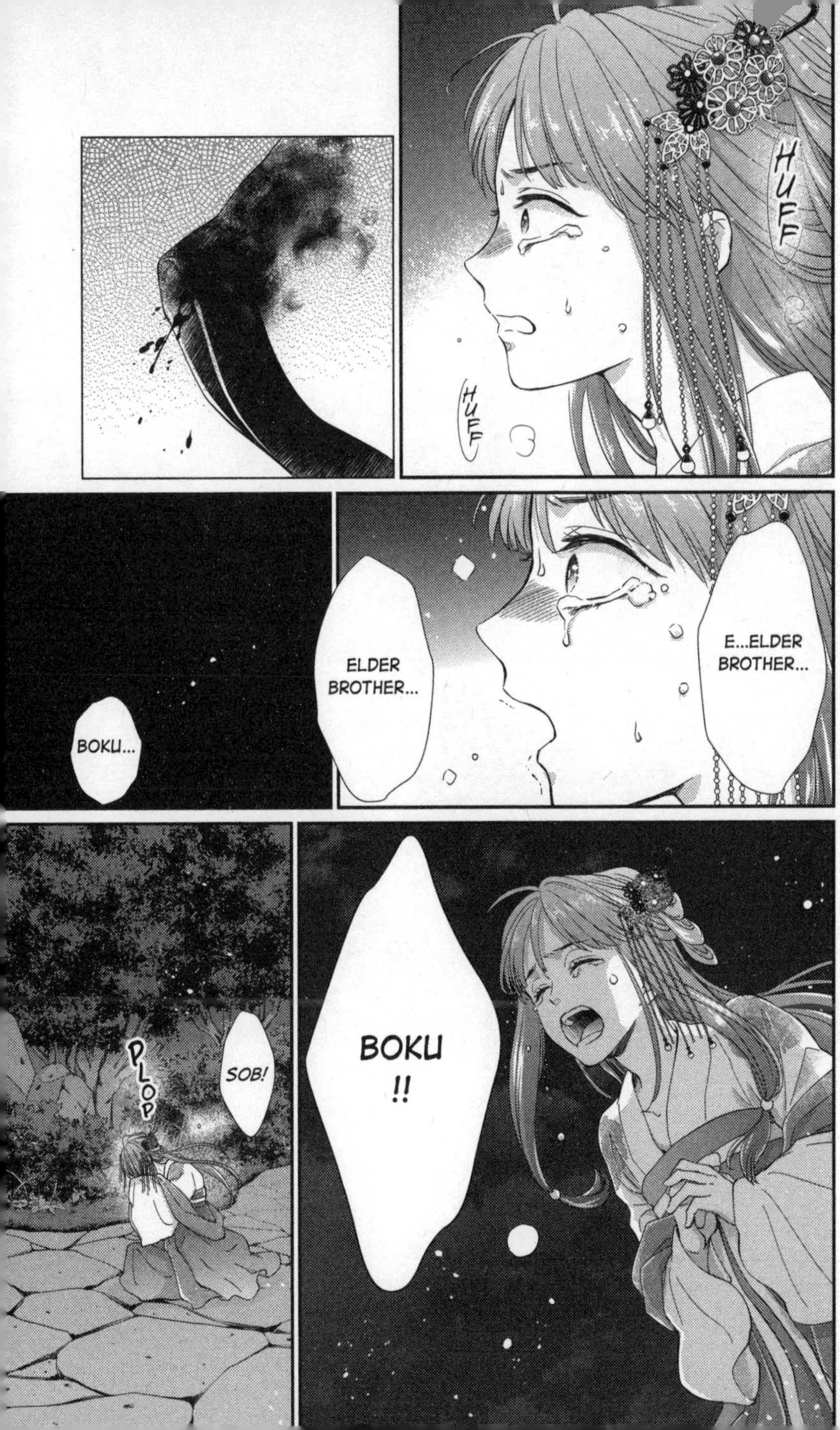
HUFF
HUFF
E...ELDER BROTHER...
ELDER BROTHER...
BOKU...
BOKU !!
SOB!
PLOP

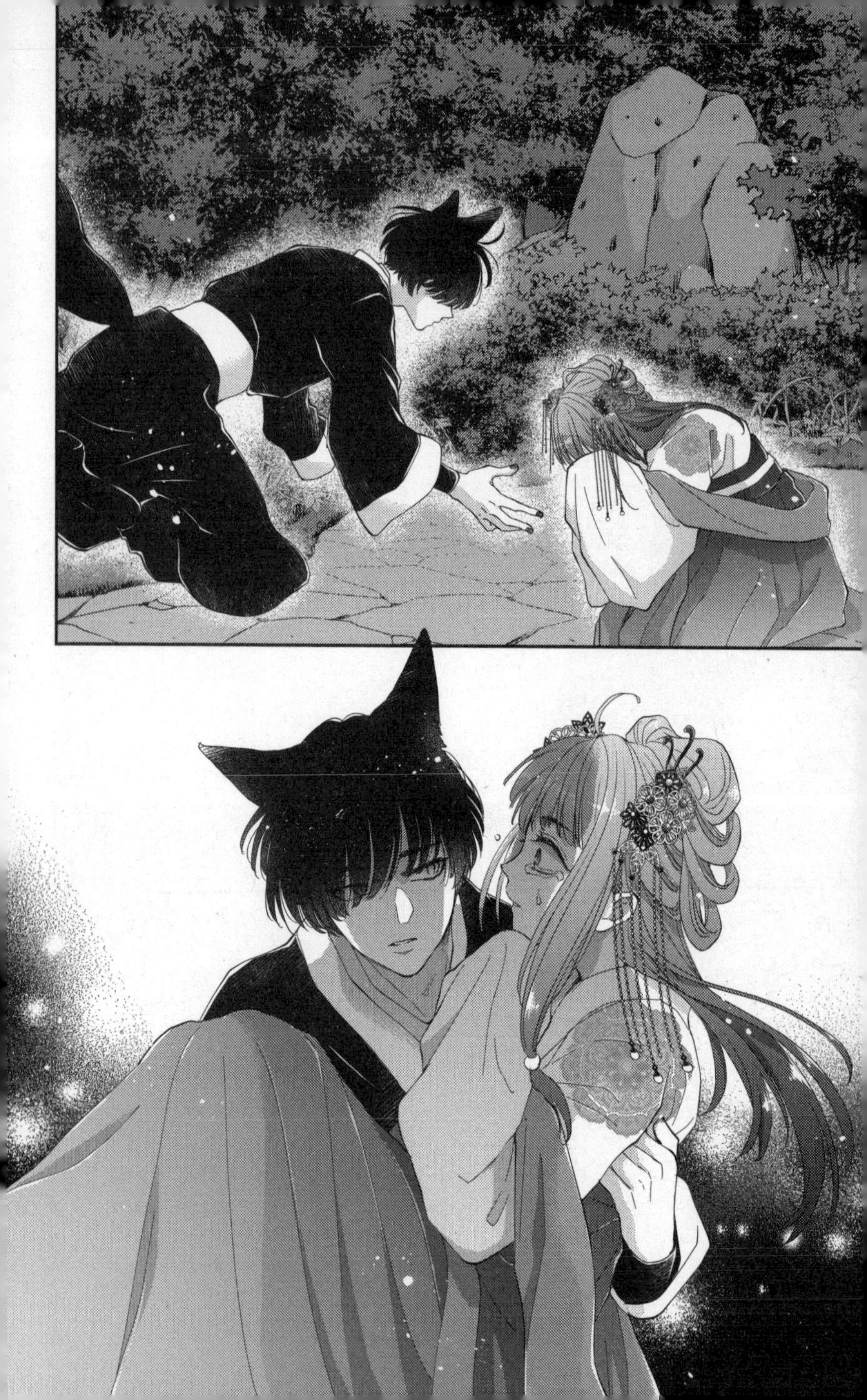

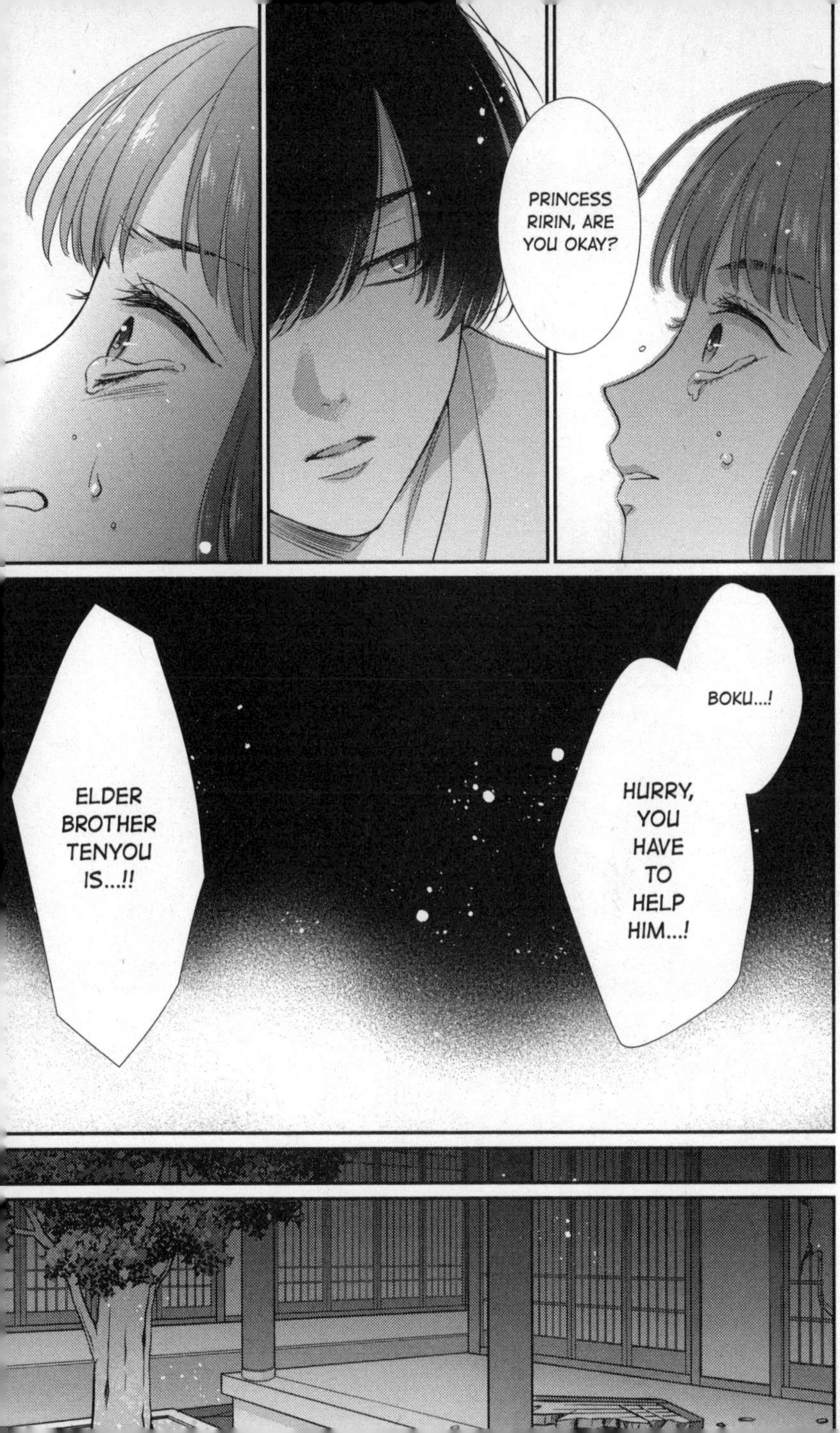
PRINCESS RIRIN, ARE YOU OKAY?
BOKU...!
HURRY, YOU HAVE TO HELP HIM...!
ELDER BROTHER TENYOU IS...!!

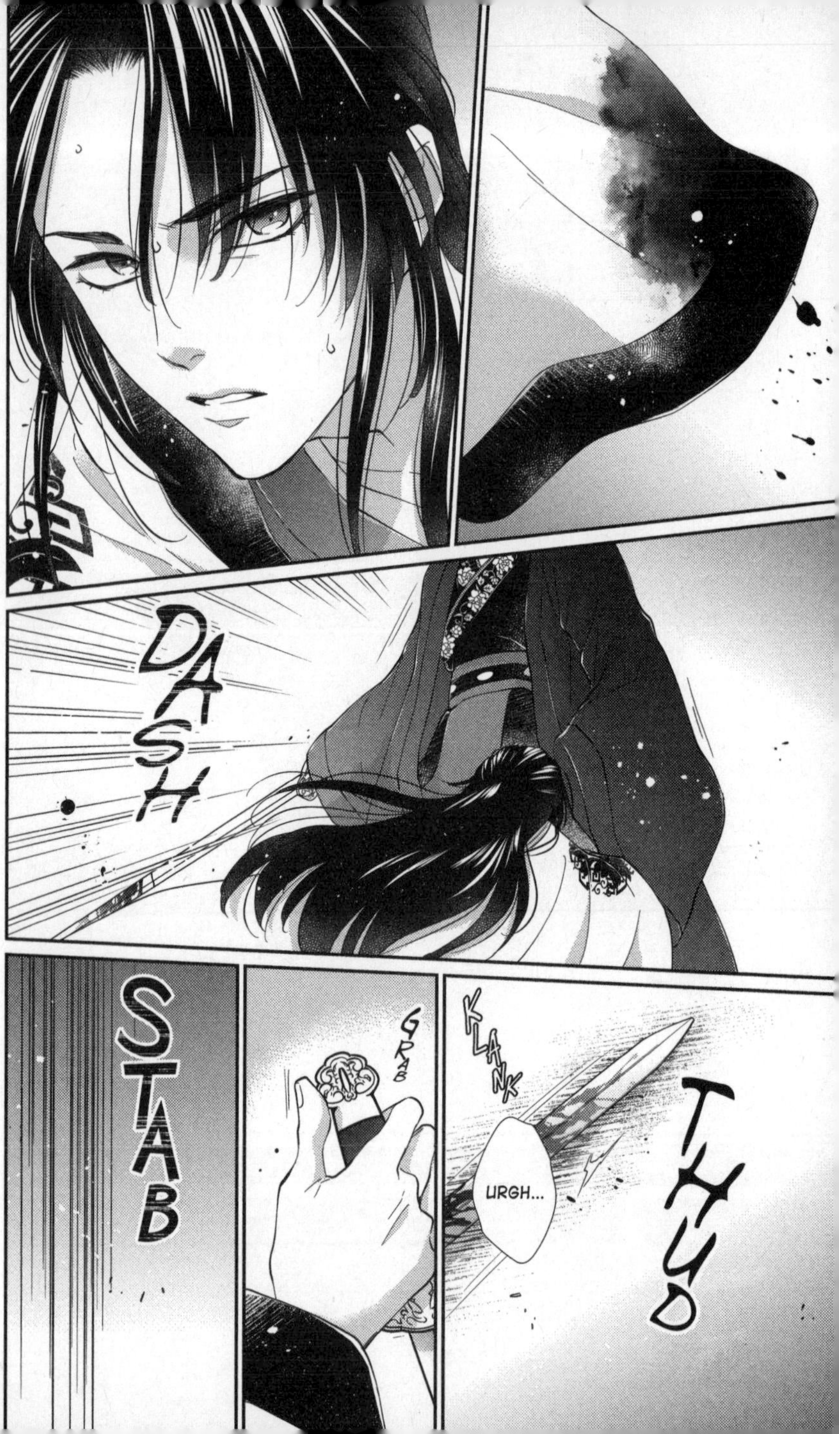
DASH
KLANK
THUD
URGH...
GRAB
STAB

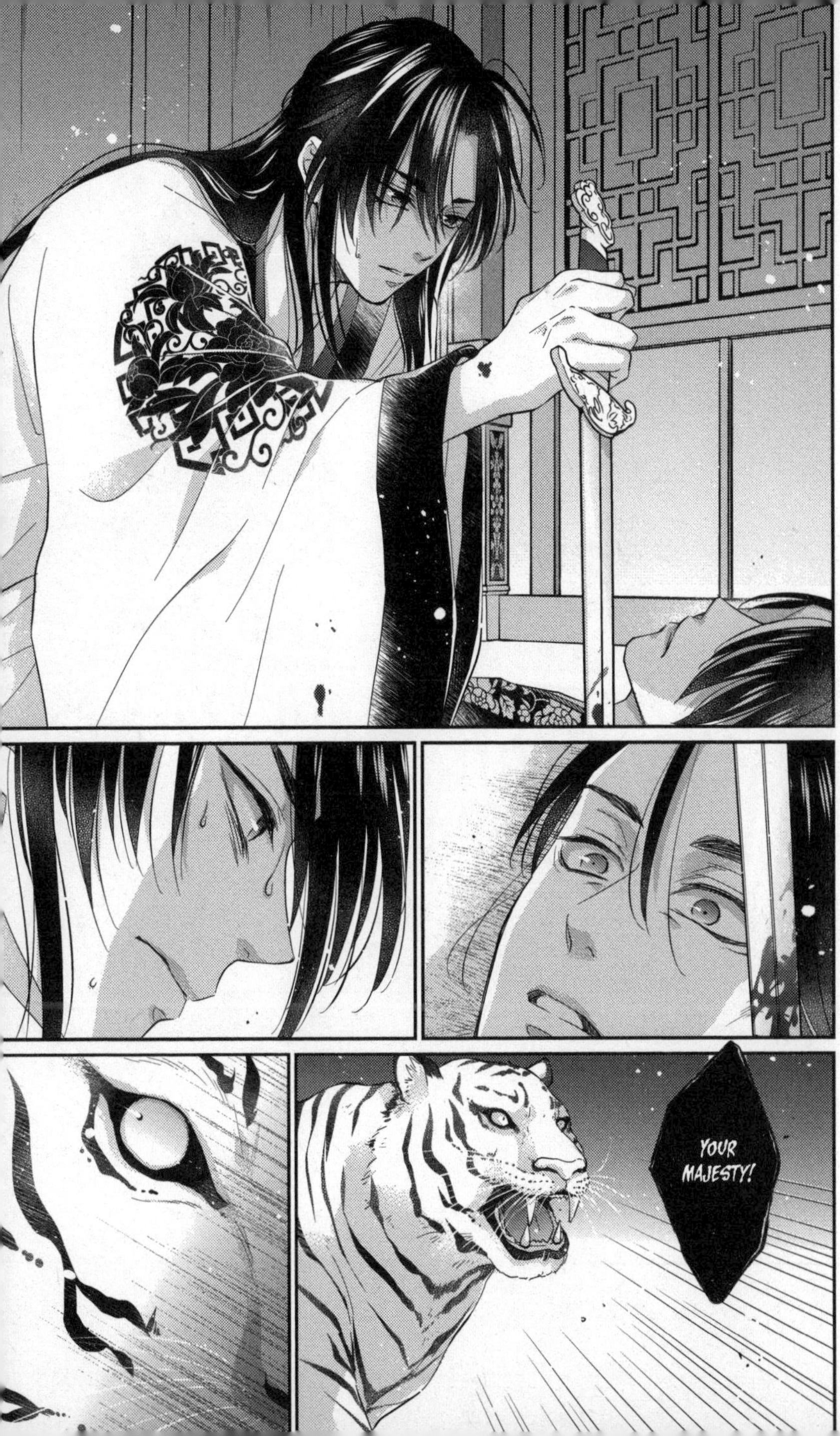
YOUR MAJESTY!

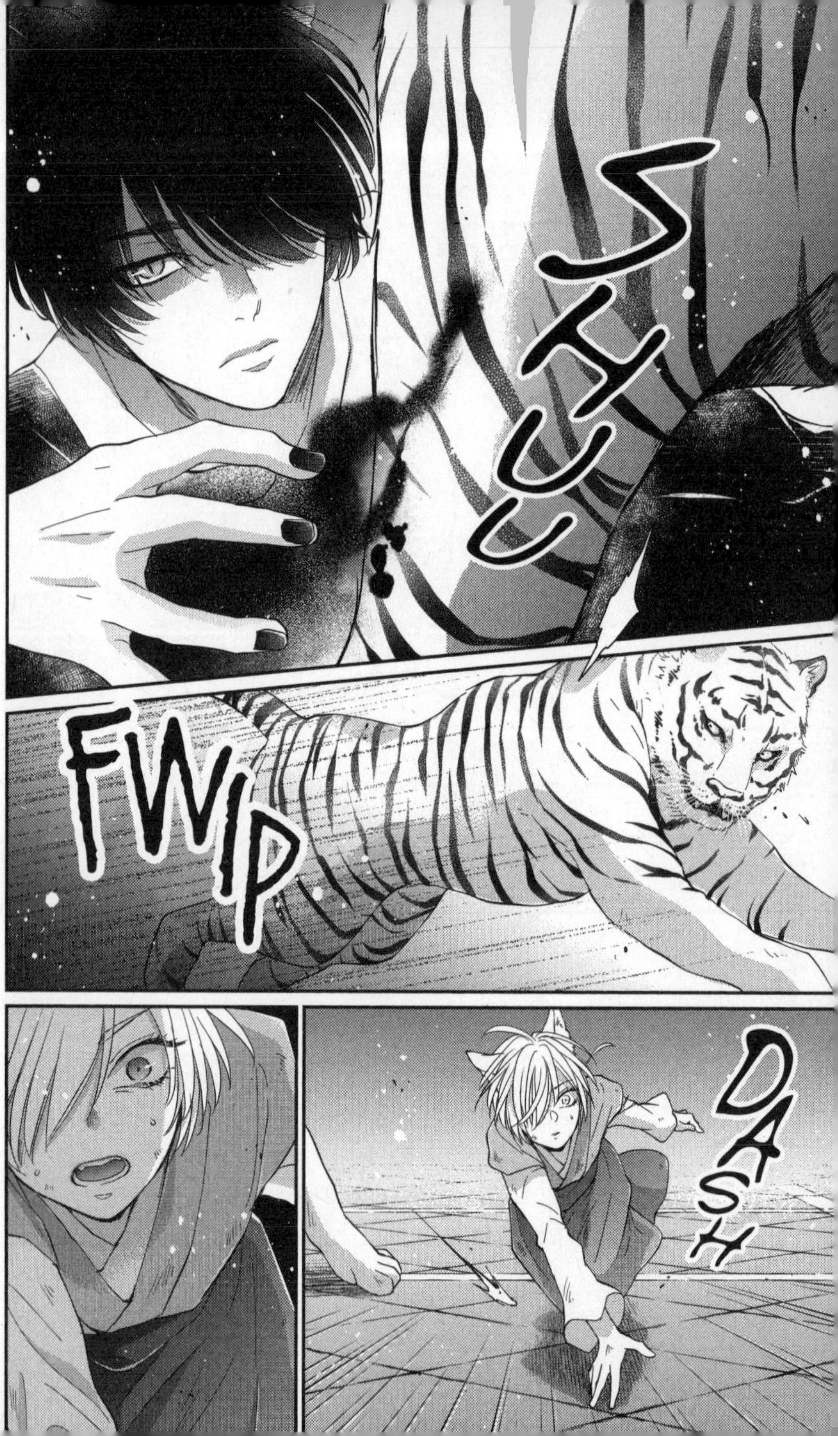
SHUU
FWIP
DASH

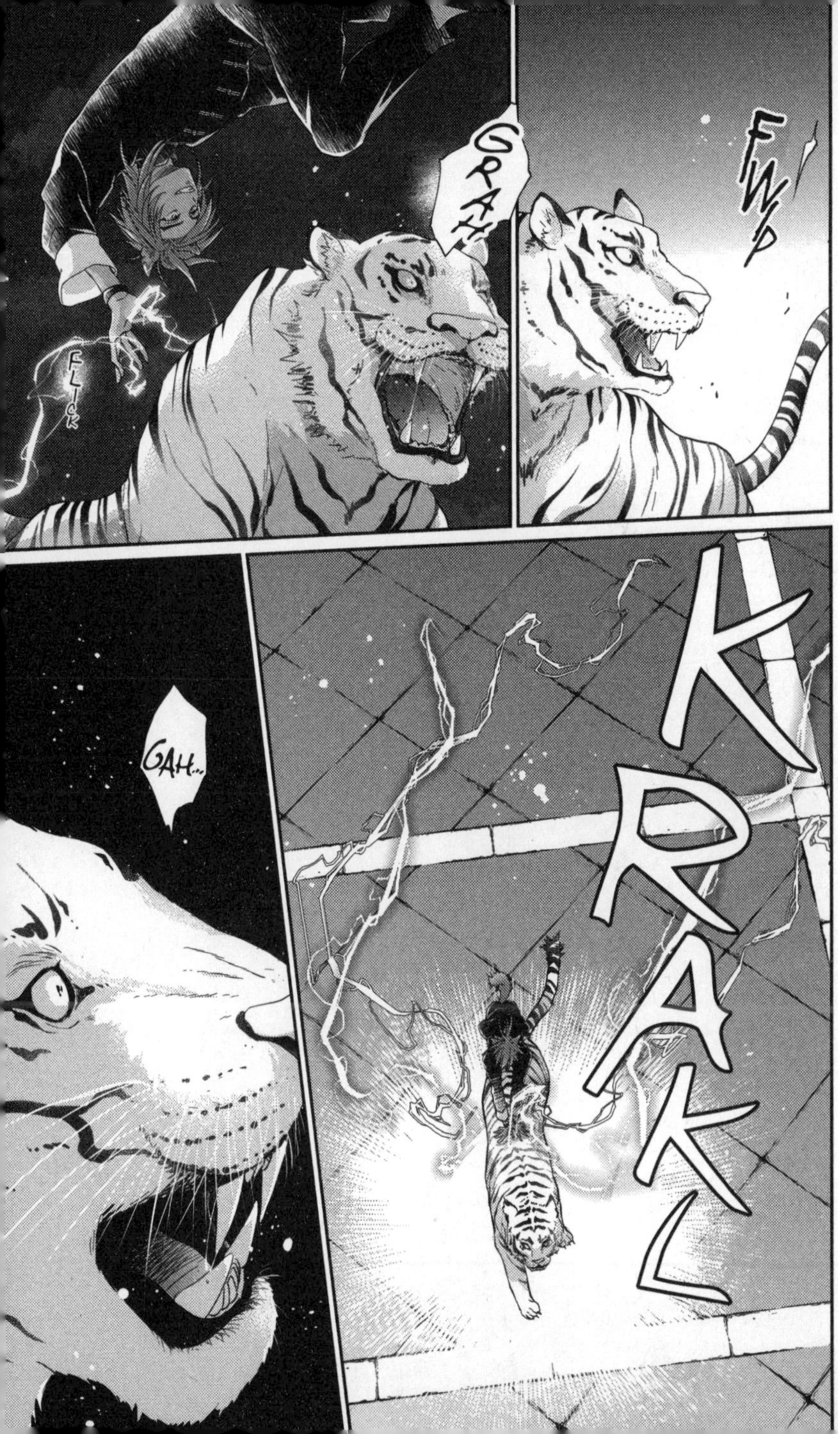
FWD
GRAH
FLICK
KRAK
GAH...

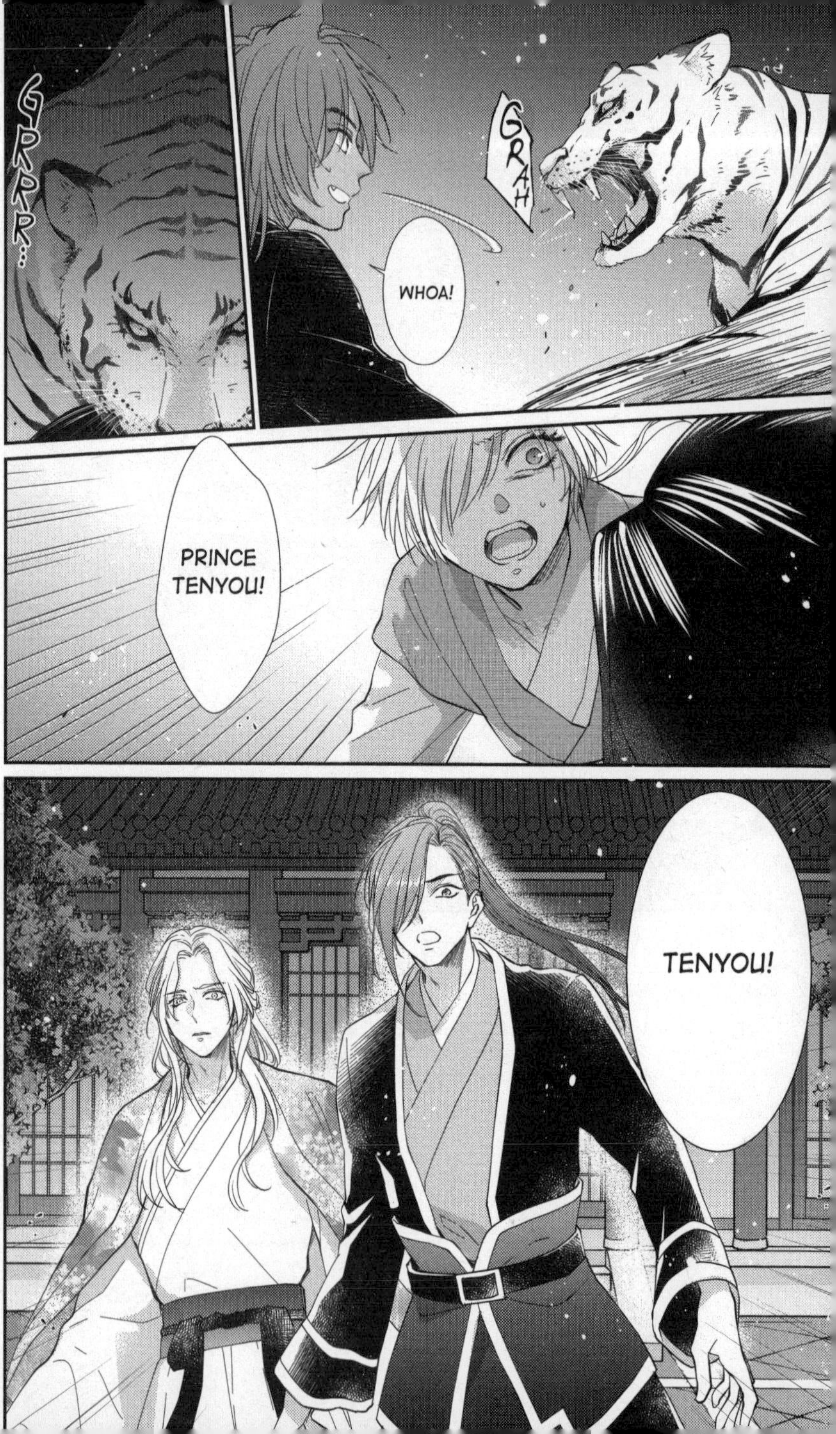
GRAH
WHOA!
GRRRR...
PRINCE TENYOU!
TENYOU!

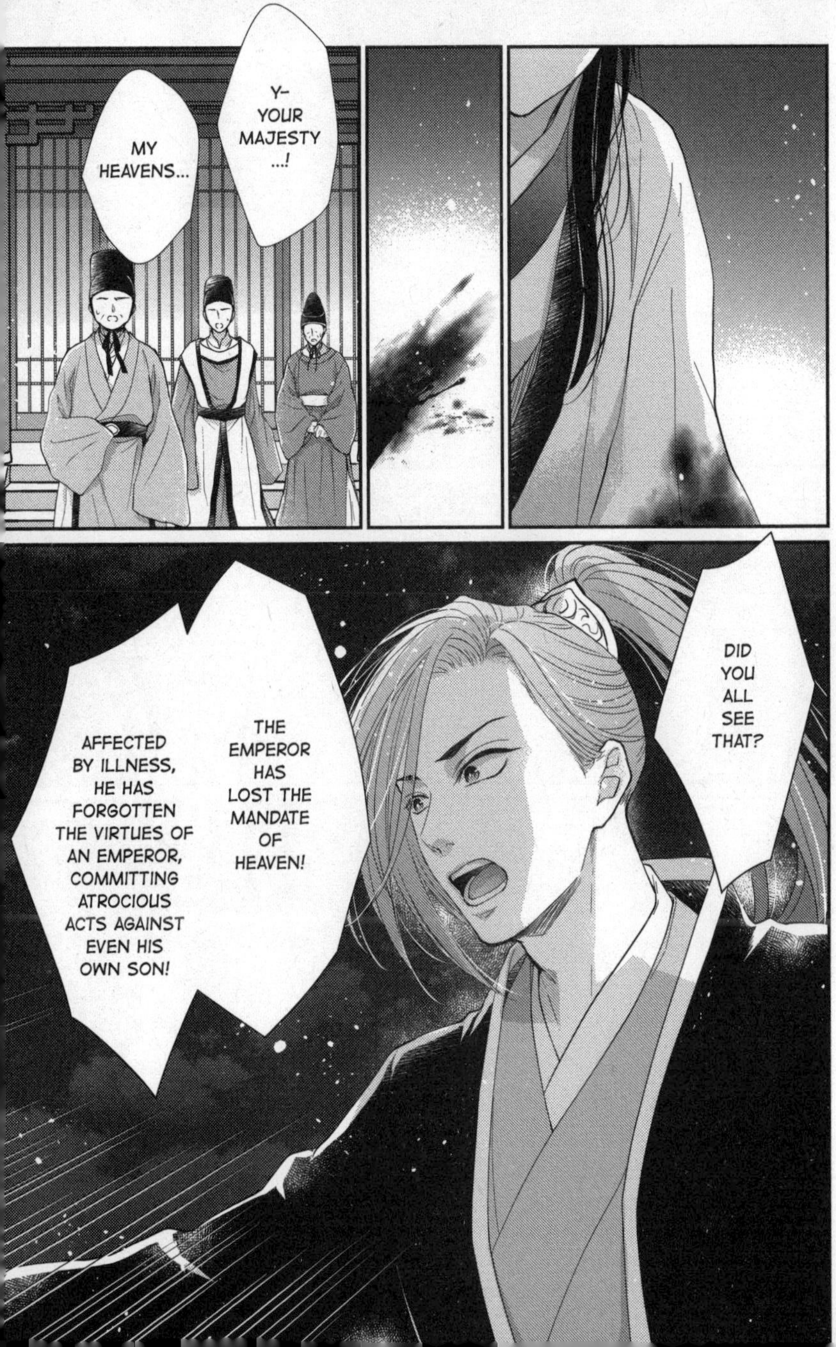
Y- YOUR MAJESTY ...!
MY HEAVENS...
DID YOU ALL SEE THAT?
THE EMPEROR HAS LOST THE MANDATE OF HEAVEN!
AFFECTED BY ILLNESS, HE HAS FORGOTTEN THE VIRTUES OF AN EMPEROR, COMMITTING ATROCIOUS ACTS AGAINST EVEN HIS OWN SON!

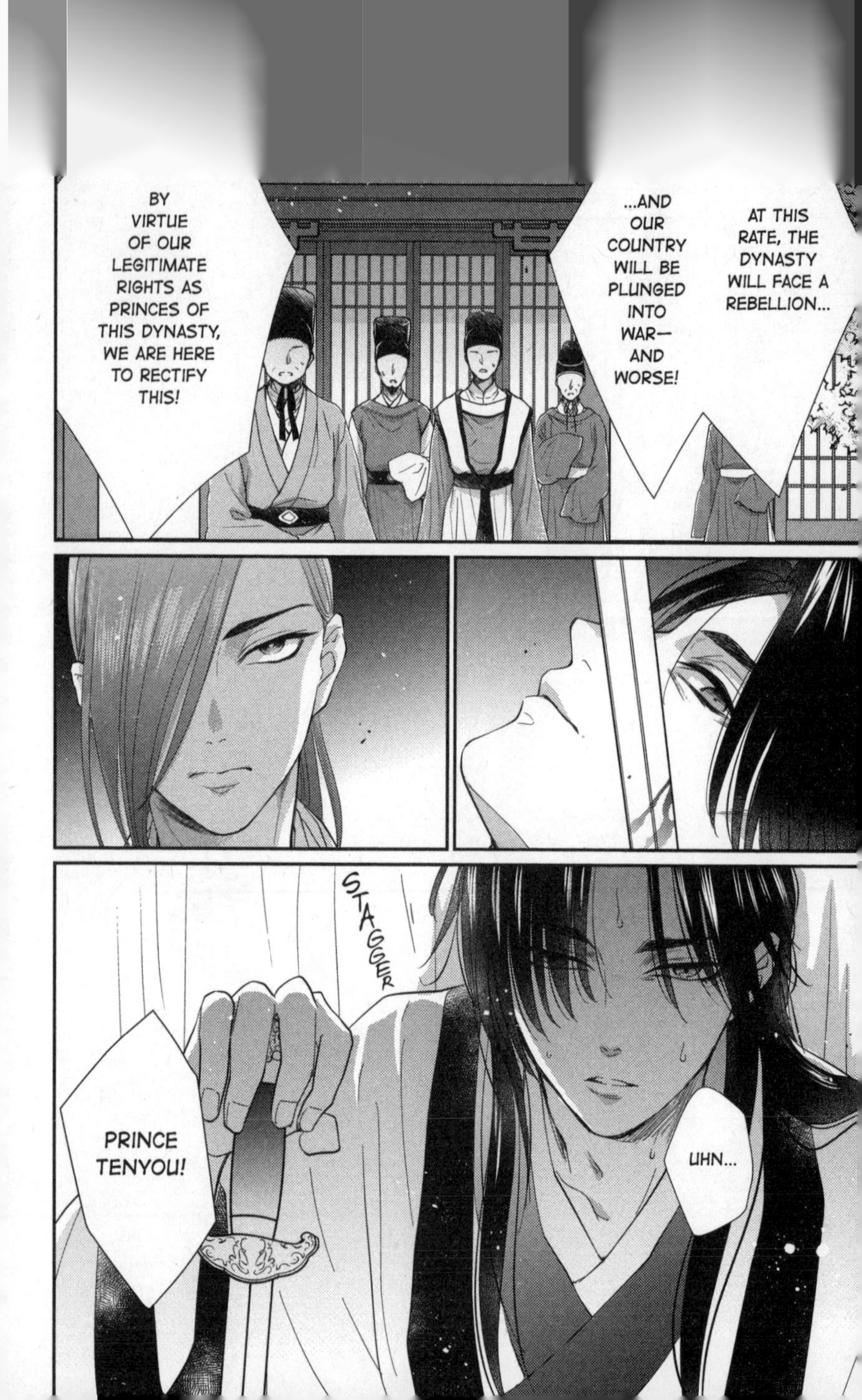
AT THIS RATE, THE DYNASTY WILL FACE A REBELLION...
...AND OUR COUNTRY WILL BE PLUNGED INTO WAR—AND WORSE!
BY VIRTUE OF OUR LEGITIMATE RIGHTS AS PRINCES OF THIS DYNASTY, WE ARE HERE TO RECTIFY THIS!
STAGGER
UHN...
PRINCE TENYOU!

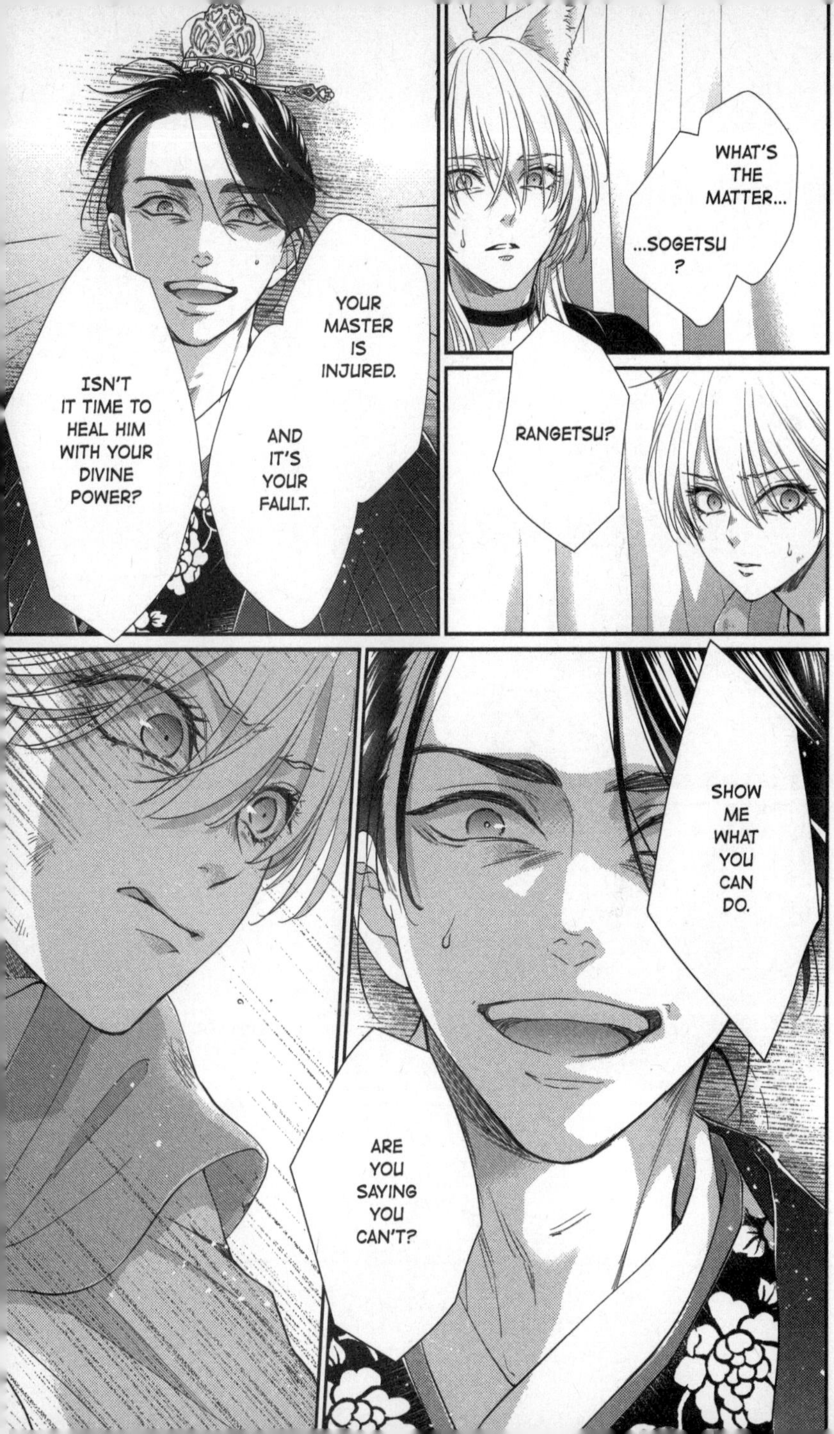
WHAT'S THE MATTER...
...SOGETSU?
RANGETSU?
YOUR MASTER IS INJURED.
AND IT'S YOUR FAULT.
ISN'T IT TIME TO HEAL HIM WITH YOUR DIVINE POWER?
SHOW ME WHAT YOU CAN DO.
ARE YOU SAYING YOU CAN'T?

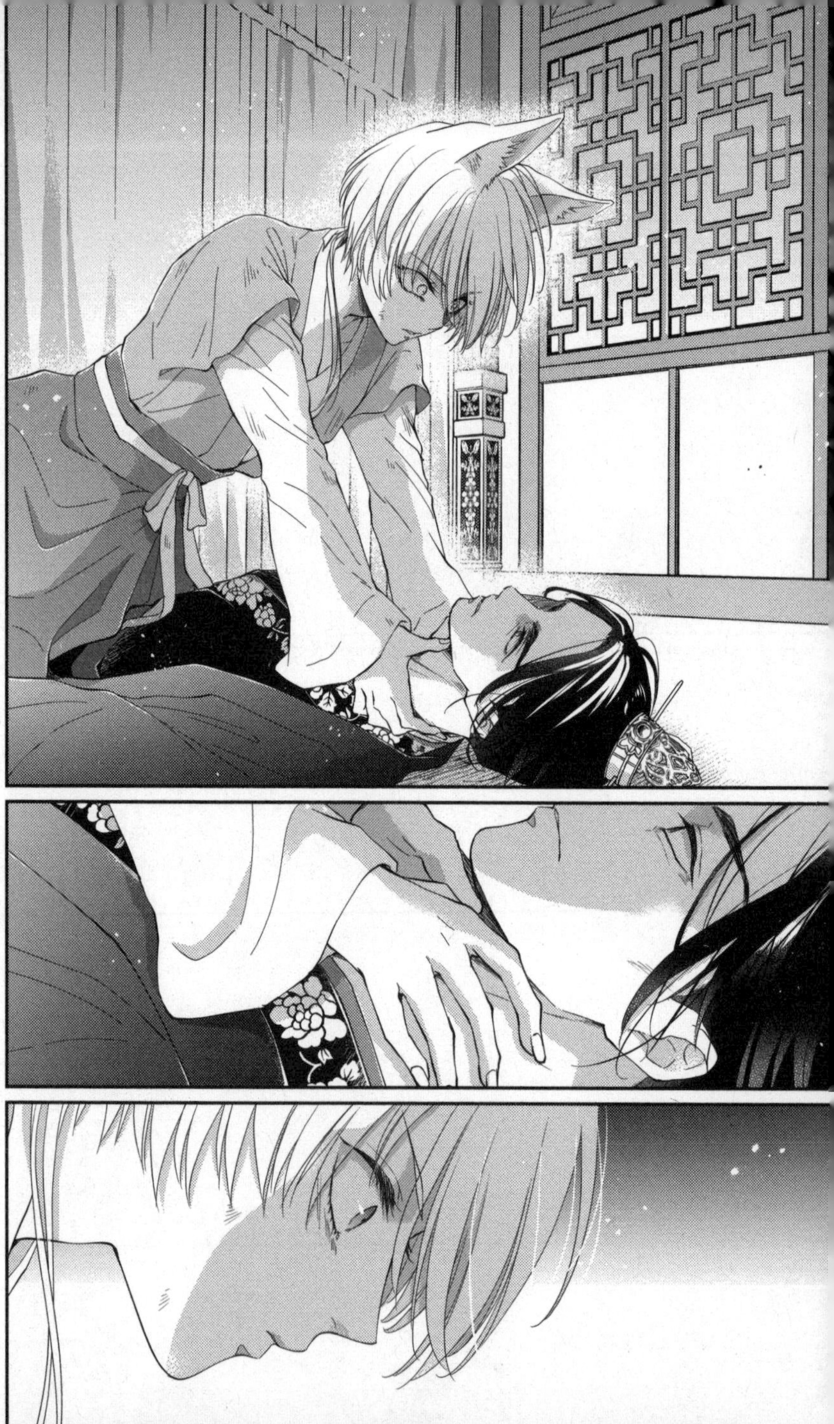

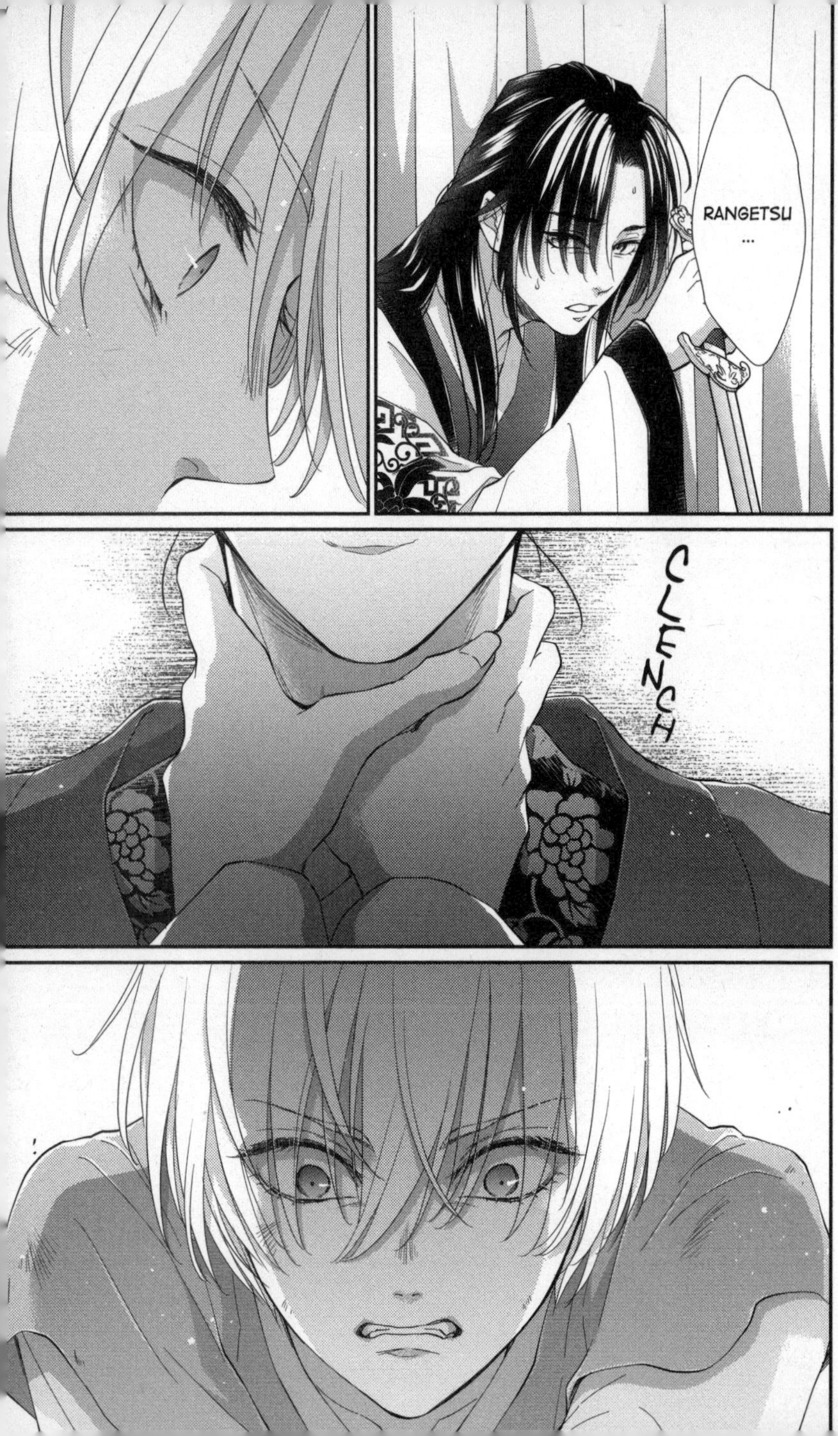
RANGETSU
...
CLENCH

WHAT'S
THE
MATTER
...?

YOU
MUST
HATE
ME.

ARE
YOU
GOING
TO KILL
ME?

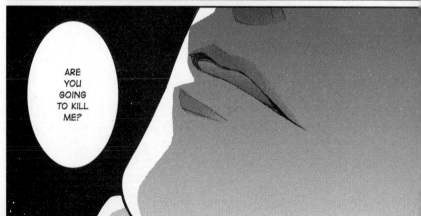

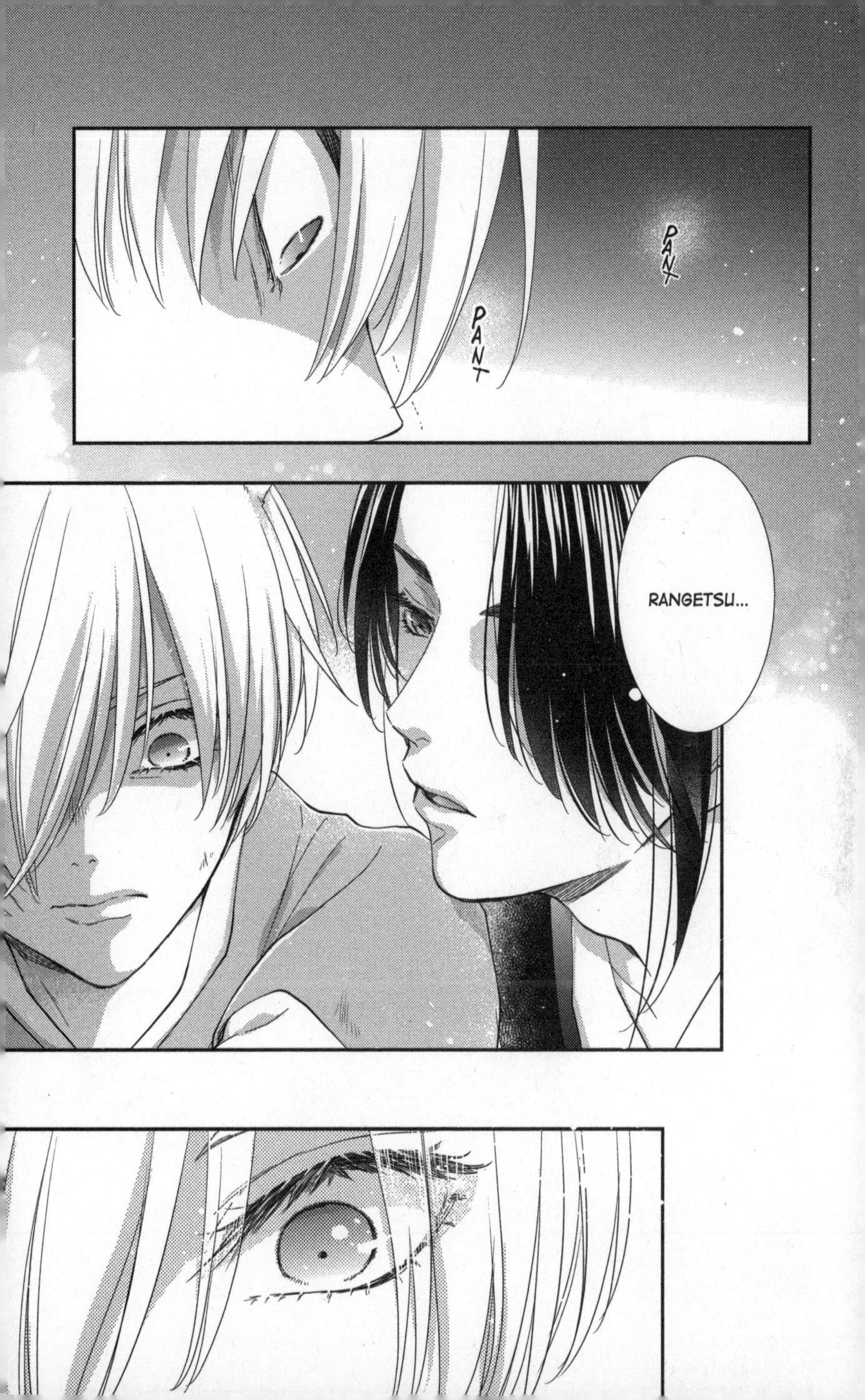
PANT
PANT
RANGETSU...

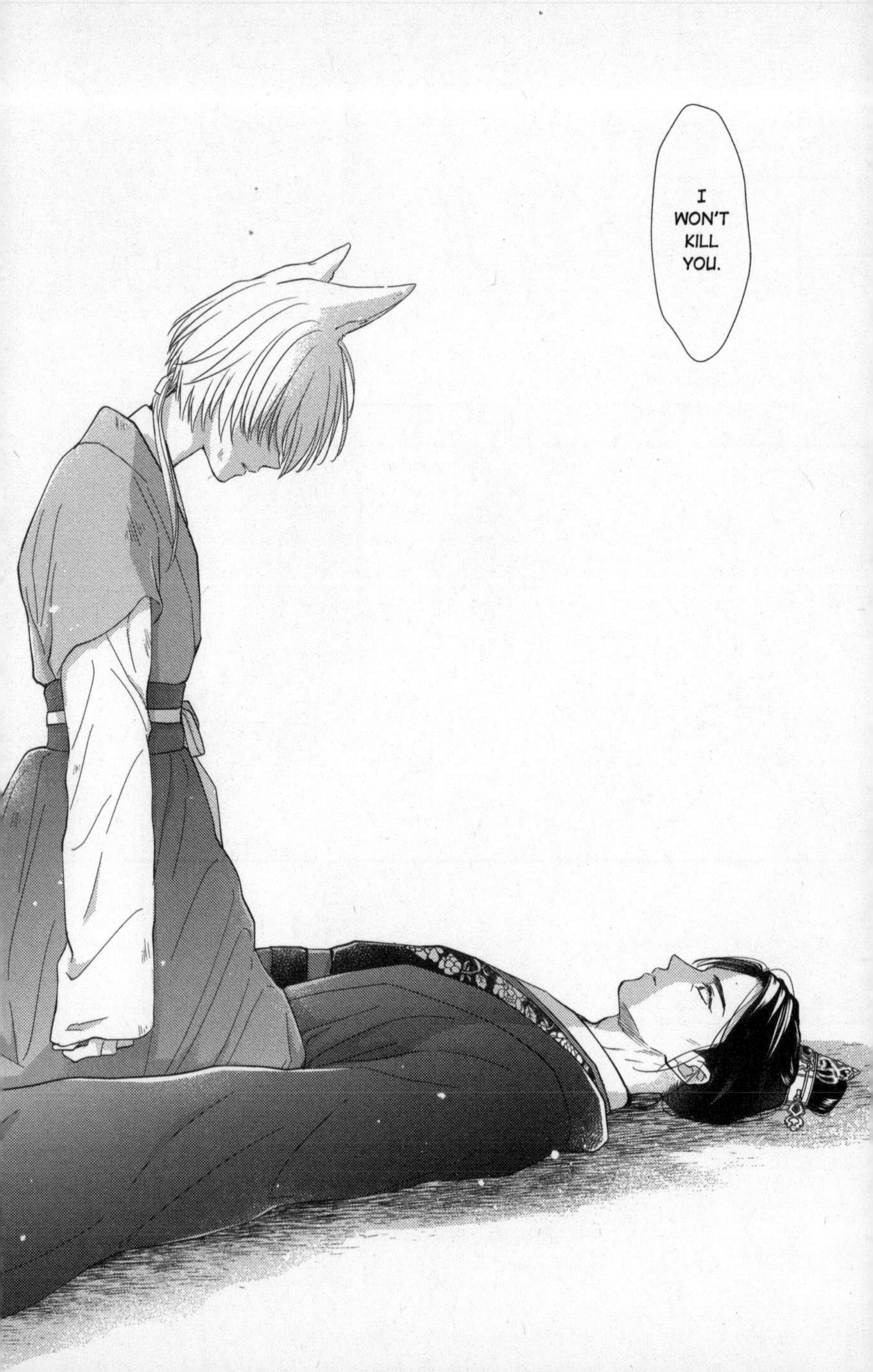
I WON'T KILL YOU.

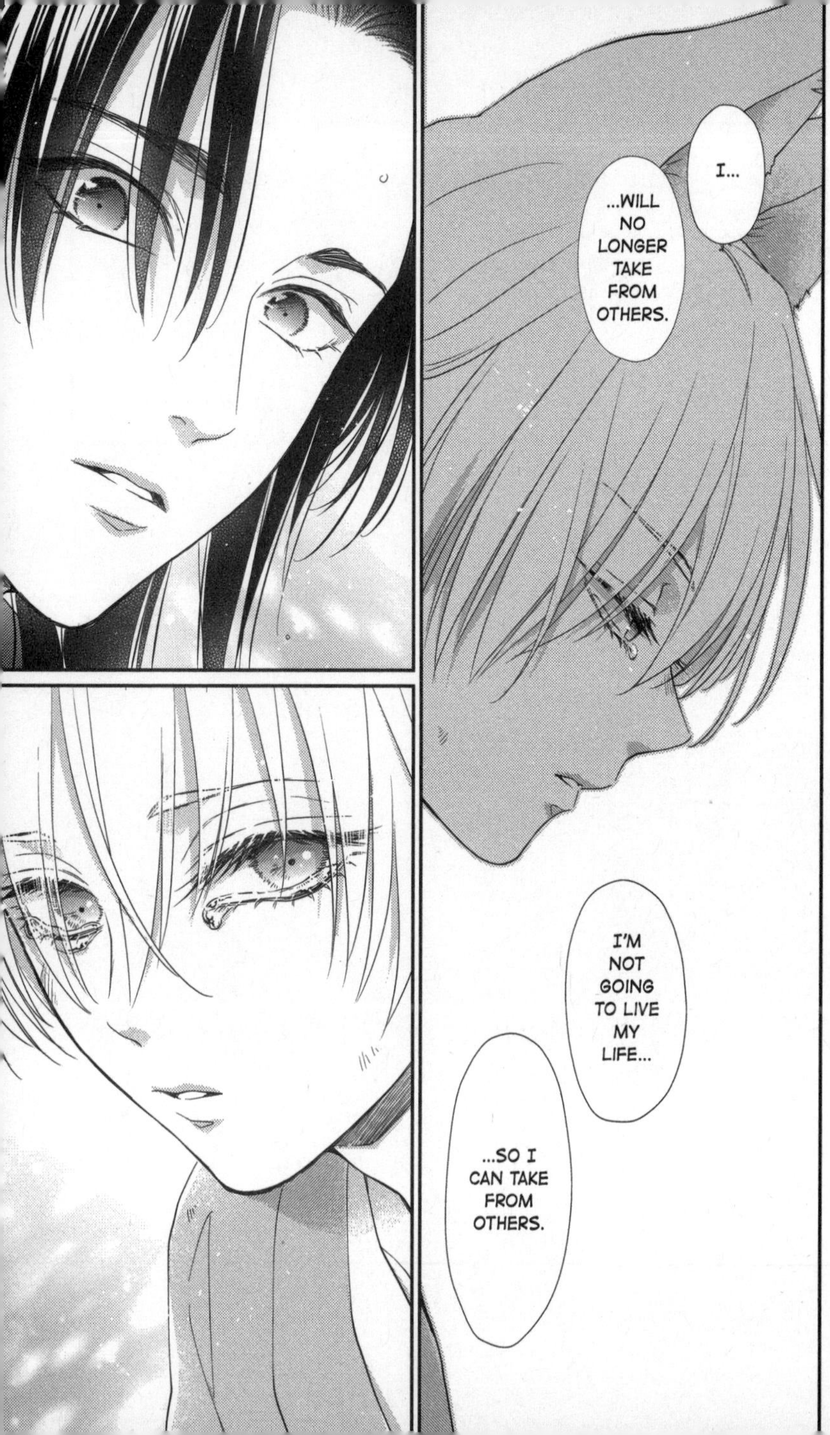
I...
...WILL NO LONGER TAKE FROM OTHERS.
I'M NOT GOING TO LIVE MY LIFE...
...SO I CAN TAKE FROM OTHERS.

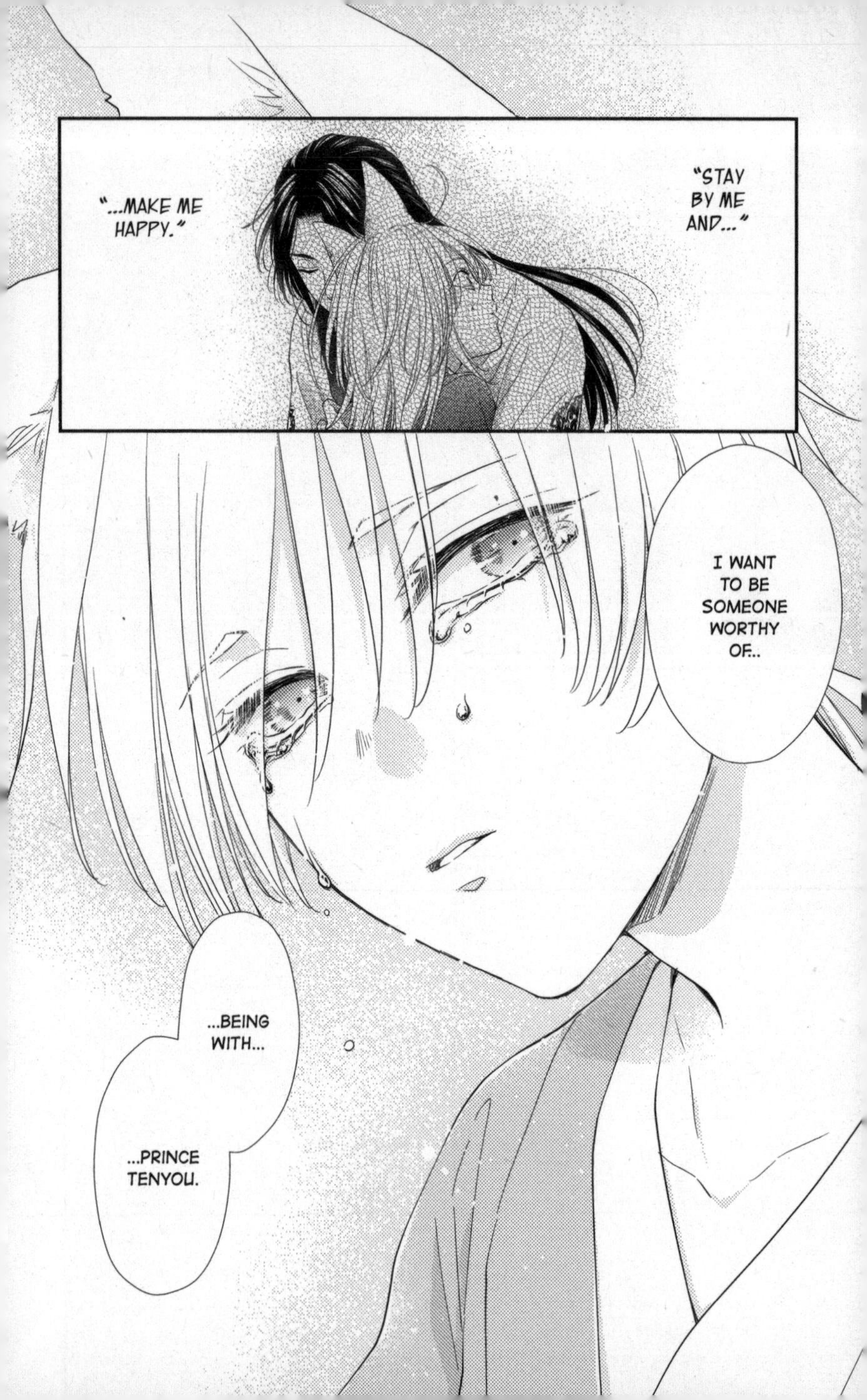
"STAY BY ME AND..."
"...MAKE ME HAPPY."
I WANT TO BE SOMEONE WORTHY OF...
...BEING WITH...
...PRINCE TENYOU.

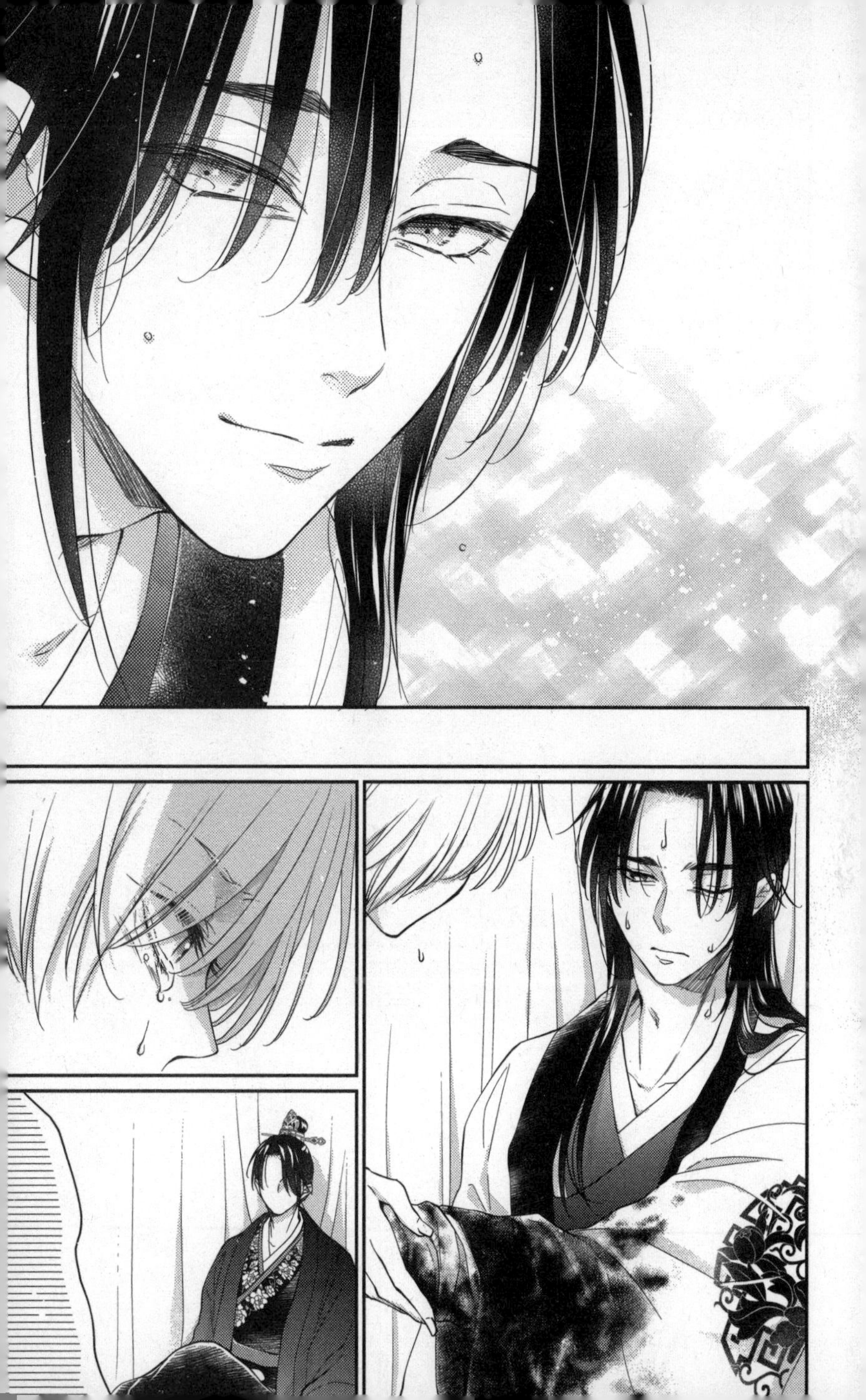

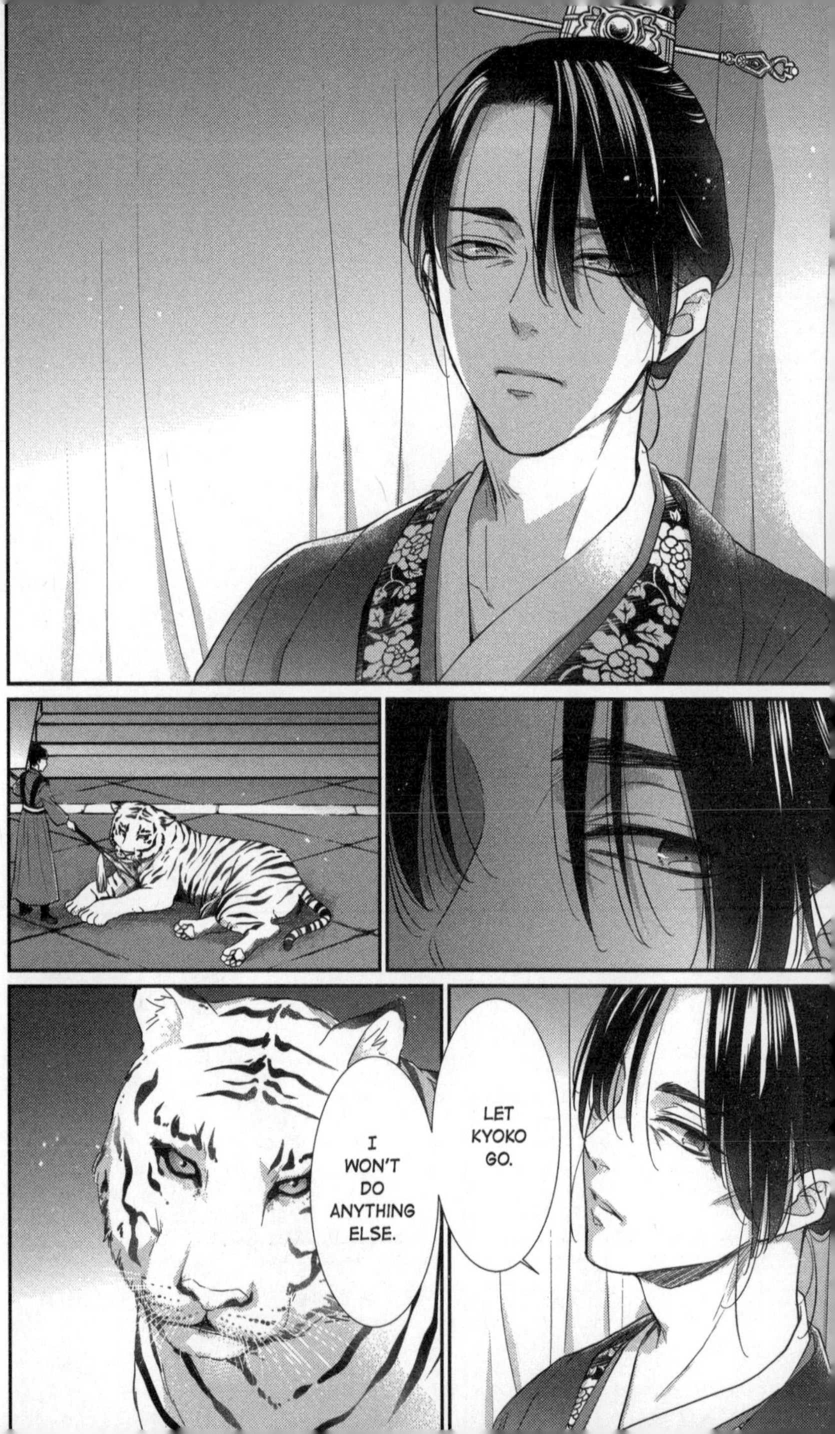
LET KYOKO GO.
I WON'T DO ANYTHING ELSE.

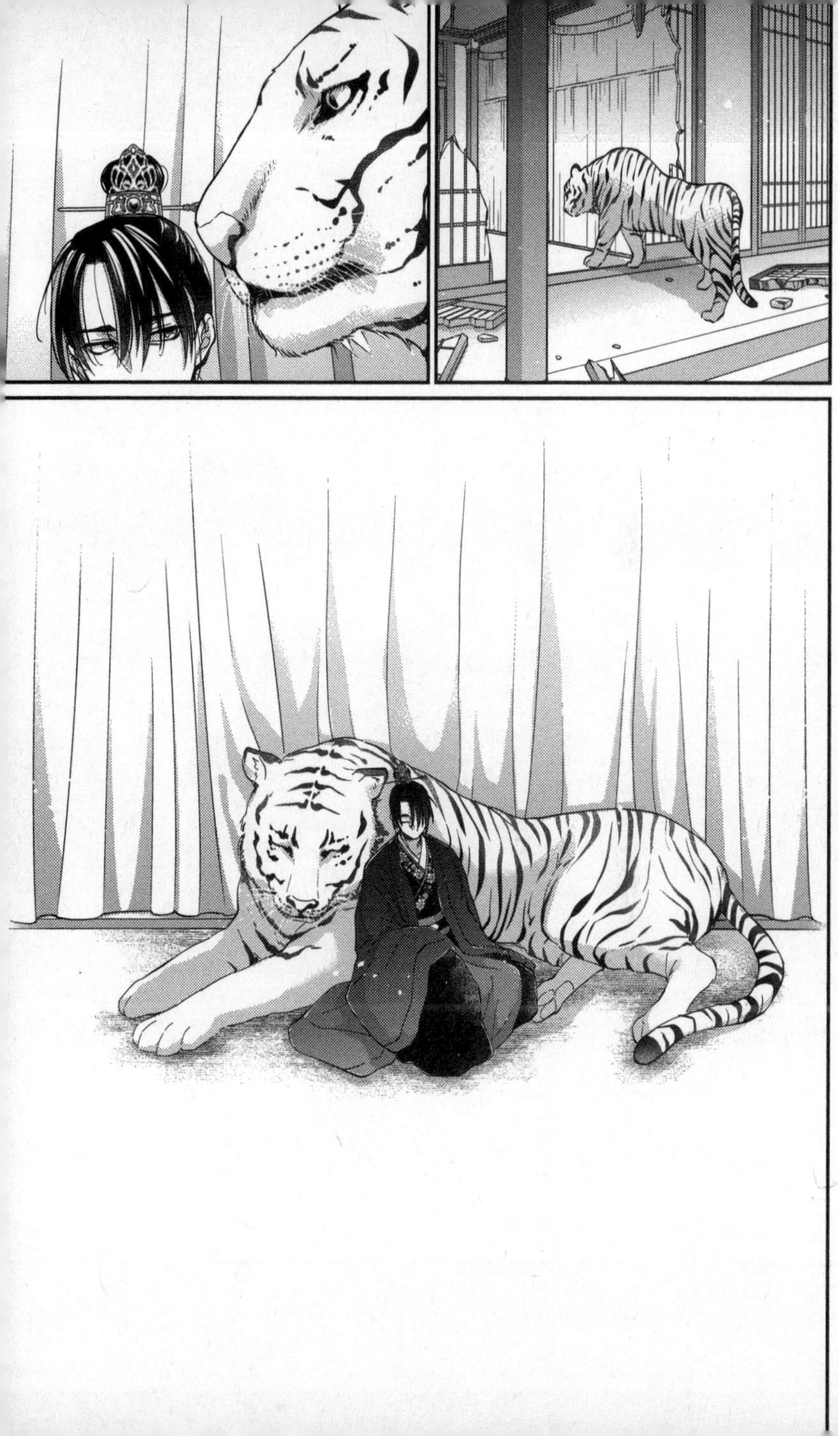

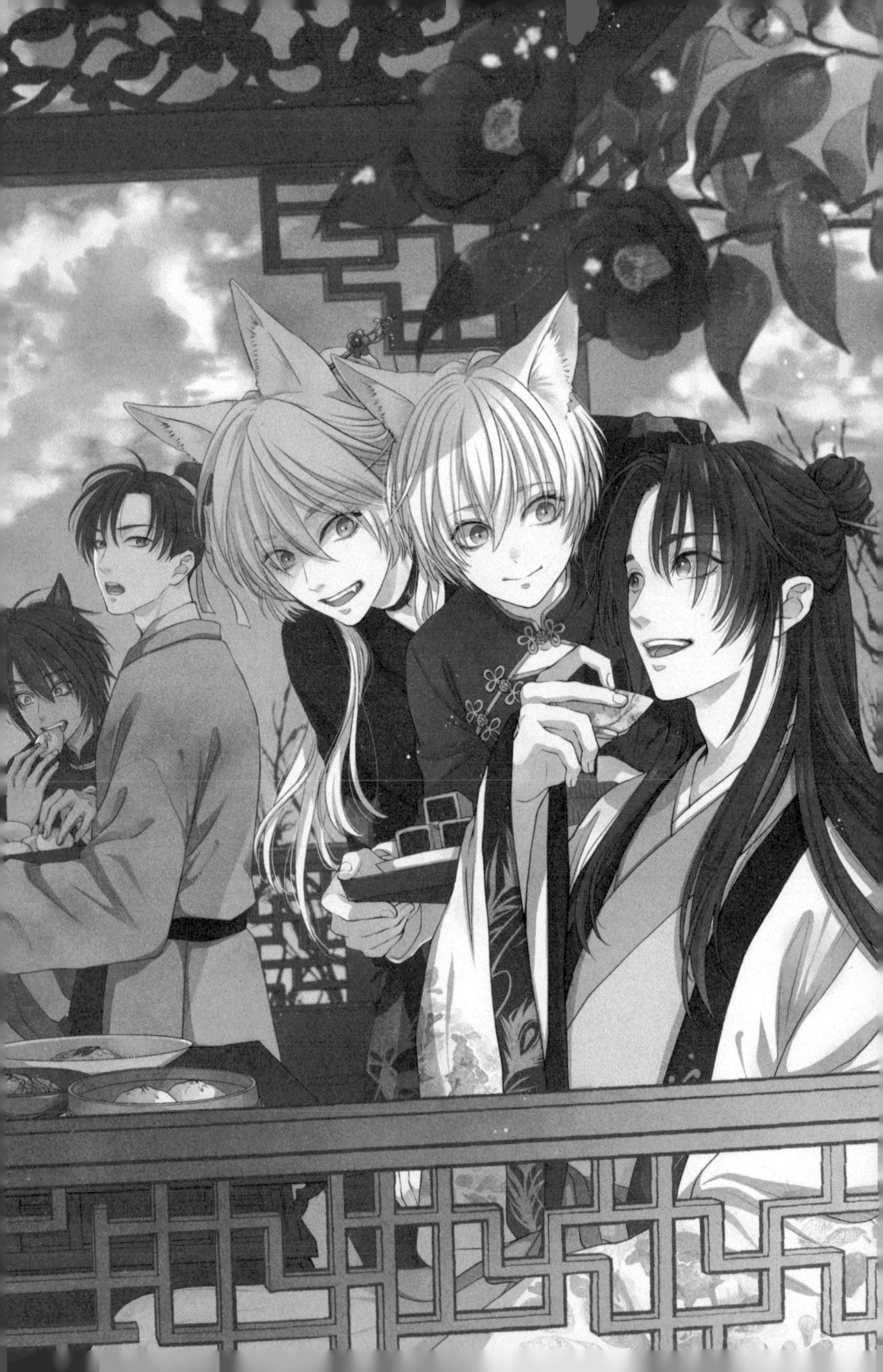

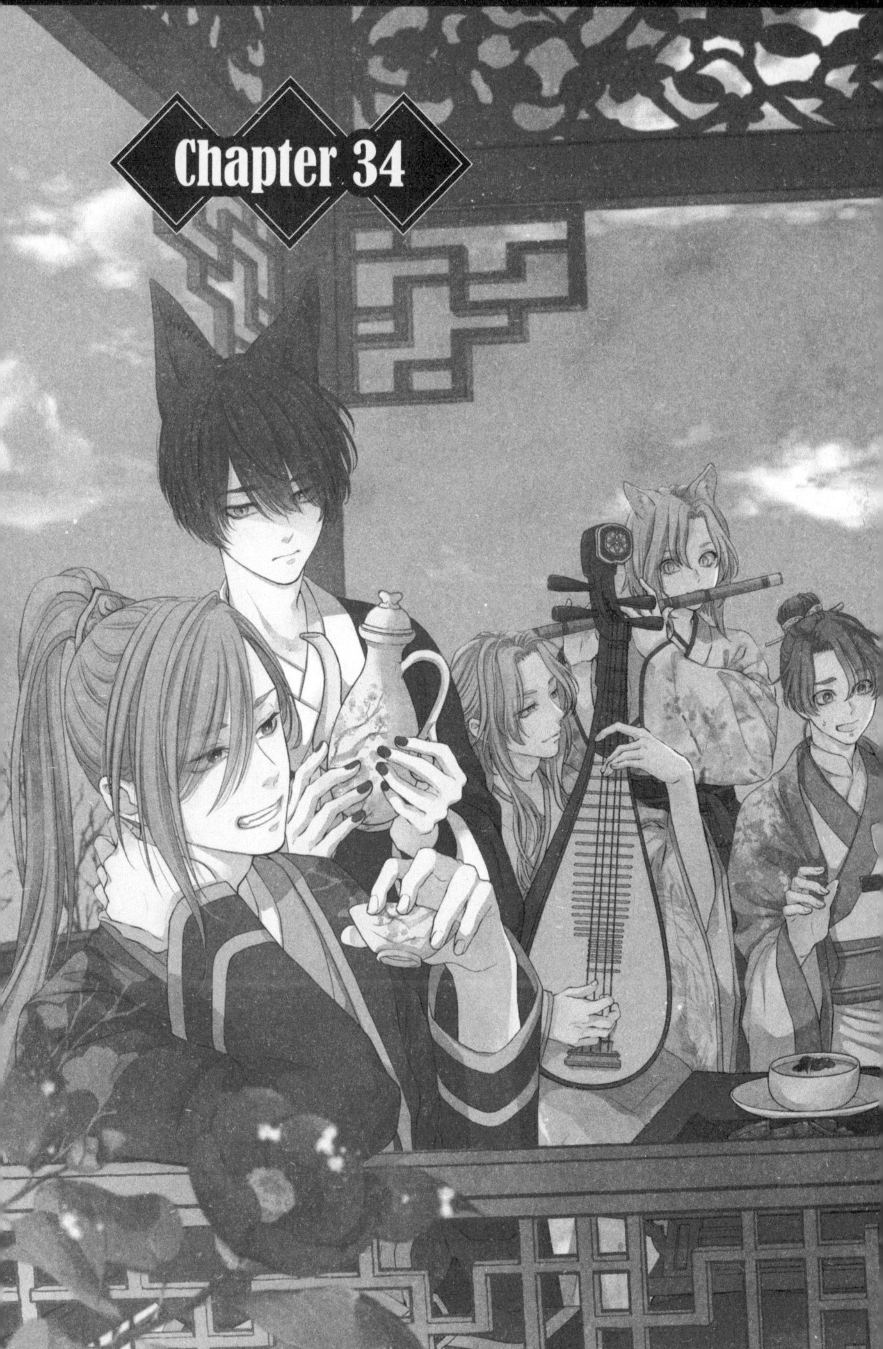
Chapter 34

THE
KING'S
Beast 麗

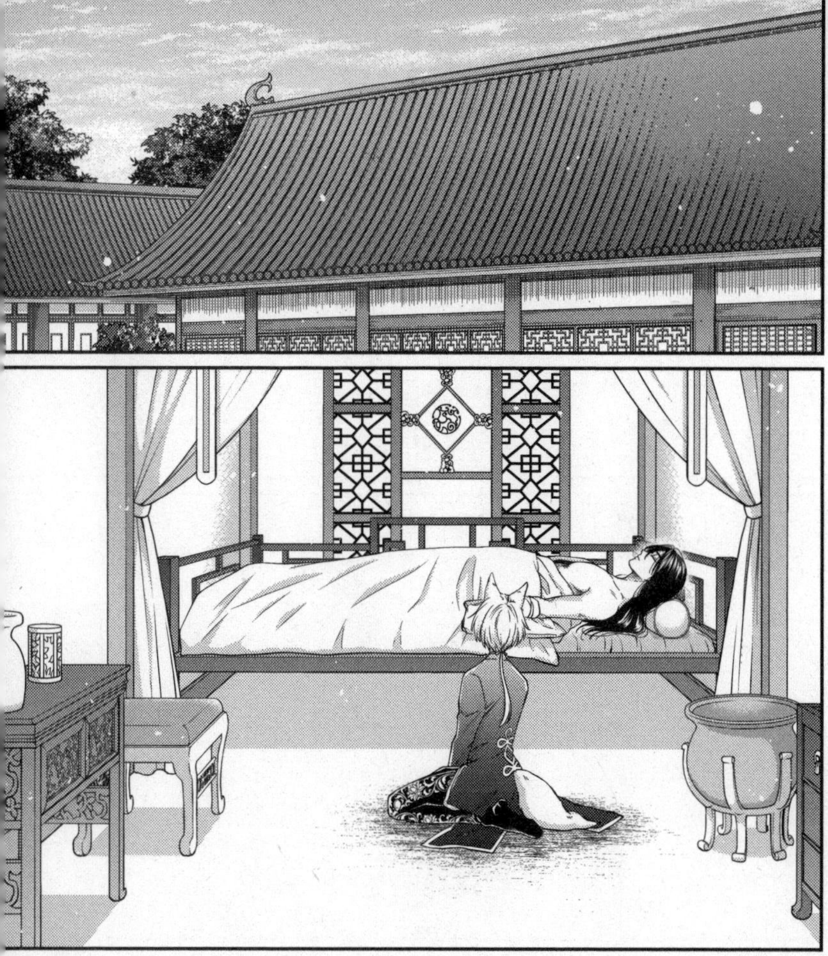

THE KING'S Beast

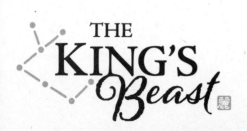

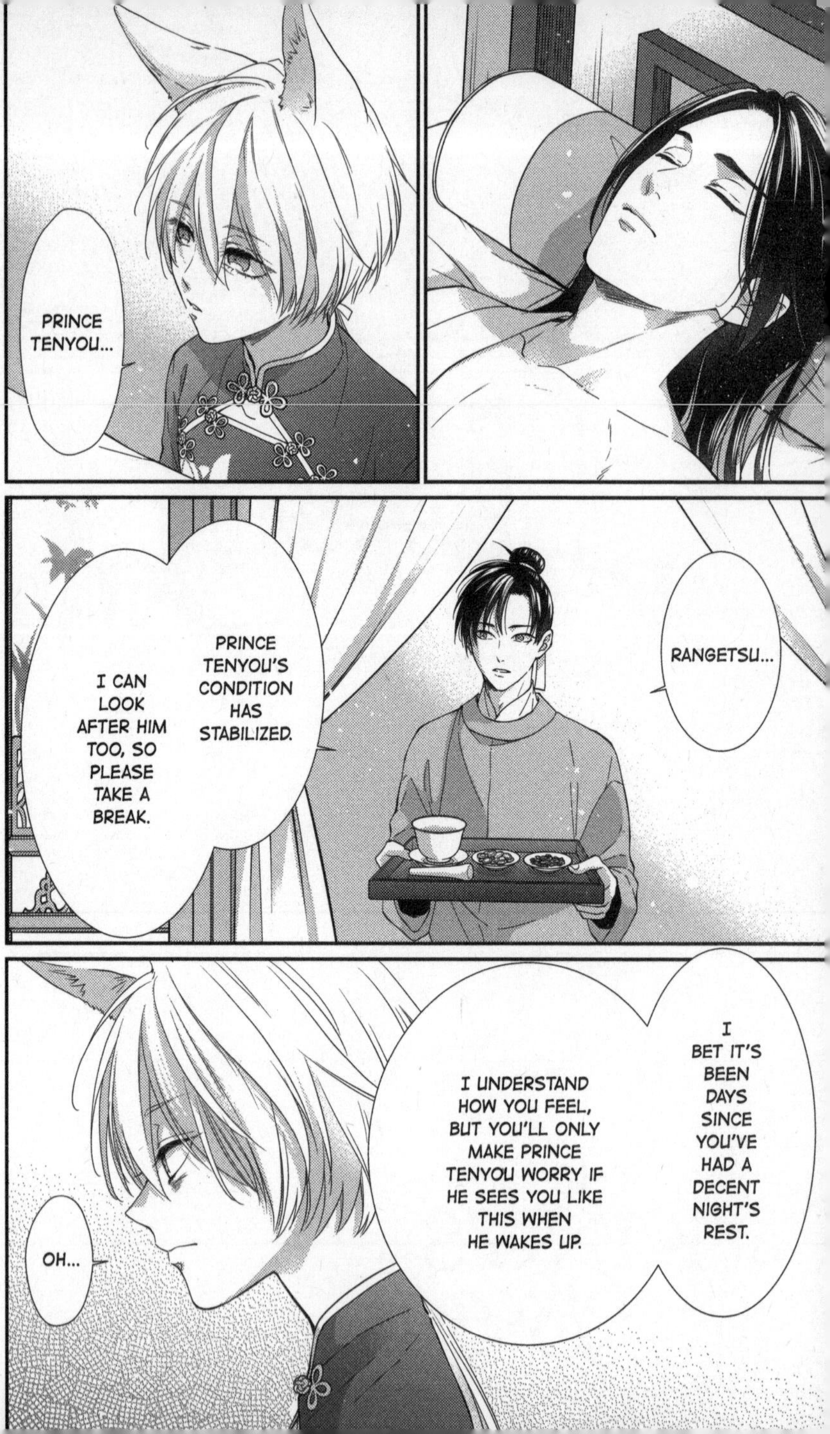
PRINCE TENYOU...
RANGETSU...
PRINCE TENYOU'S CONDITION HAS STABILIZED.
I CAN LOOK AFTER HIM TOO, SO PLEASE TAKE A BREAK.
I BET IT'S BEEN DAYS SINCE YOU'VE HAD A DECENT NIGHT'S REST.
I UNDERSTAND HOW YOU FEEL, BUT YOU'LL ONLY MAKE PRINCE TENYOU WORRY IF HE SEES YOU LIKE THIS WHEN HE WAKES UP.
OH...

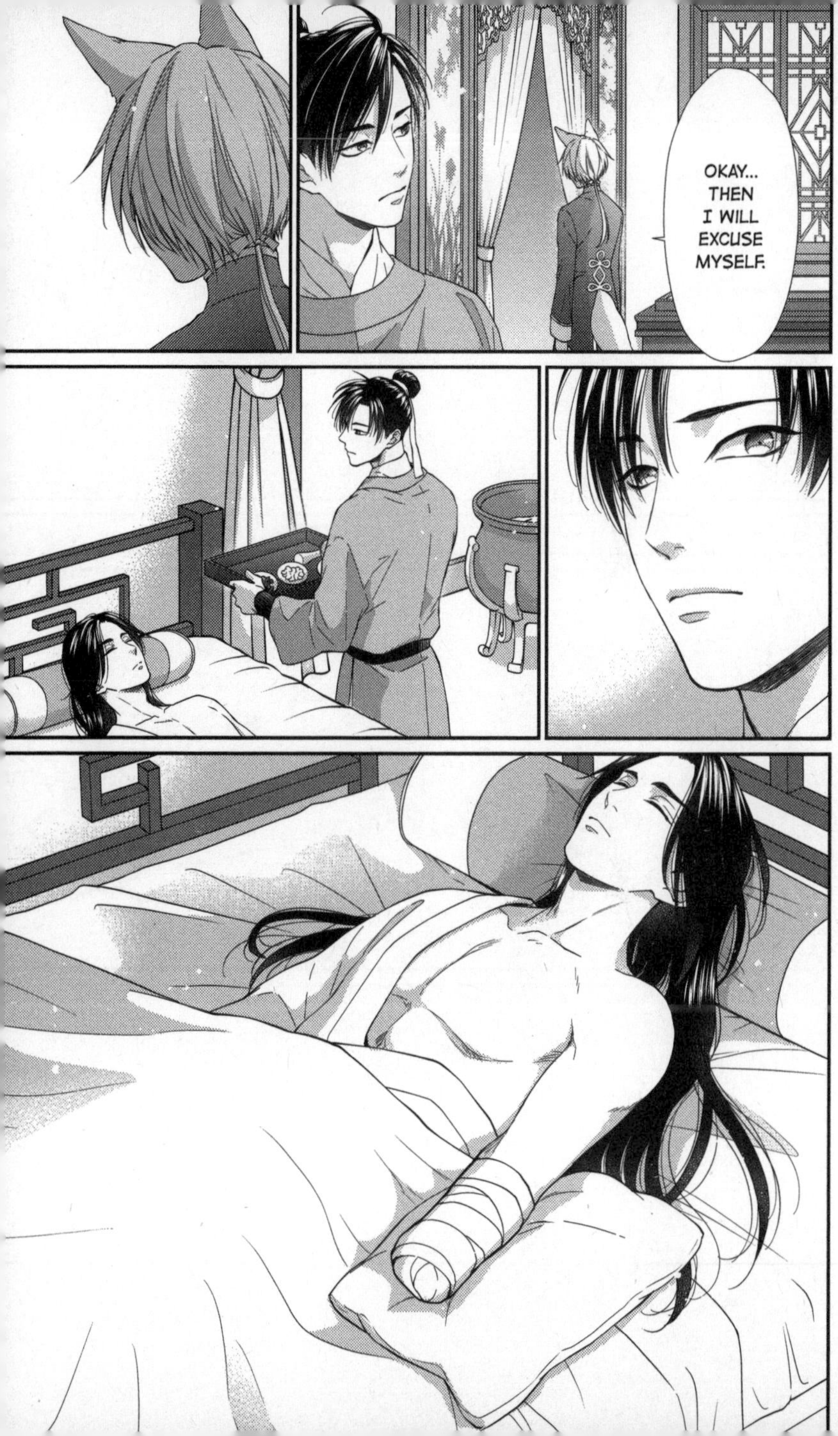
OKAY... THEN I WILL EXCUSE MYSELF.

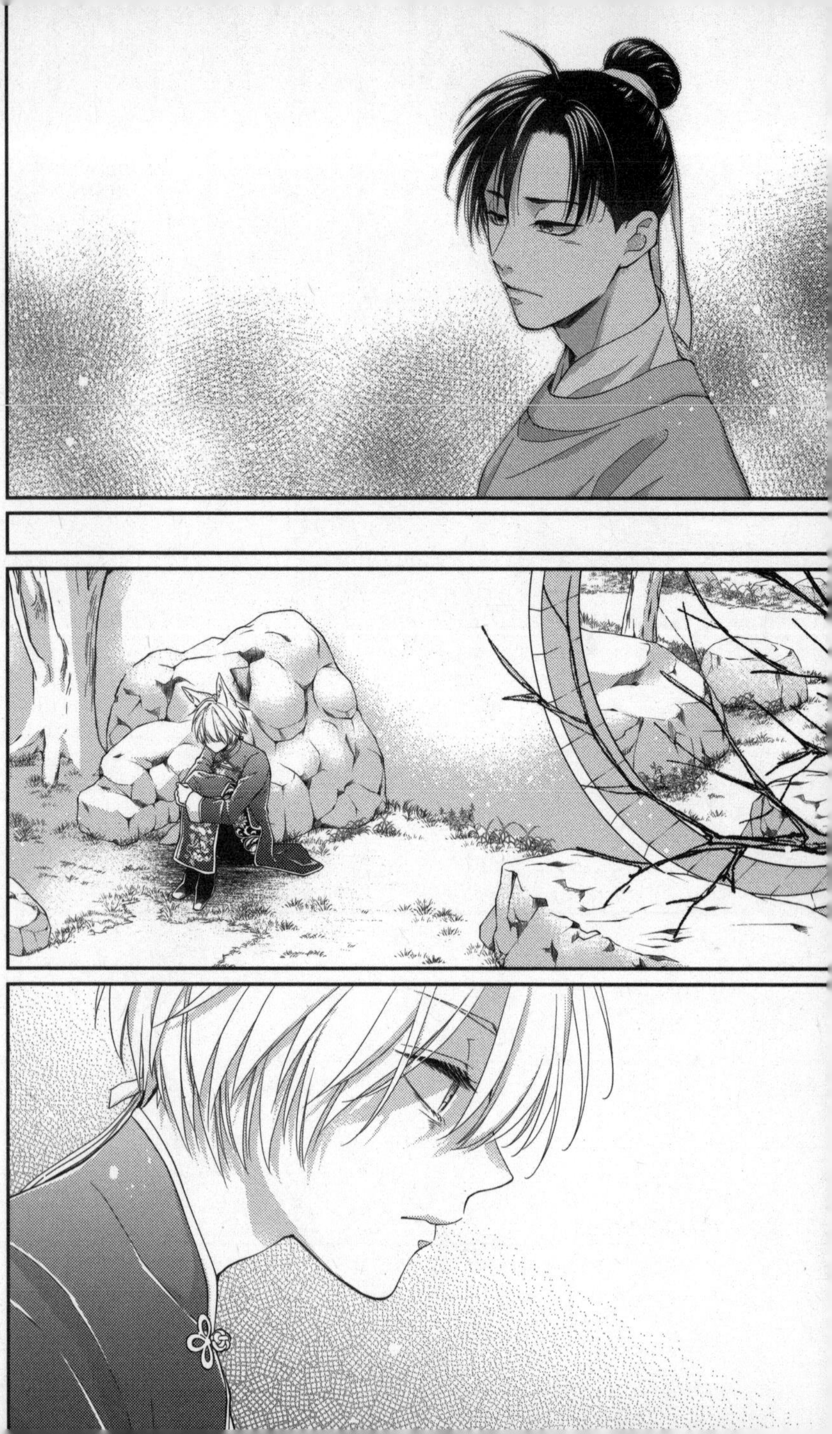

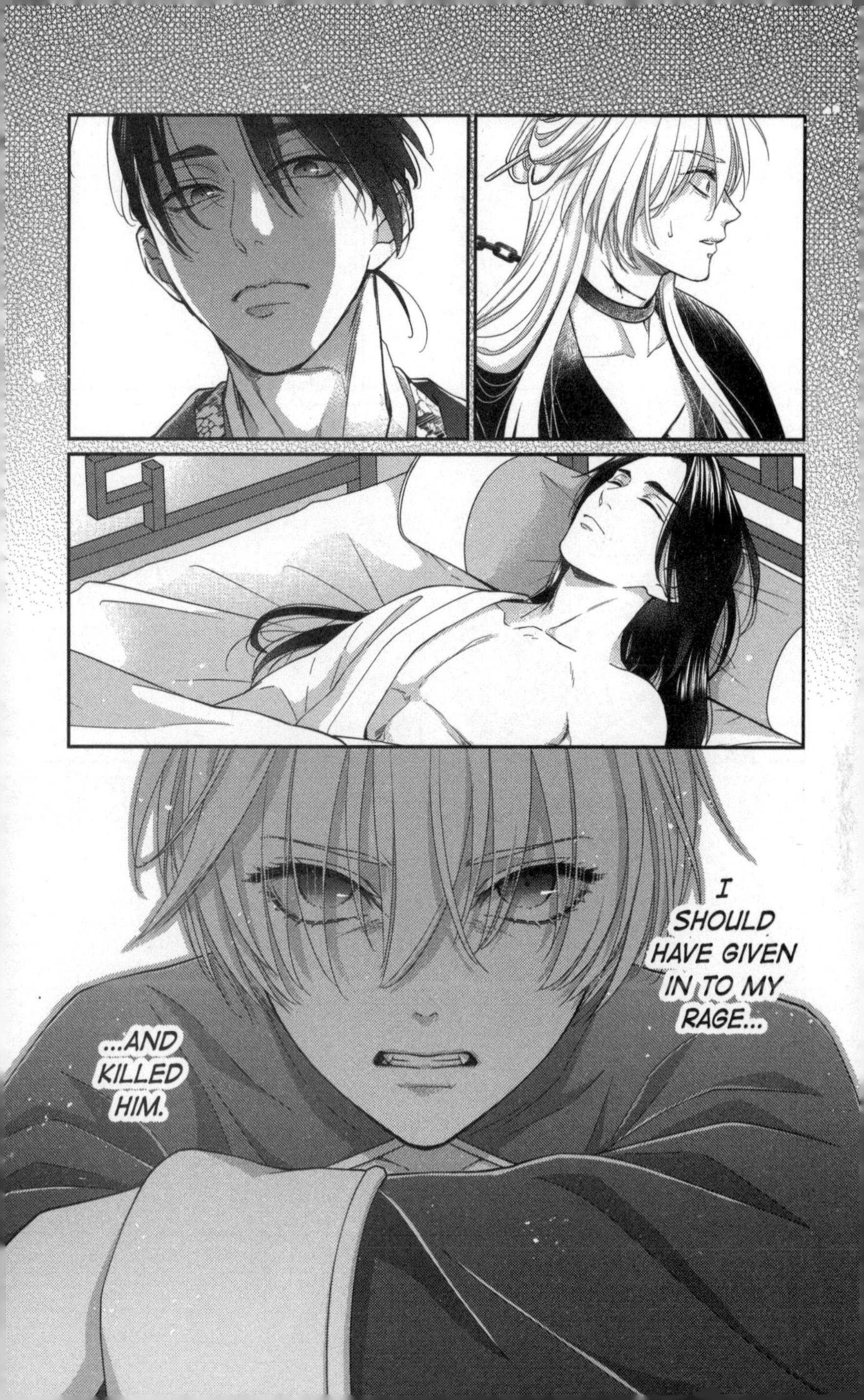
I SHOULD HAVE GIVEN IN TO MY RAGE...
...AND KILLED HIM.

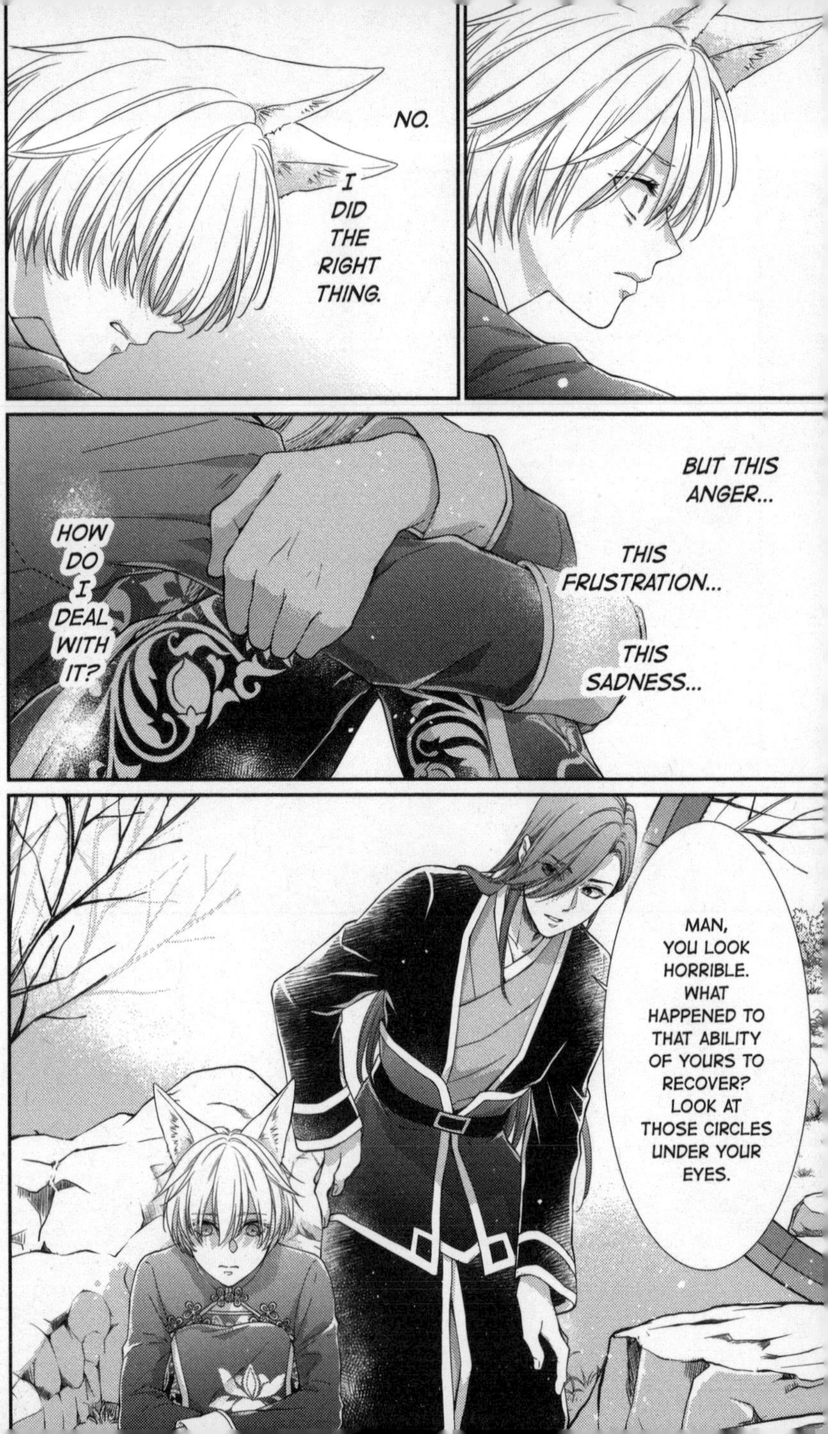
NO.
I DID THE RIGHT THING.
BUT THIS ANGER...
THIS FRUSTRATION...
THIS SADNESS...
HOW DO I DEAL WITH IT?
MAN, YOU LOOK HORRIBLE. WHAT HAPPENED TO THAT ABILITY OF YOURS TO RECOVER? LOOK AT THOSE CIRCLES UNDER YOUR EYES.

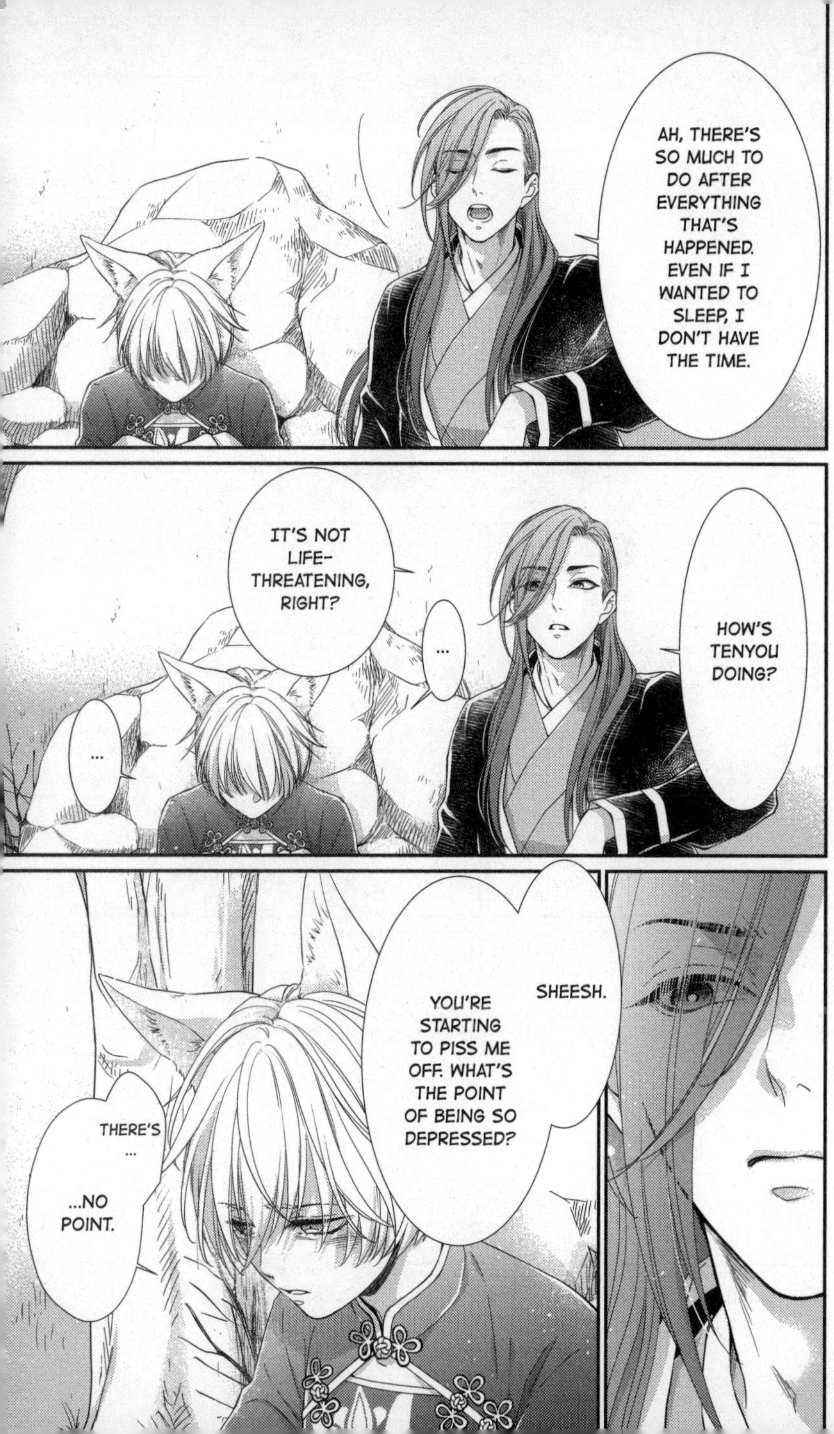
AH, THERE'S SO MUCH TO DO AFTER EVERYTHING THAT'S HAPPENED. EVEN IF I WANTED TO SLEEP, I DON'T HAVE THE TIME.
HOW'S TENYOU DOING?
...
IT'S NOT LIFE-THREATENING, RIGHT?
...
SHEESH.
YOU'RE STARTING TO PISS ME OFF. WHAT'S THE POINT OF BEING SO DEPRESSED?
THERE'S ...
...NO POINT.

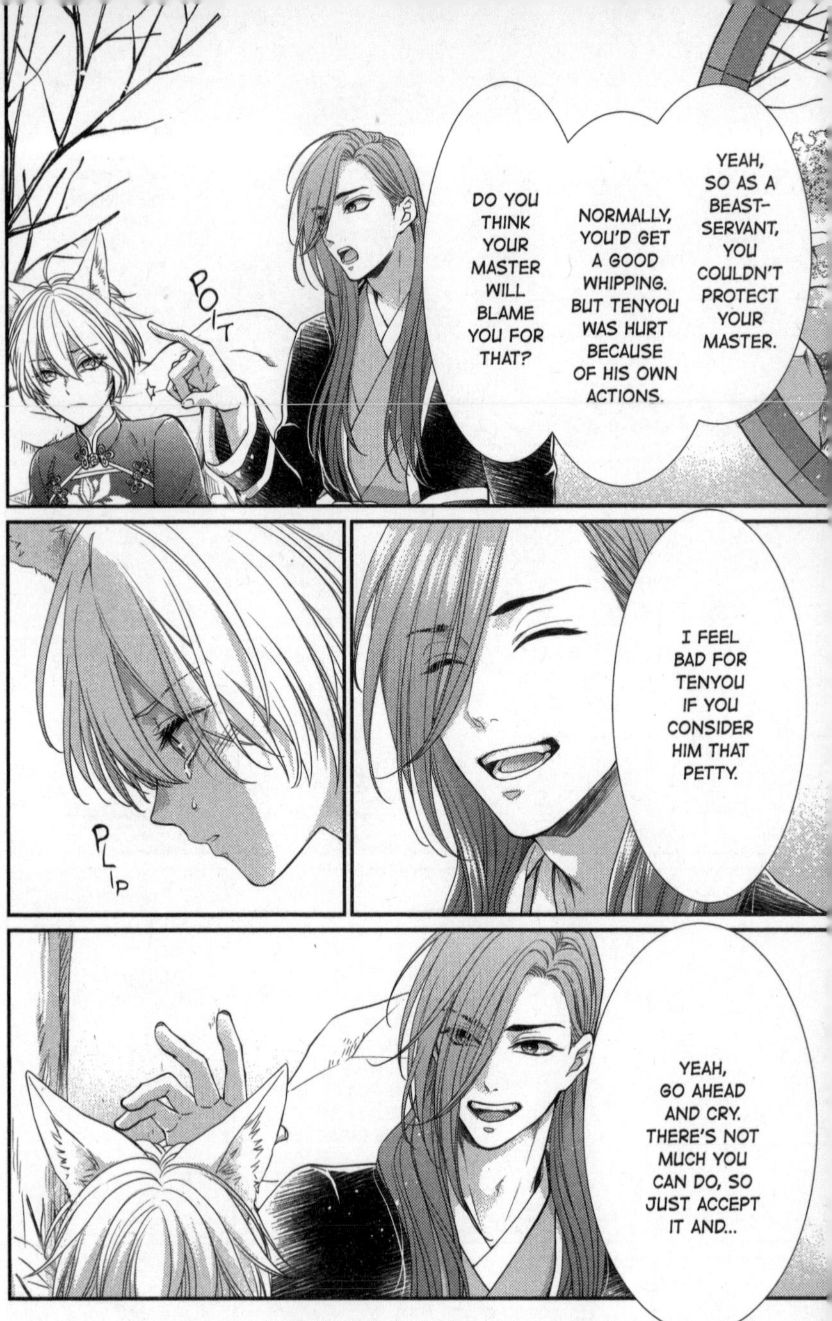
YEAH, SO AS A BEAST-SERVANT, YOU COULDN'T PROTECT YOUR MASTER.
NORMALLY, YOU'D GET A GOOD WHIPPING. BUT TENYOU WAS HURT BECAUSE OF HIS OWN ACTIONS.
DO YOU THINK YOUR MASTER WILL BLAME YOU FOR THAT?
POIT
I FEEL BAD FOR TENYOU IF YOU CONSIDER HIM THAT PETTY.
PLIP
YEAH, GO AHEAD AND CRY. THERE'S NOT MUCH YOU CAN DO, SO JUST ACCEPT IT AND...

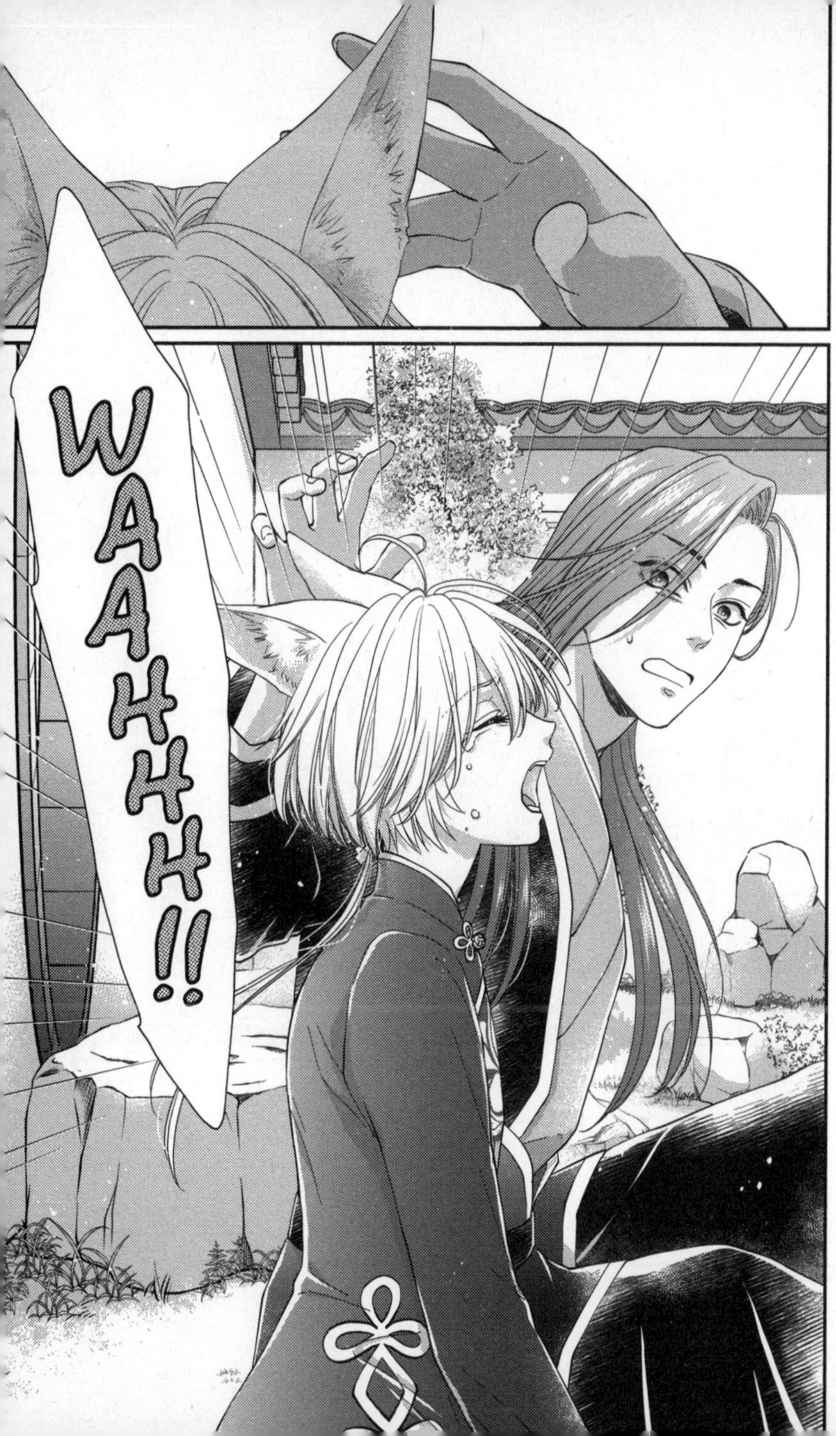
WAAHHH!!

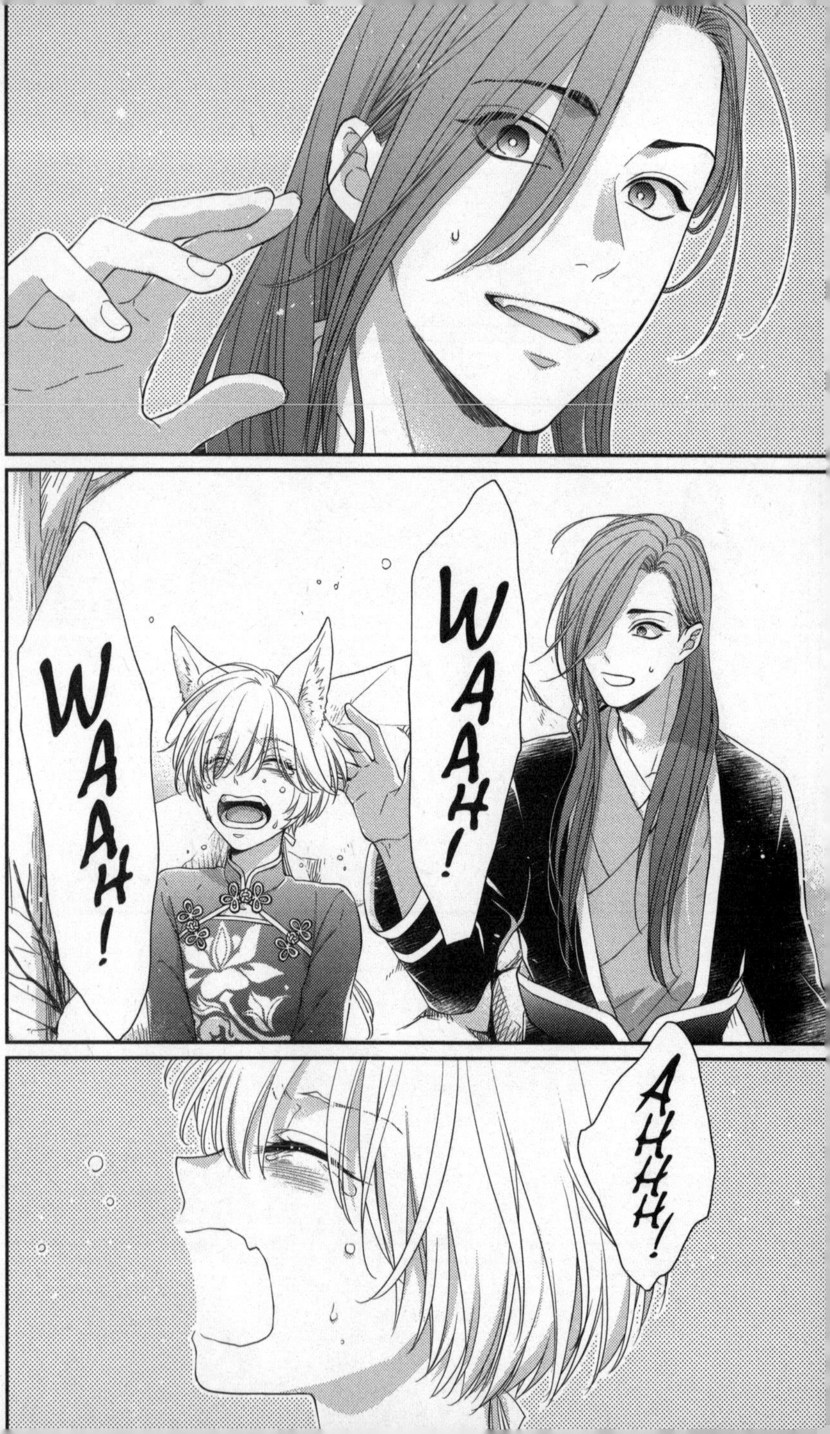
WAAAH!
WAAAH!
AHHHH!

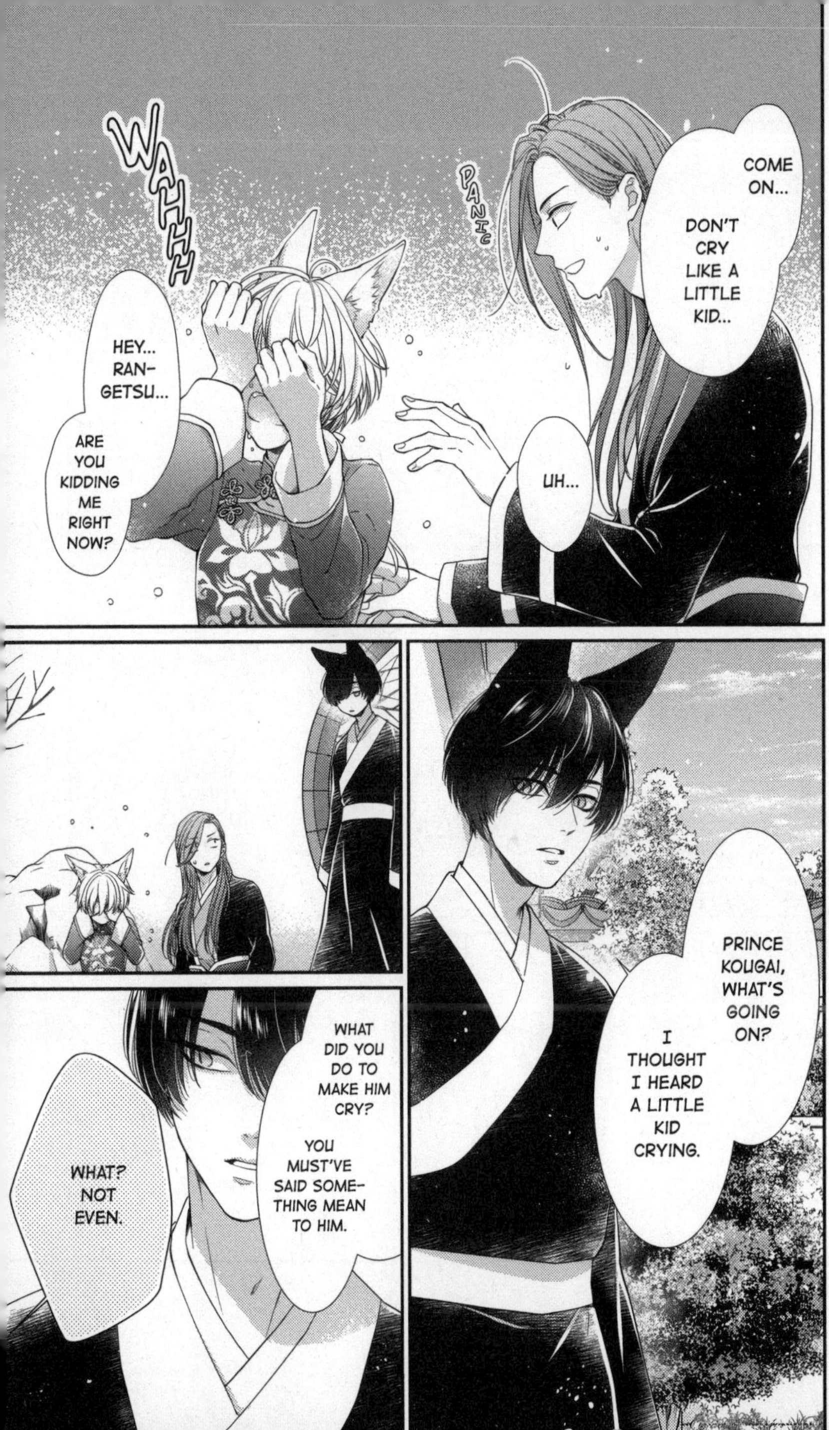
COME ON...
DON'T CRY LIKE A LITTLE KID...
PANIC
WAHHHH
UH...
HEY... RAN-GETSU...
ARE YOU KIDDING ME RIGHT NOW?
PRINCE KOUGAI, WHAT'S GOING ON?
I THOUGHT I HEARD A LITTLE KID CRYING.
WHAT DID YOU DO TO MAKE HIM CRY?
YOU MUST'VE SAID SOME-THING MEAN TO HIM.
WHAT? NOT EVEN.

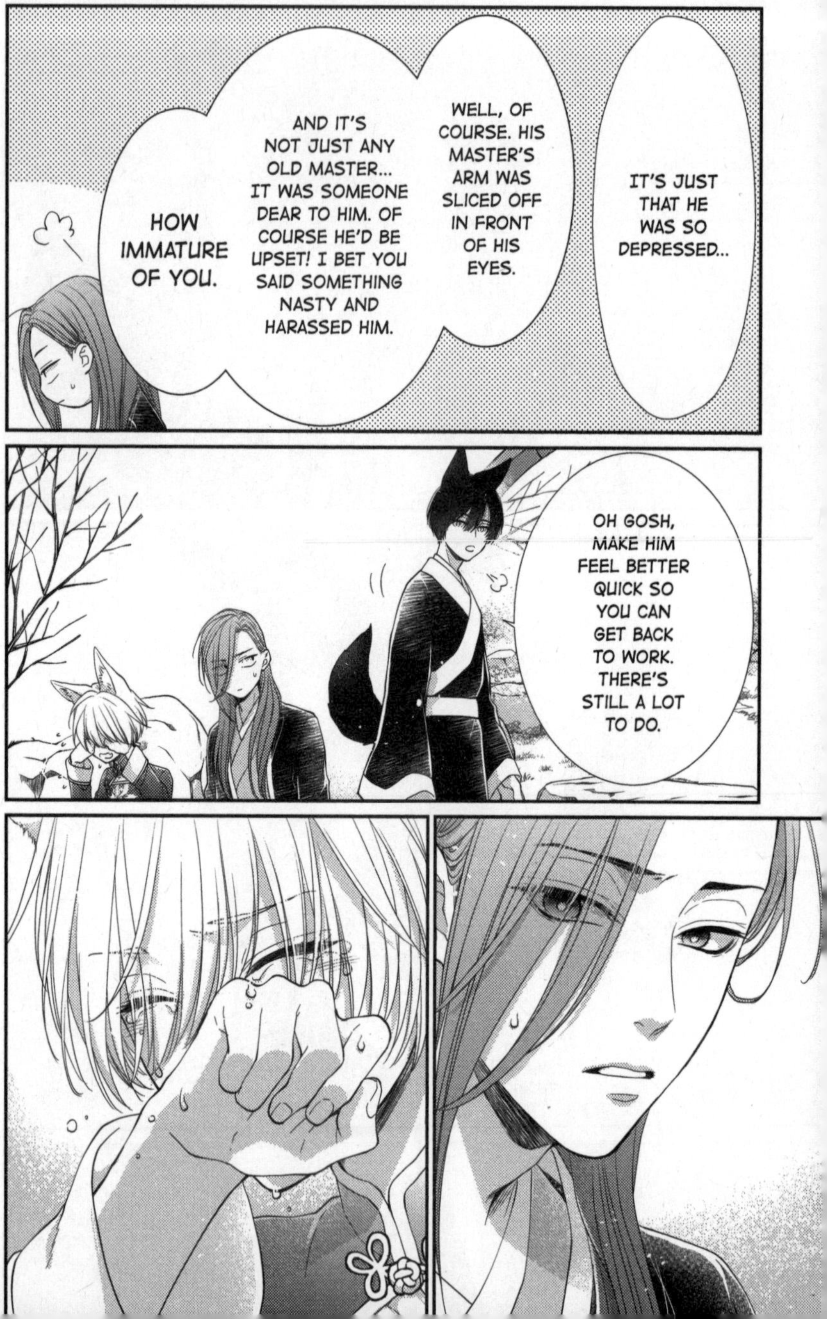
IT'S JUST THAT HE WAS SO DEPRESSED...
WELL, OF COURSE. HIS MASTER'S ARM WAS SLICED OFF IN FRONT OF HIS EYES.
AND IT'S NOT JUST ANY OLD MASTER... IT WAS SOMEONE DEAR TO HIM. OF COURSE HE'D BE UPSET! I BET YOU SAID SOMETHING NASTY AND HARASSED HIM.
HOW IMMATURE OF YOU.
OH GOSH, MAKE HIM FEEL BETTER QUICK SO YOU CAN GET BACK TO WORK. THERE'S STILL A LOT TO DO.

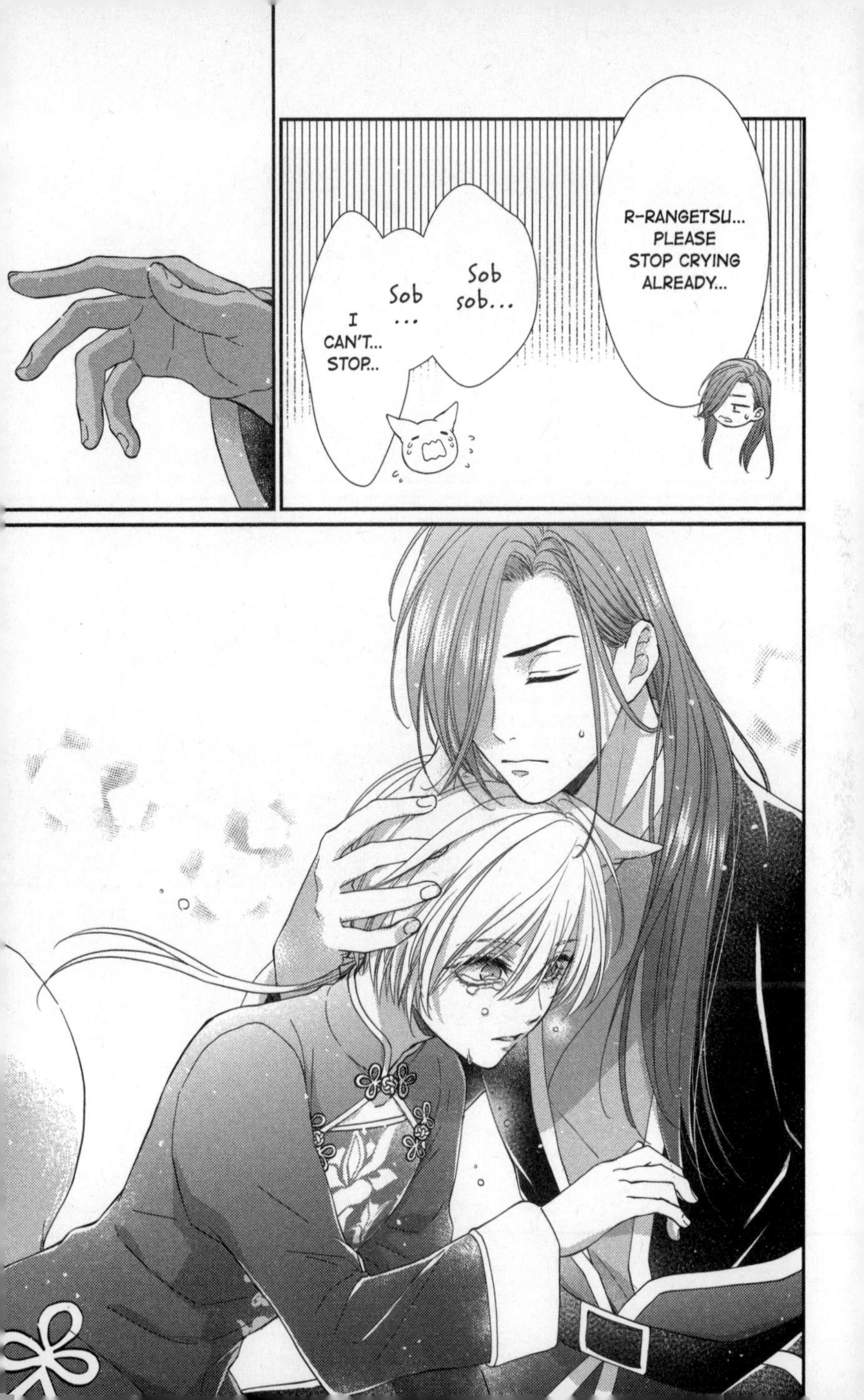
R-RANGETSU... PLEASE STOP CRYING ALREADY...
Sob sob...
Sob ...
I CAN'T... STOP...

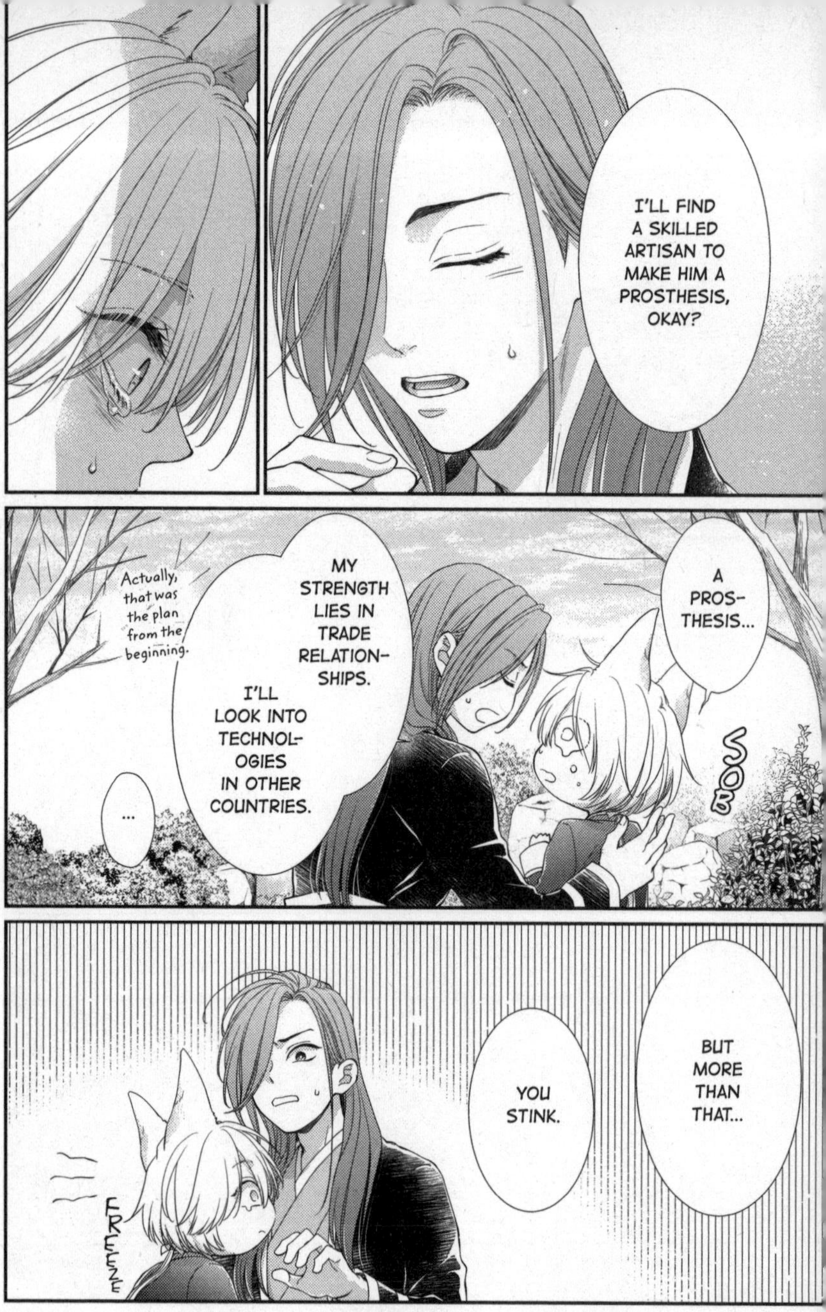

I'LL FIND A SKILLED ARTISAN TO MAKE HIM A PROSTHESIS, OKAY?
A PROS-THESIS...
SOB
MY STRENGTH LIES IN TRADE RELATION-SHIPS.
I'LL LOOK INTO TECHNOL-OGIES IN OTHER COUNTRIES.
Actually, that was the plan from the beginning.
...
BUT MORE THAN THAT...
YOU STINK.
FREEZE

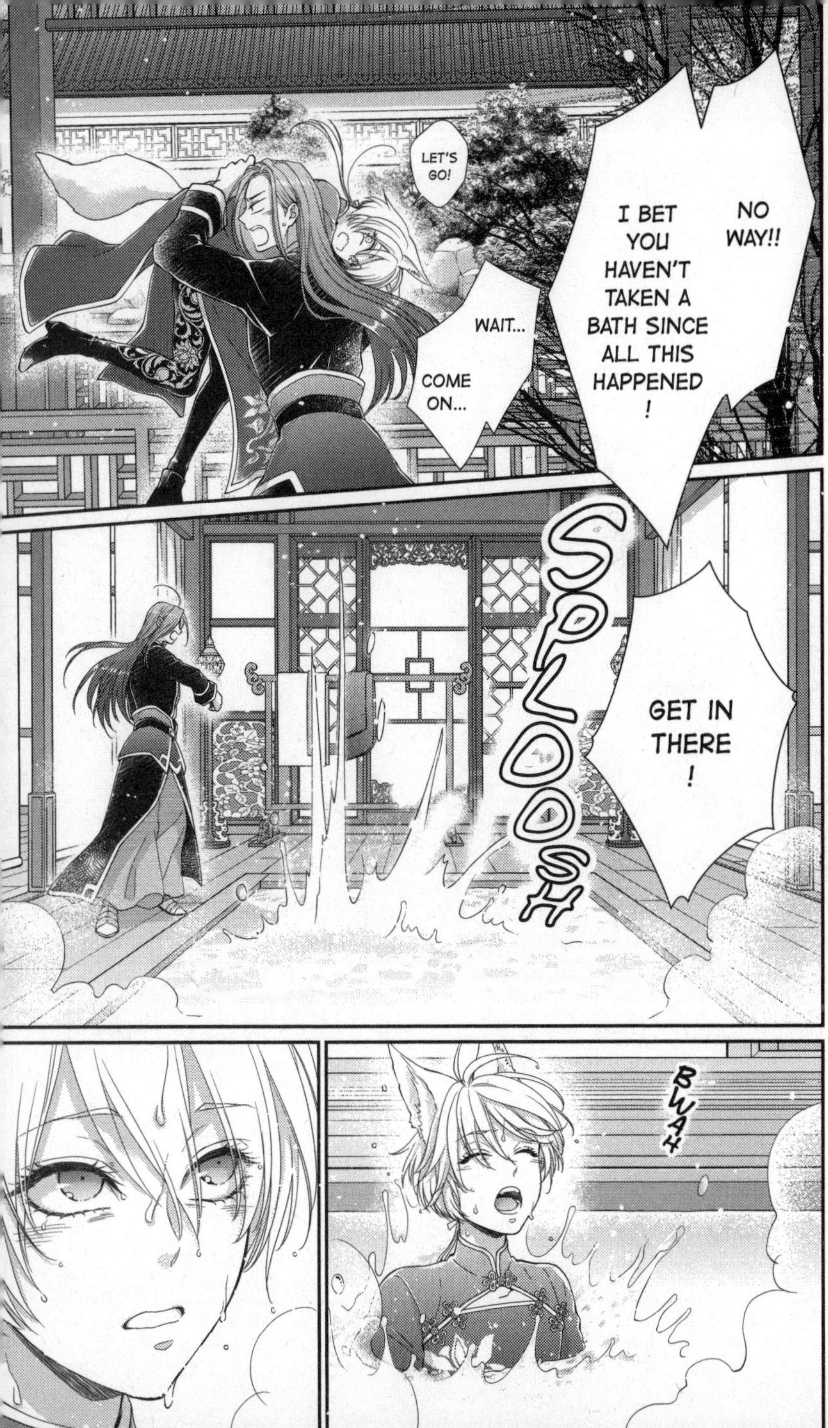
NO WAY!!
I BET YOU HAVEN'T TAKEN A BATH SINCE ALL THIS HAPPENED!
LET'S GO!
WAIT...
COME ON...
GET IN THERE!
SPLOOSH
BWAH

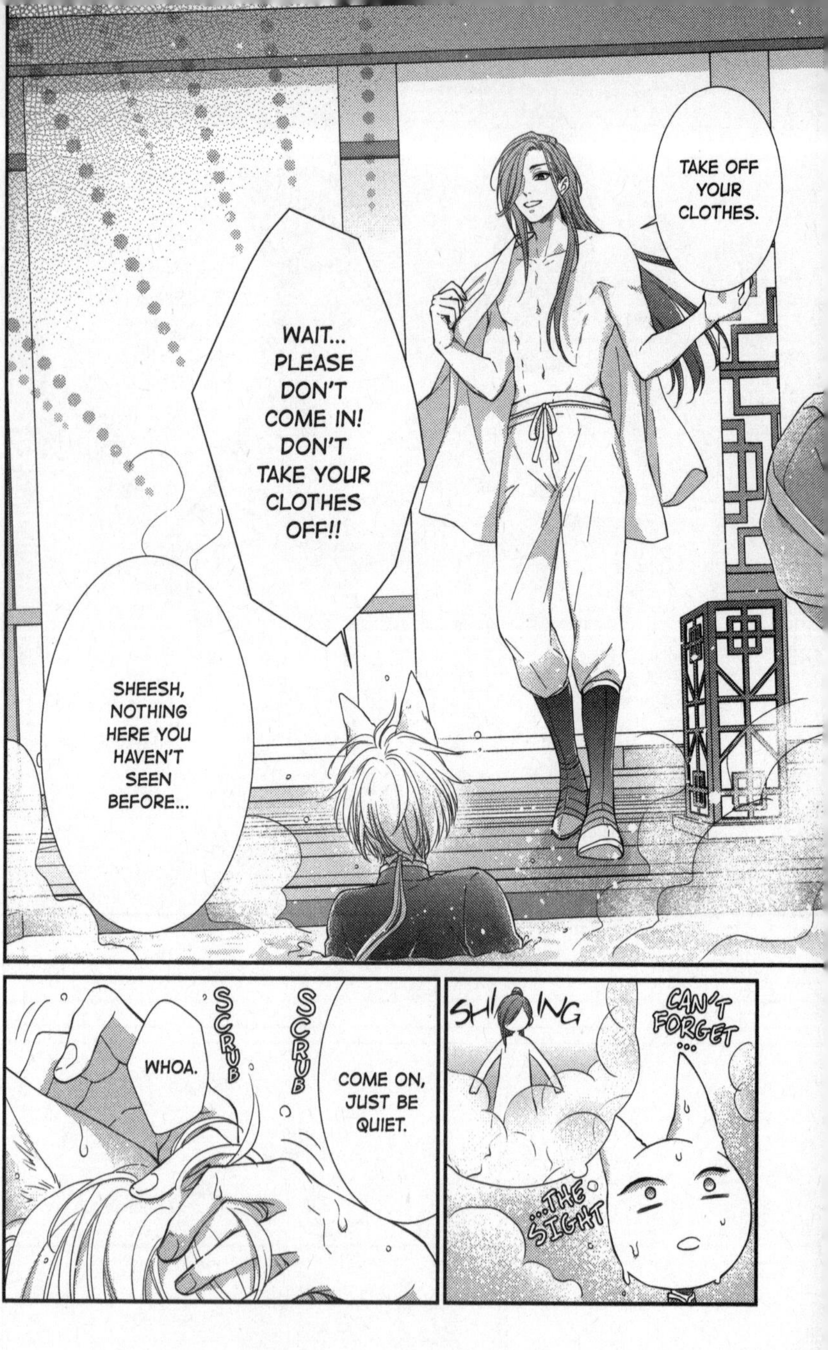
TAKE OFF YOUR CLOTHES.
WAIT... PLEASE DON'T COME IN! DON'T TAKE YOUR CLOTHES OFF!!
SHEESH, NOTHING HERE YOU HAVEN'T SEEN BEFORE...
SHIING
CAN'T FORGET...
...THE SIGHT
SCRUB
COME ON, JUST BE QUIET.
SCRUB
WHOA.

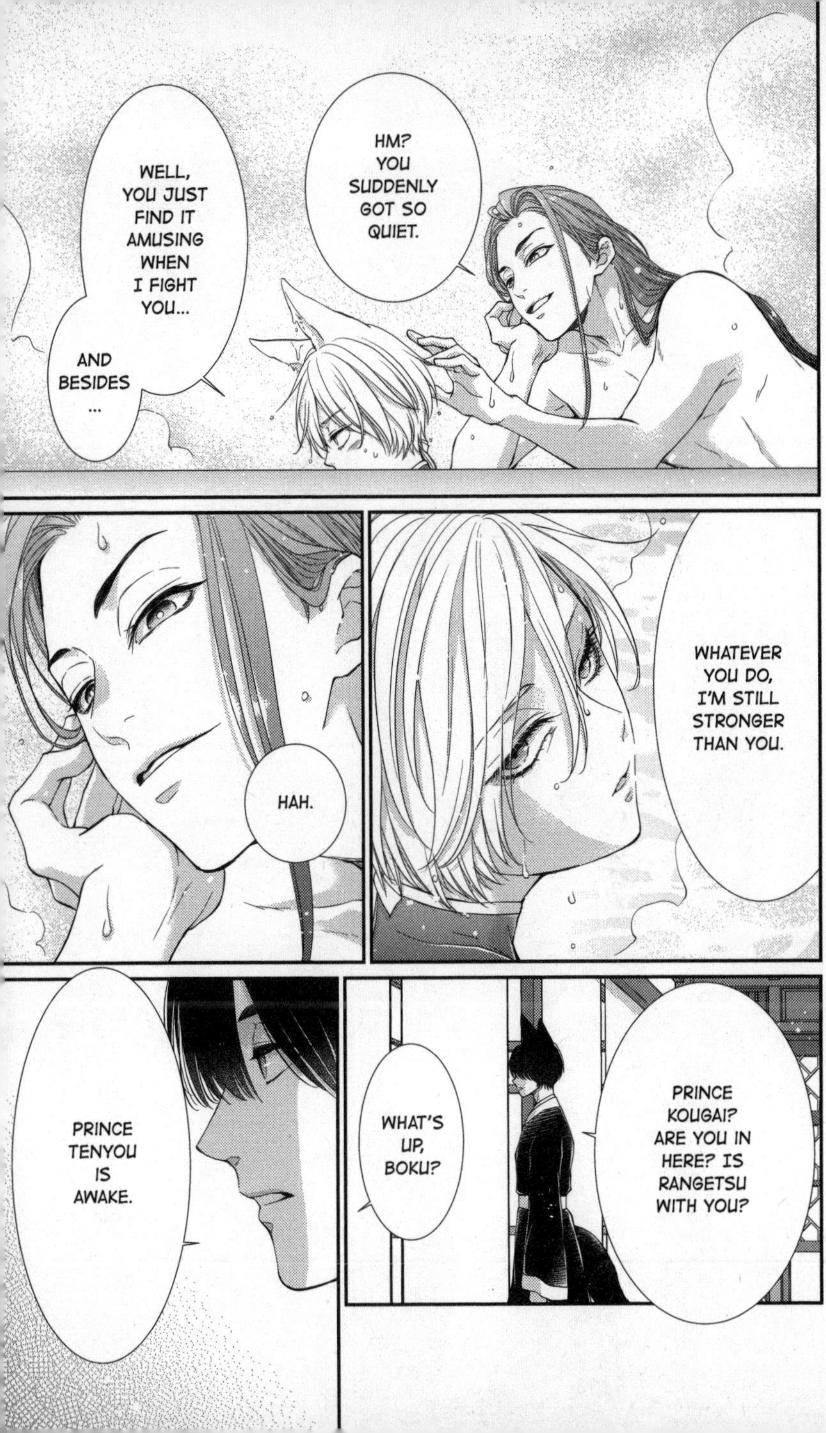
HM? YOU SUDDENLY GOT SO QUIET.
WELL, YOU JUST FIND IT AMUSING WHEN I FIGHT YOU...
AND BESIDES ...
WHATEVER YOU DO, I'M STILL STRONGER THAN YOU.
HAH.
PRINCE KOUGAI? ARE YOU IN HERE? IS RANGETSU WITH YOU?
WHAT'S UP, BOKU?
PRINCE TENYOU IS AWAKE.

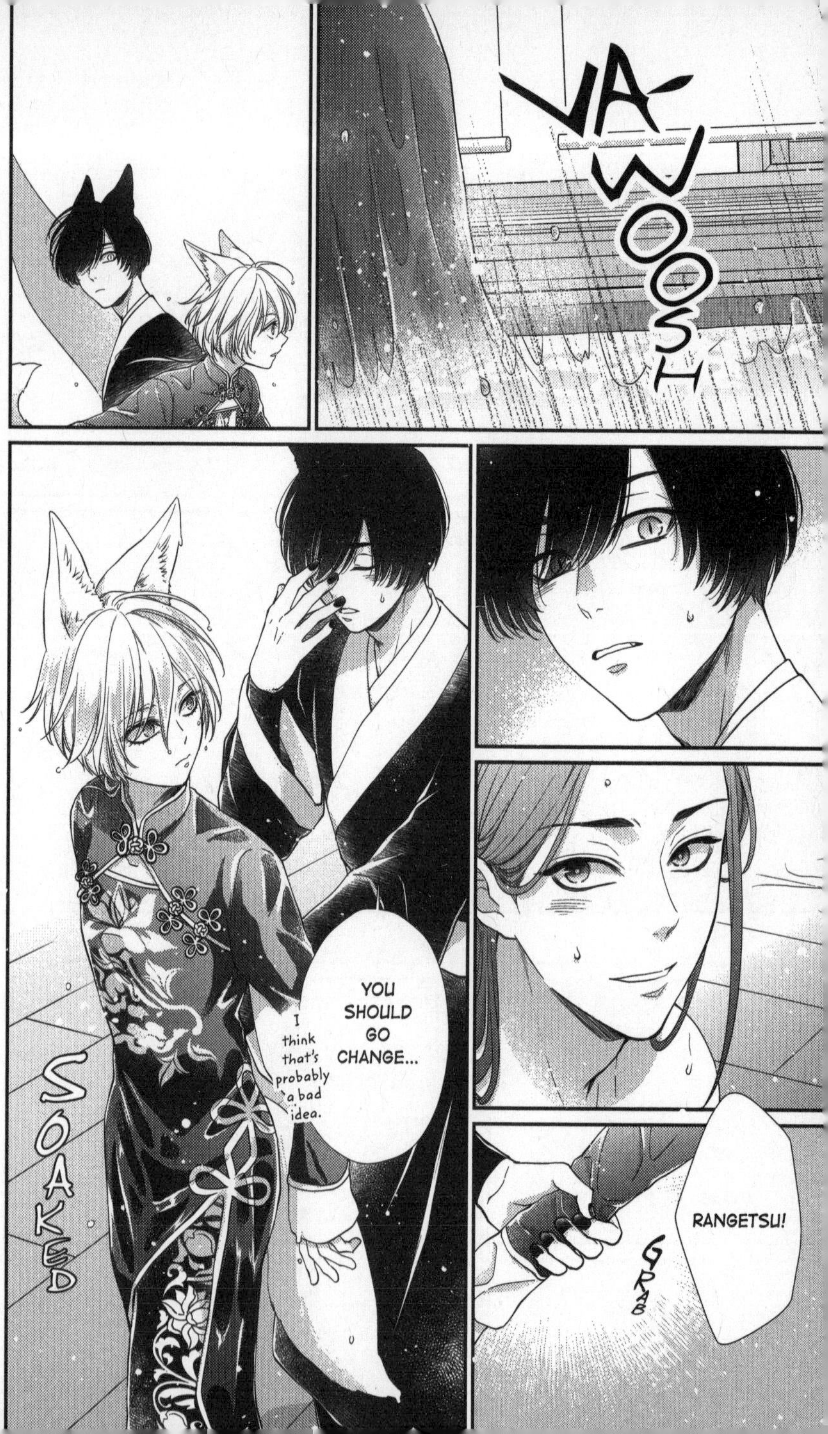
VAWOOSH
RANGETSU!
GRAB
YOU SHOULD GO CHANGE...
I think that's probably a bad idea.
SOAKED

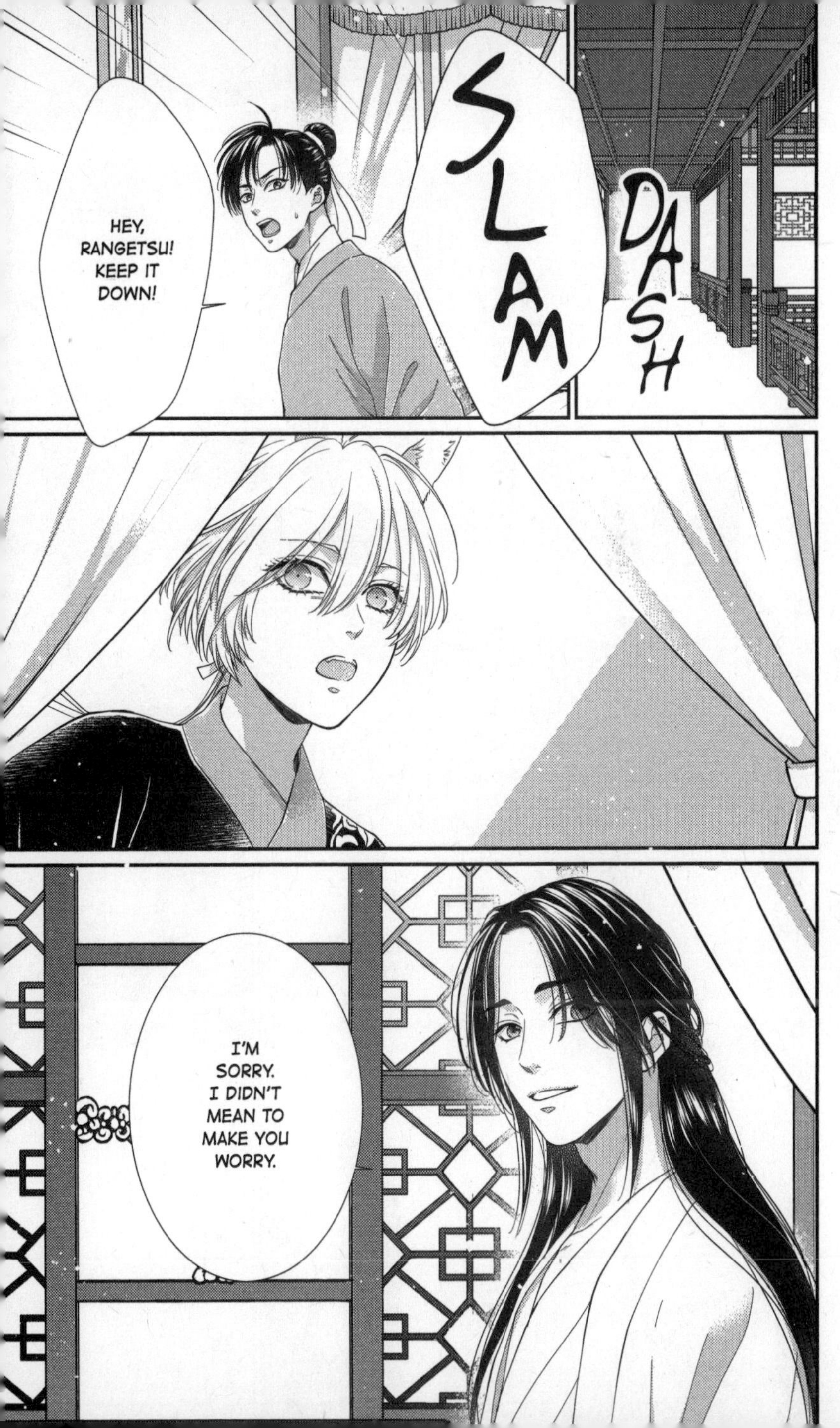
DASH
SLAM
HEY, RANGETSU! KEEP IT DOWN!
I'M SORRY. I DIDN'T MEAN TO MAKE YOU WORRY.

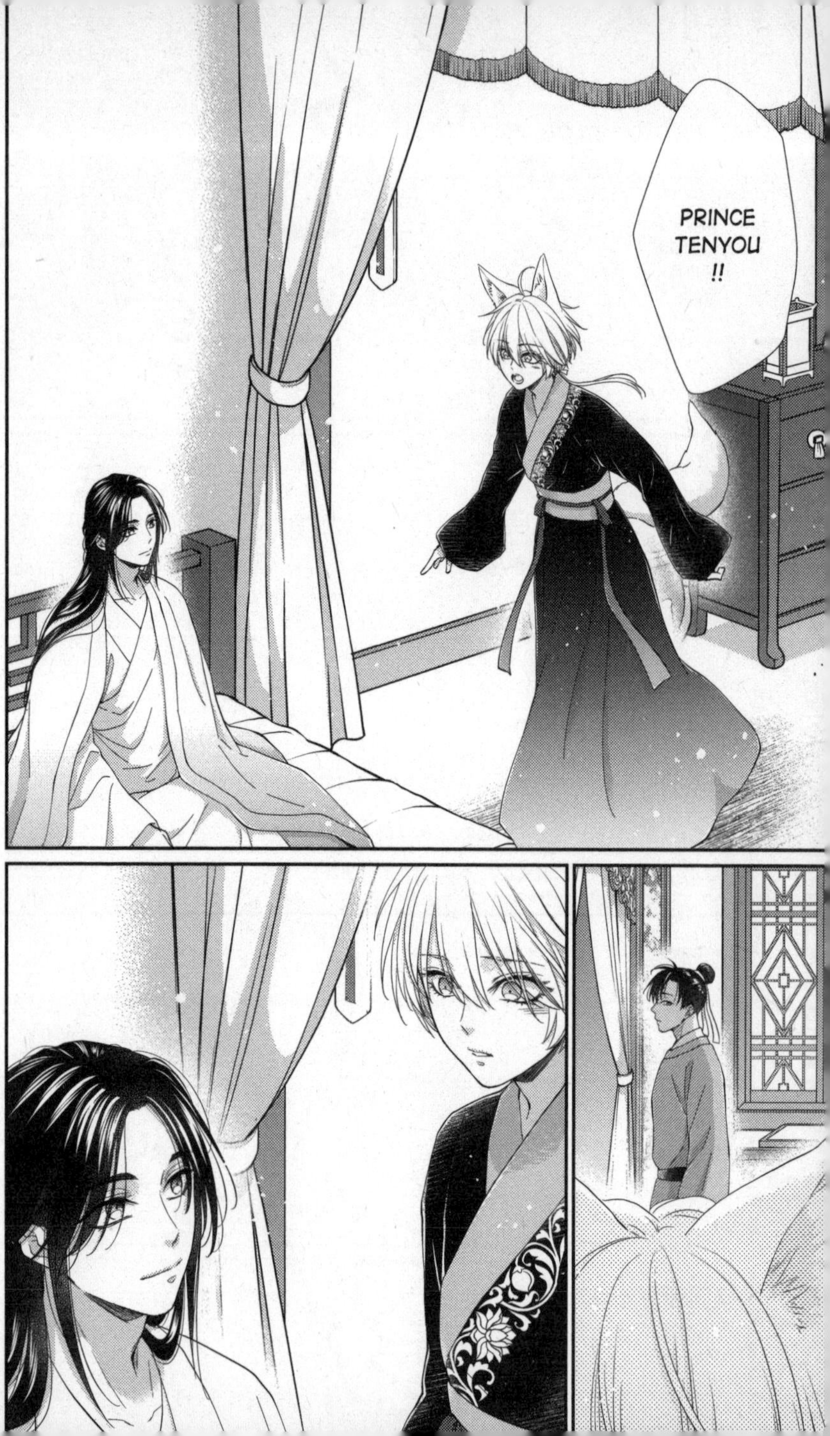
PRINCE TENYOU !!

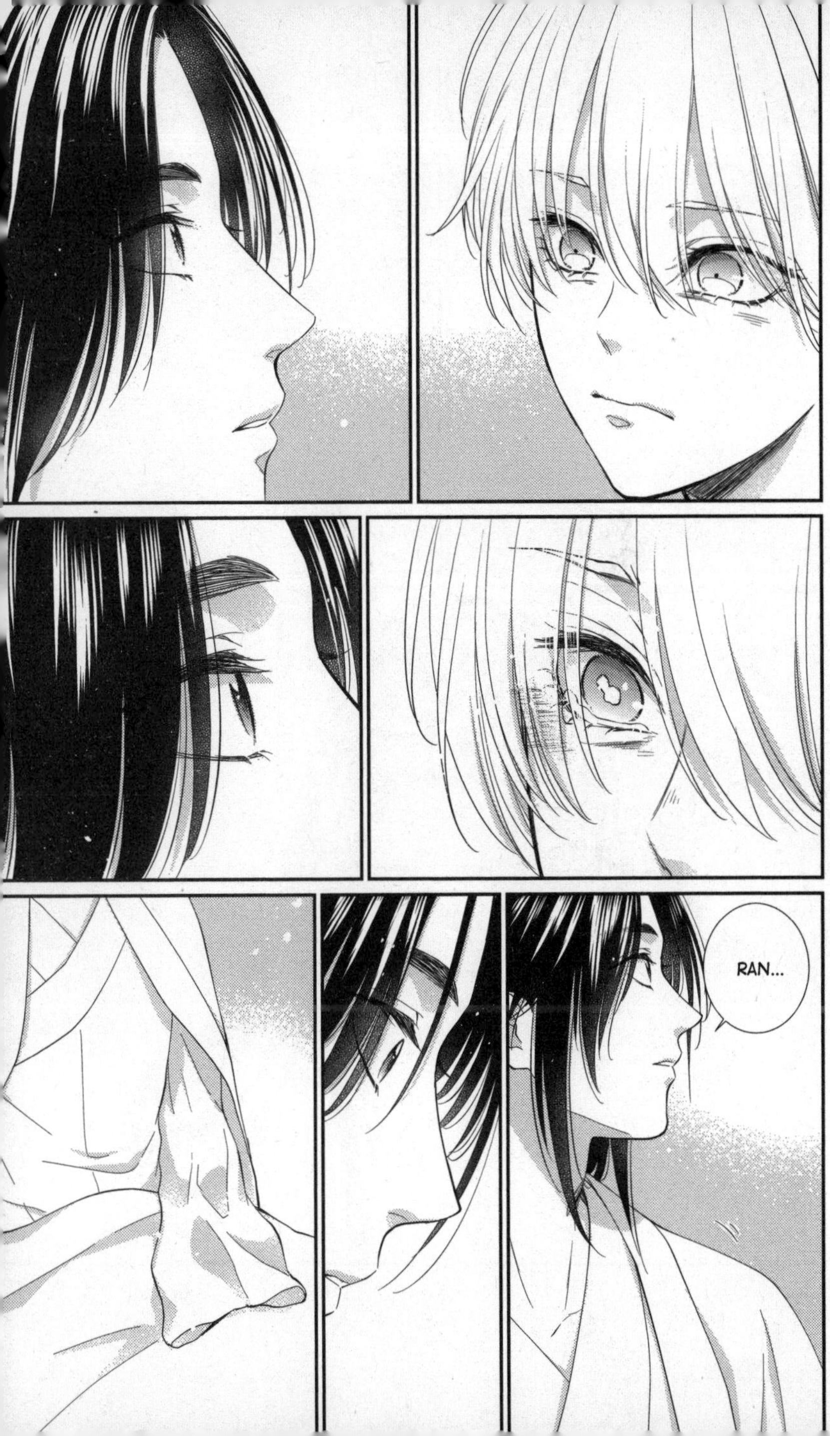
RAN...

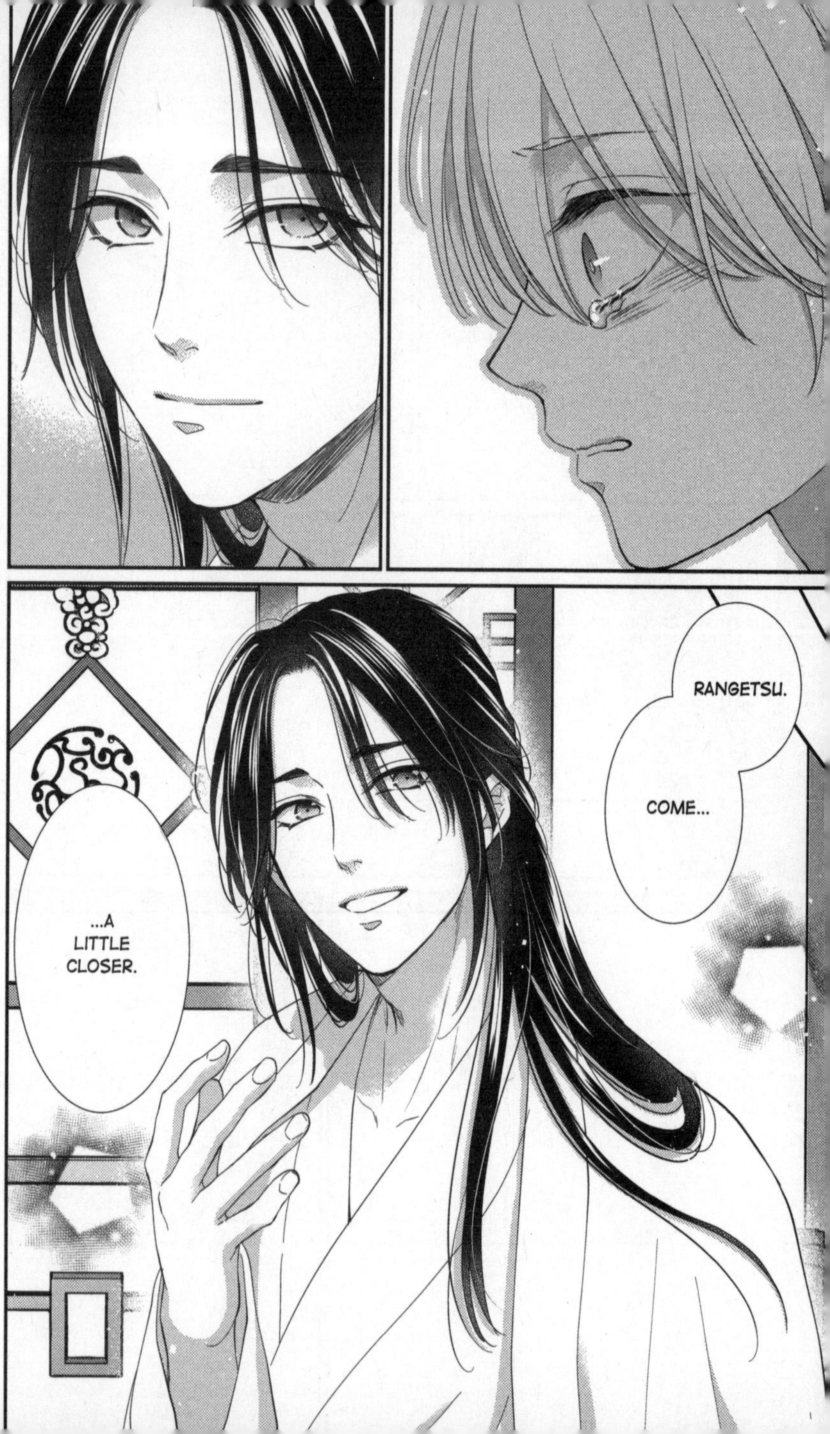
RANGETSU.
COME...
...A LITTLE CLOSER.

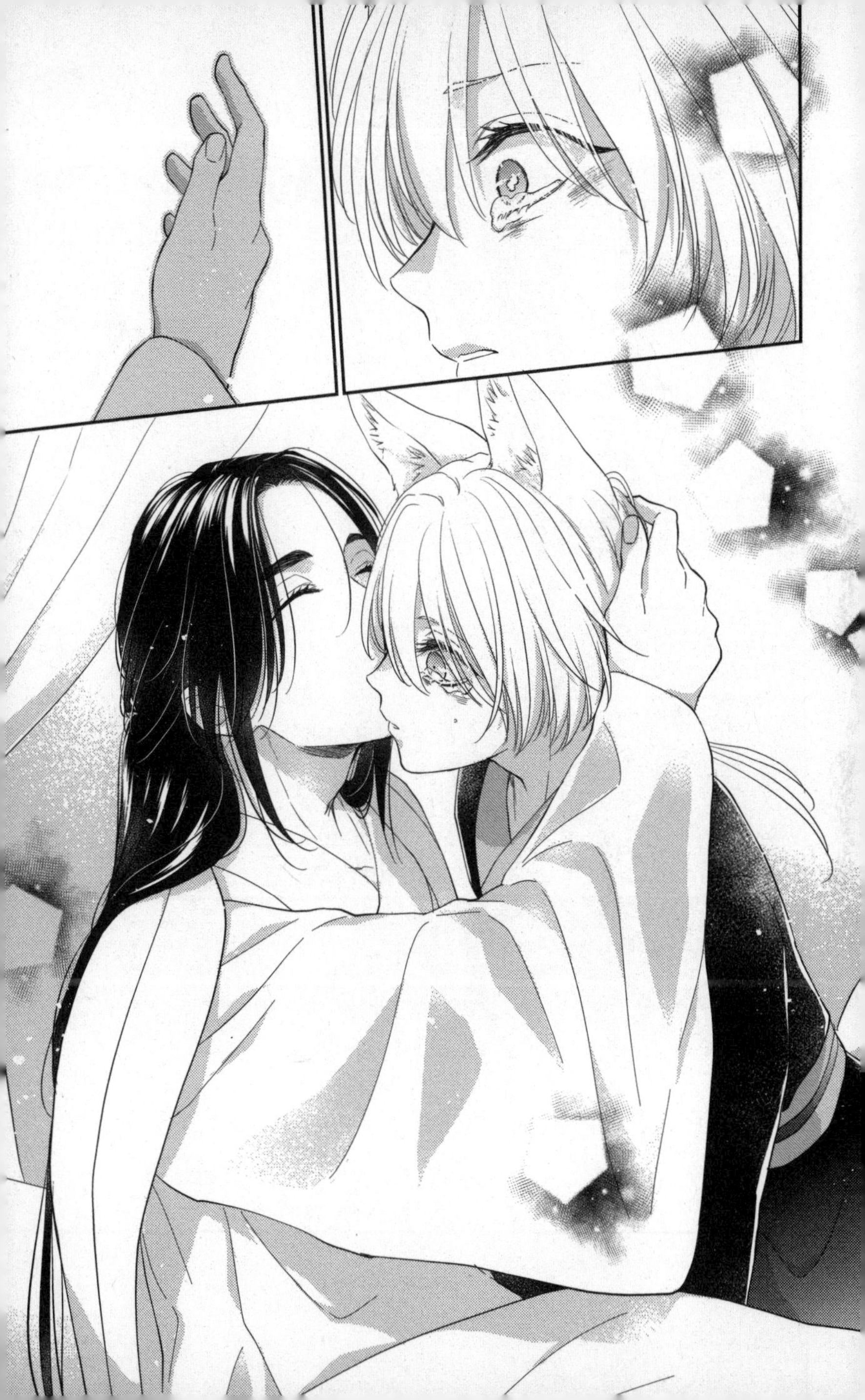

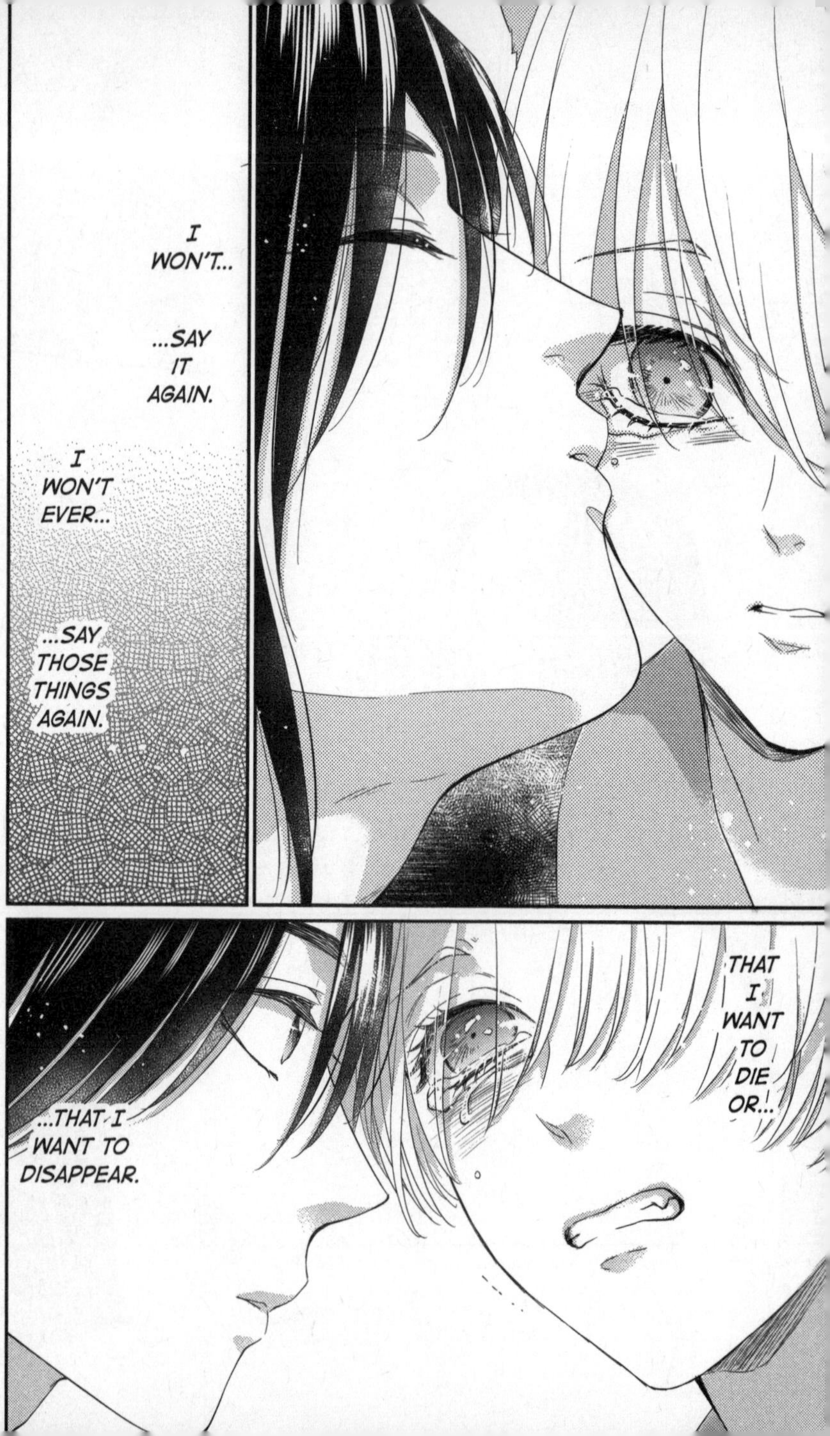
I WON'T...
...SAY IT AGAIN.
I WON'T EVER...
...SAY THOSE THINGS AGAIN.
THAT I WANT TO DIE OR...
...THAT I WANT TO DISAPPEAR.

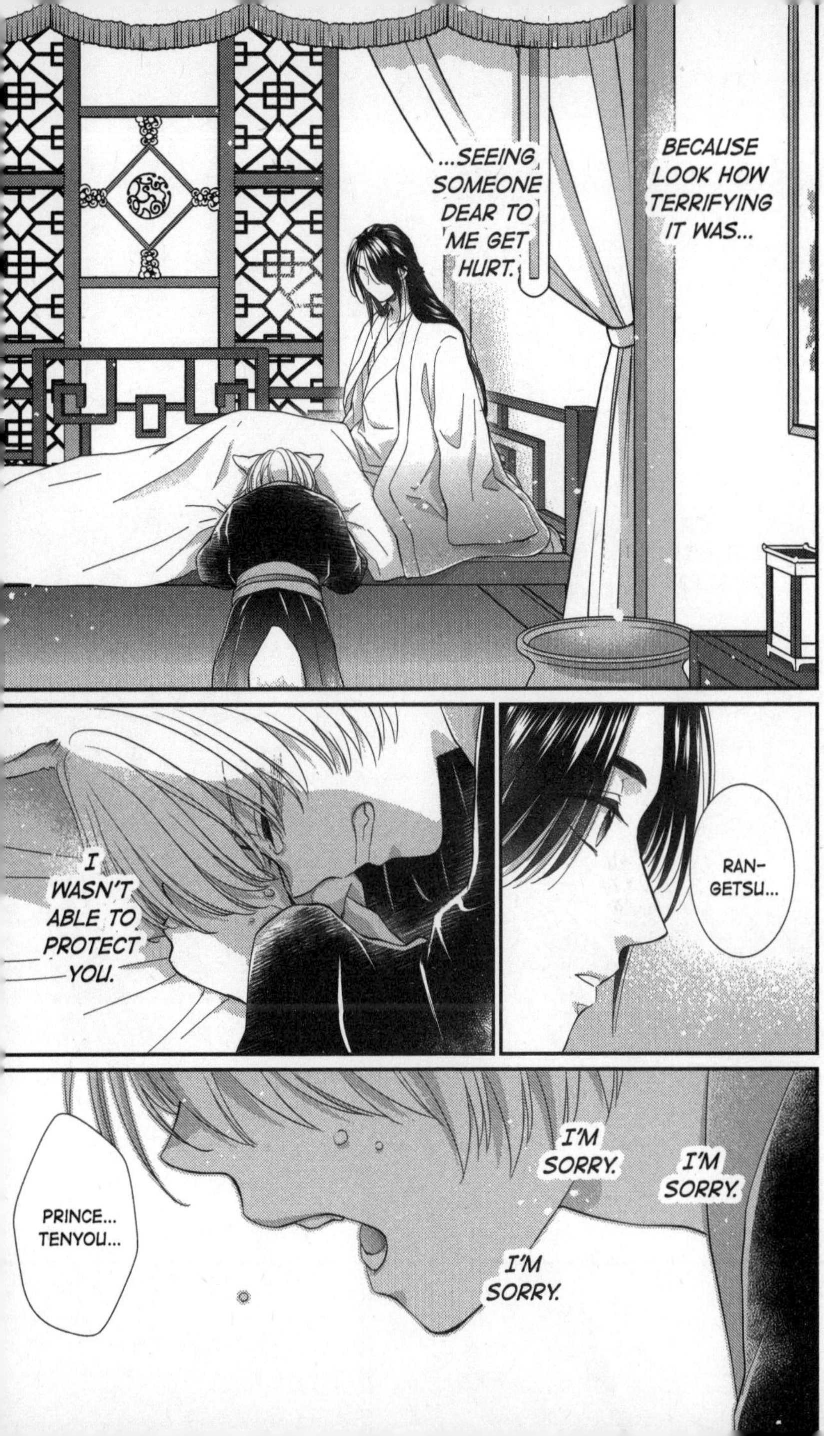
BECAUSE LOOK HOW TERRIFYING IT WAS...
...SEEING SOMEONE DEAR TO ME GET HURT.
RAN-GETSU...
I WASN'T ABLE TO PROTECT YOU.
I'M SORRY.
I'M SORRY.
I'M SORRY.
PRINCE... TENYOU...

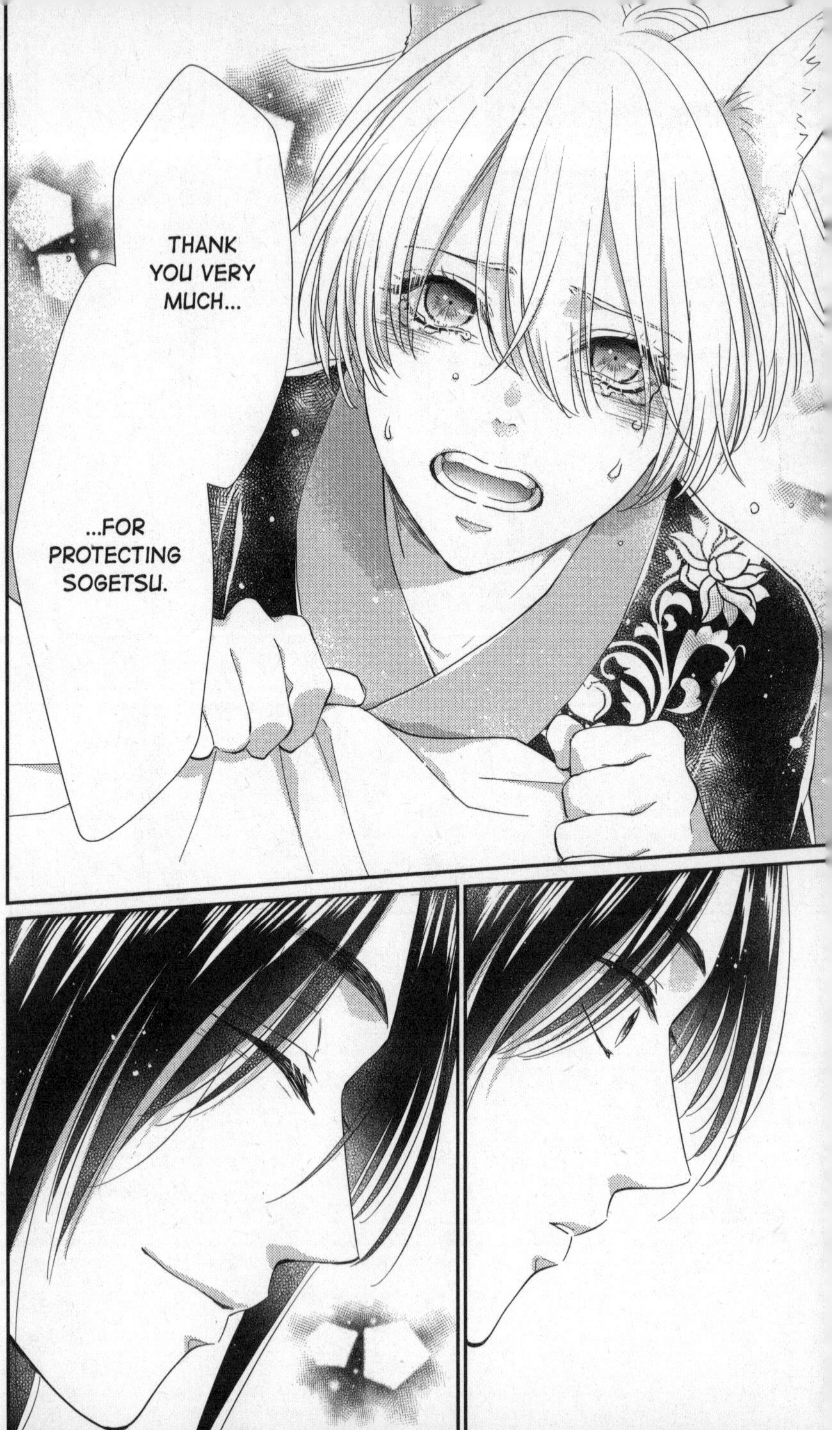
THANK YOU VERY MUCH...
...FOR PROTECTING SOGETSU.

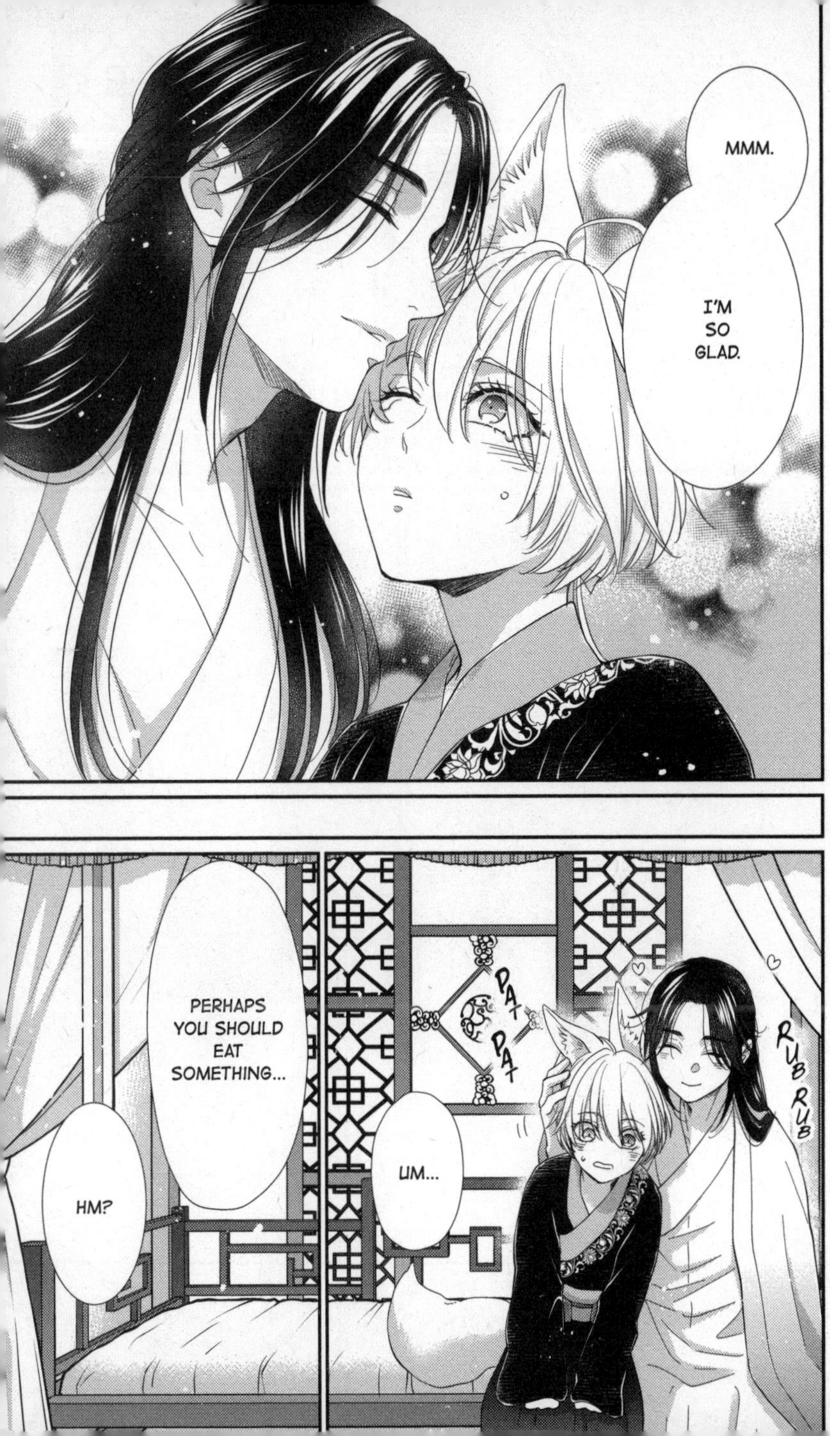

MMM.
I'M SO GLAD.
RUB RUB
PAT PAT
PERHAPS YOU SHOULD EAT SOMETHING...
UM...
HM?

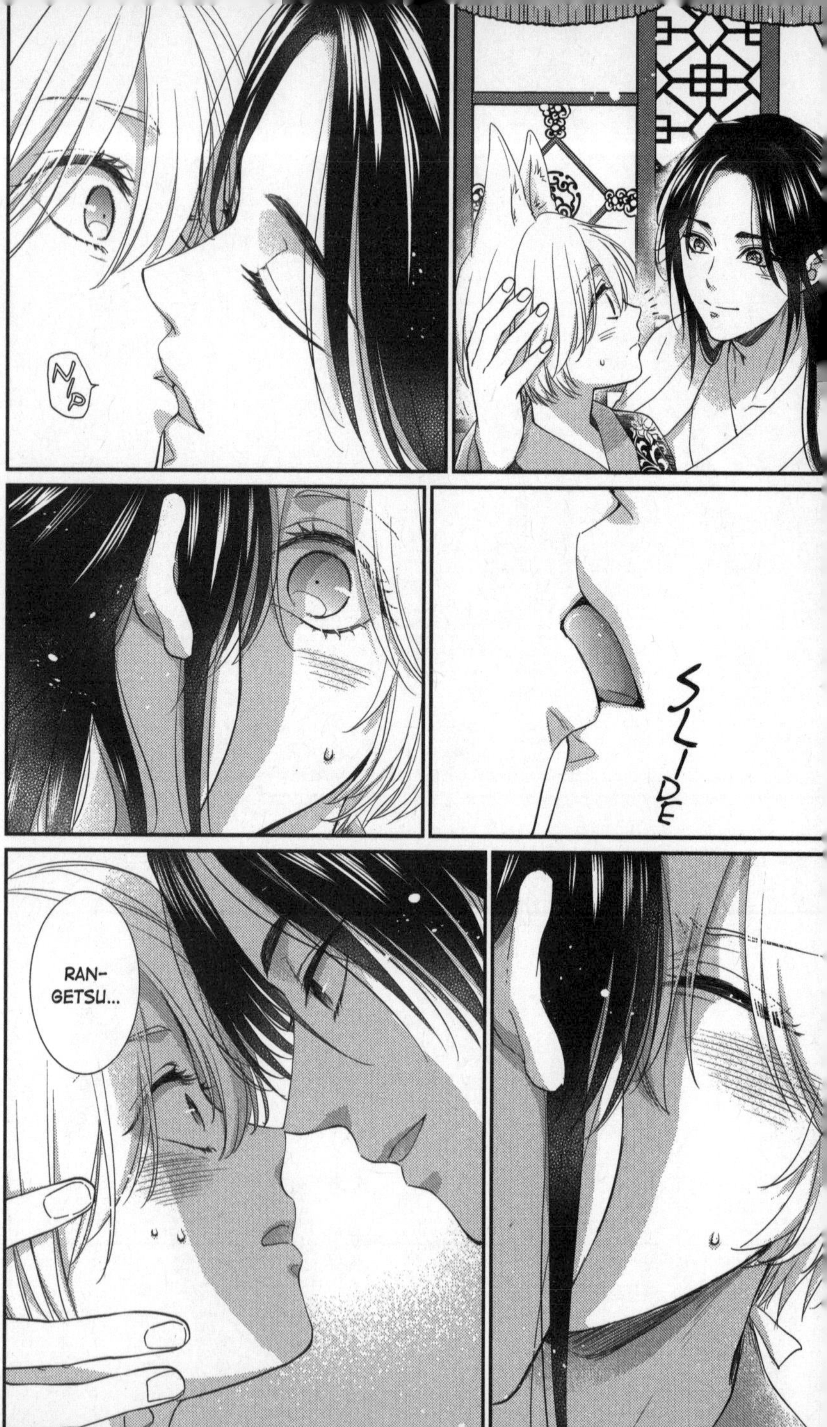
NIP
SLIDE
RAN-GETSU...

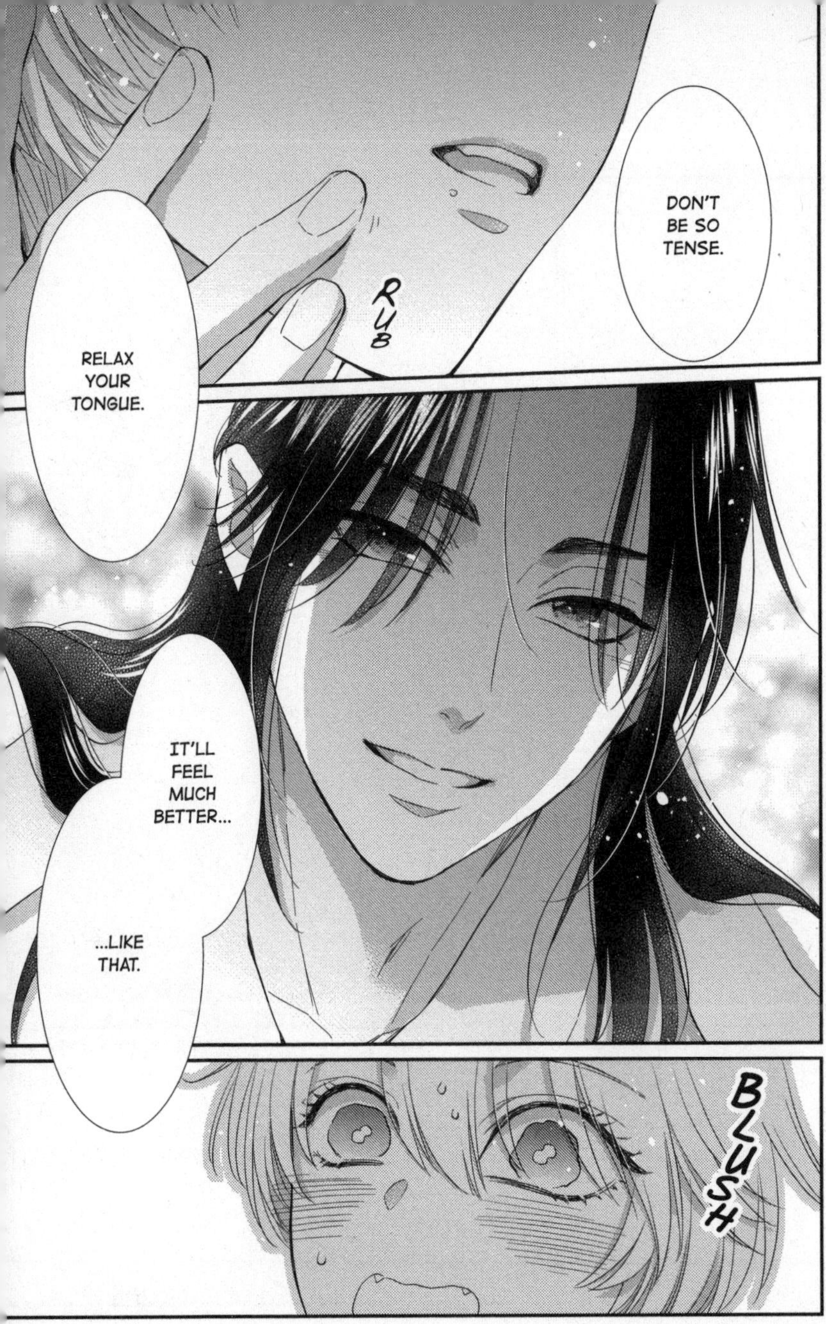
DON'T BE SO TENSE.
RUB
RELAX YOUR TONGUE.
IT'LL FEEL MUCH BETTER...
...LIKE THAT.
BLUSH

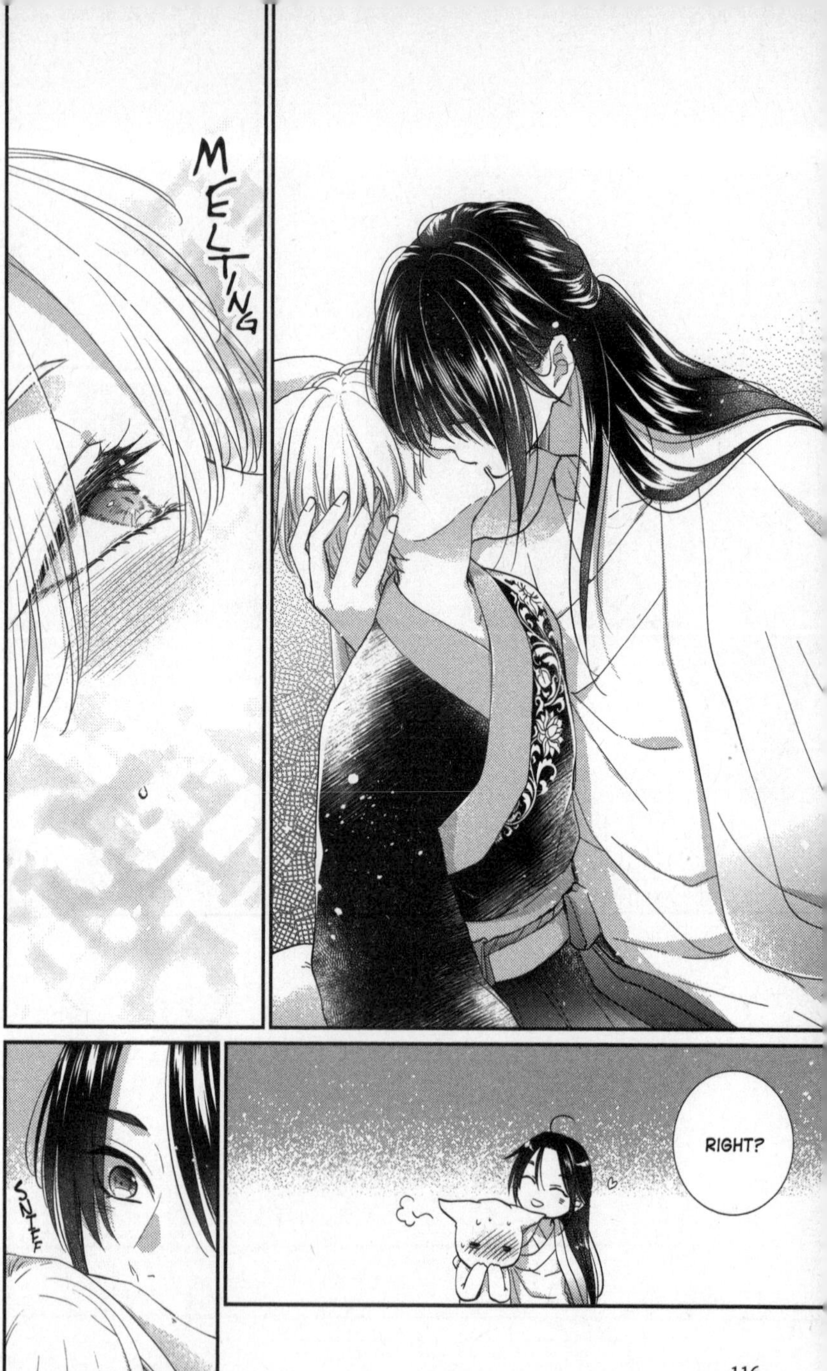
MELTING
RIGHT?
SNIFF

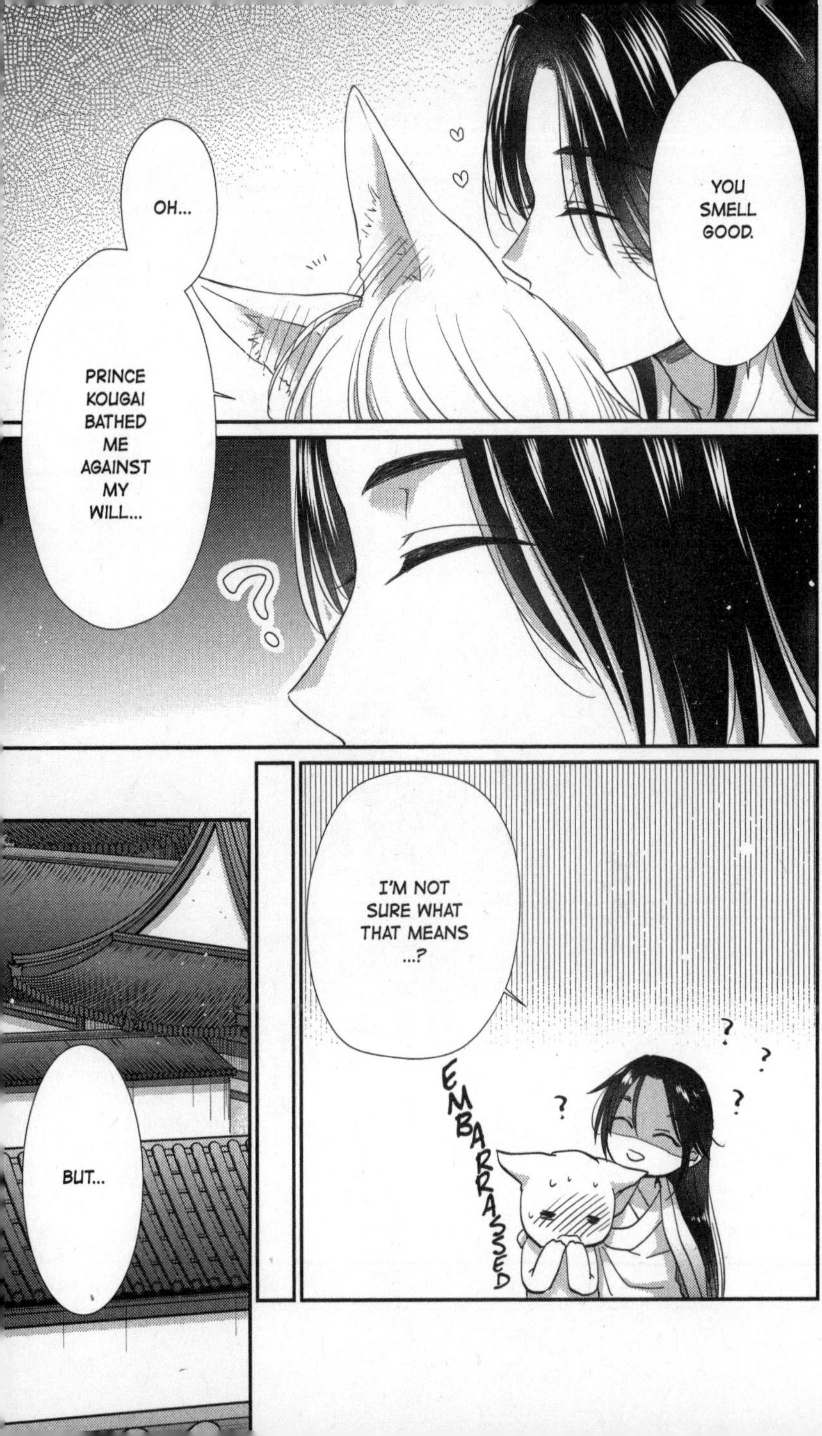
YOU SMELL GOOD.
OH...
PRINCE KOUGAI BATHED ME AGAINST MY WILL...
I'M NOT SURE WHAT THAT MEANS ...?
EMBARRASSED
BUT...

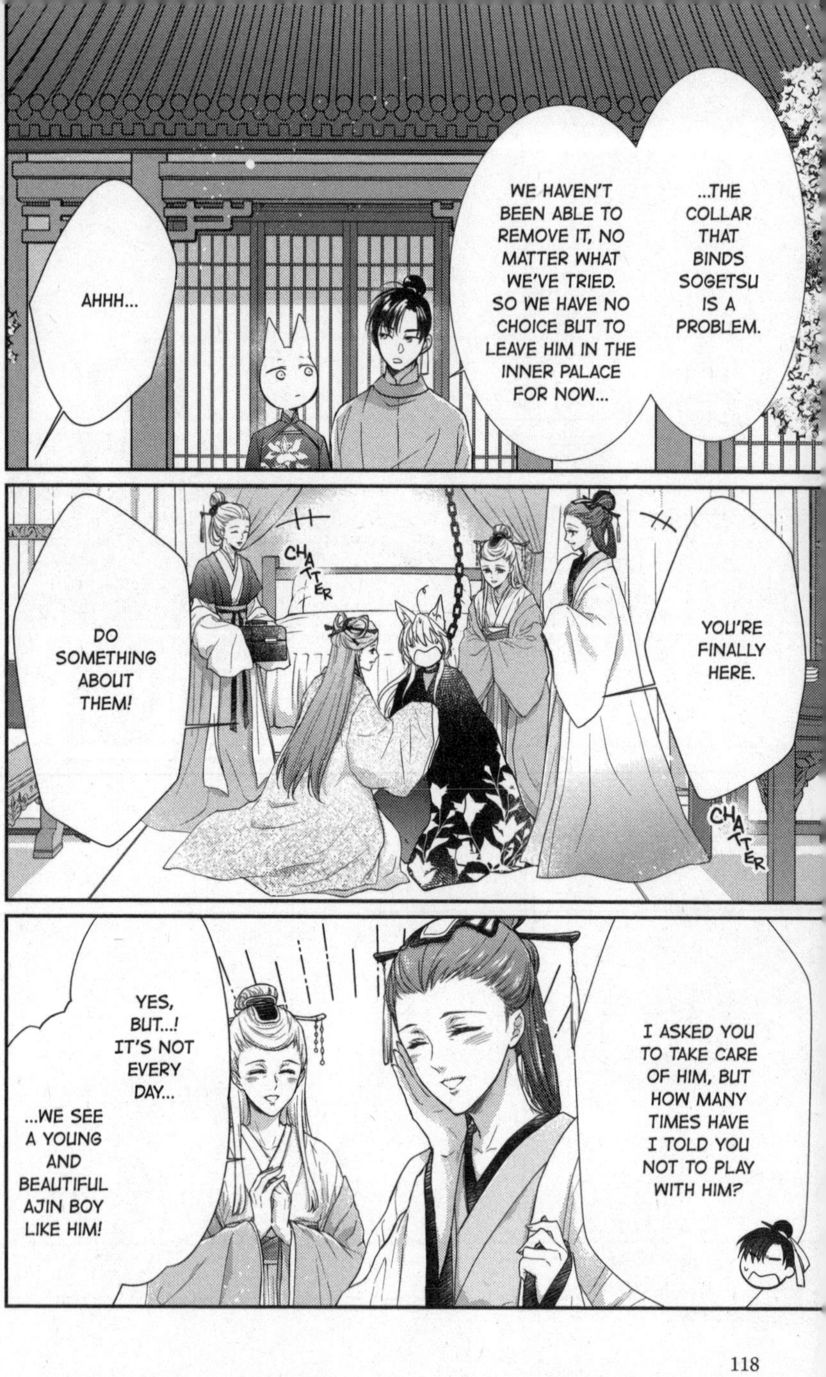
...THE COLLAR THAT BINDS SOGETSU IS A PROBLEM.
WE HAVEN'T BEEN ABLE TO REMOVE IT, NO MATTER WHAT WE'VE TRIED. SO WE HAVE NO CHOICE BUT TO LEAVE HIM IN THE INNER PALACE FOR NOW...
AHHH...
YOU'RE FINALLY HERE.
CHATTER
CHATTER
DO SOMETHING ABOUT THEM!
I ASKED YOU TO TAKE CARE OF HIM, BUT HOW MANY TIMES HAVE I TOLD YOU NOT TO PLAY WITH HIM?
YES, BUT...! IT'S NOT EVERY DAY...
...WE SEE A YOUNG AND BEAUTIFUL AJIN BOY LIKE HIM!

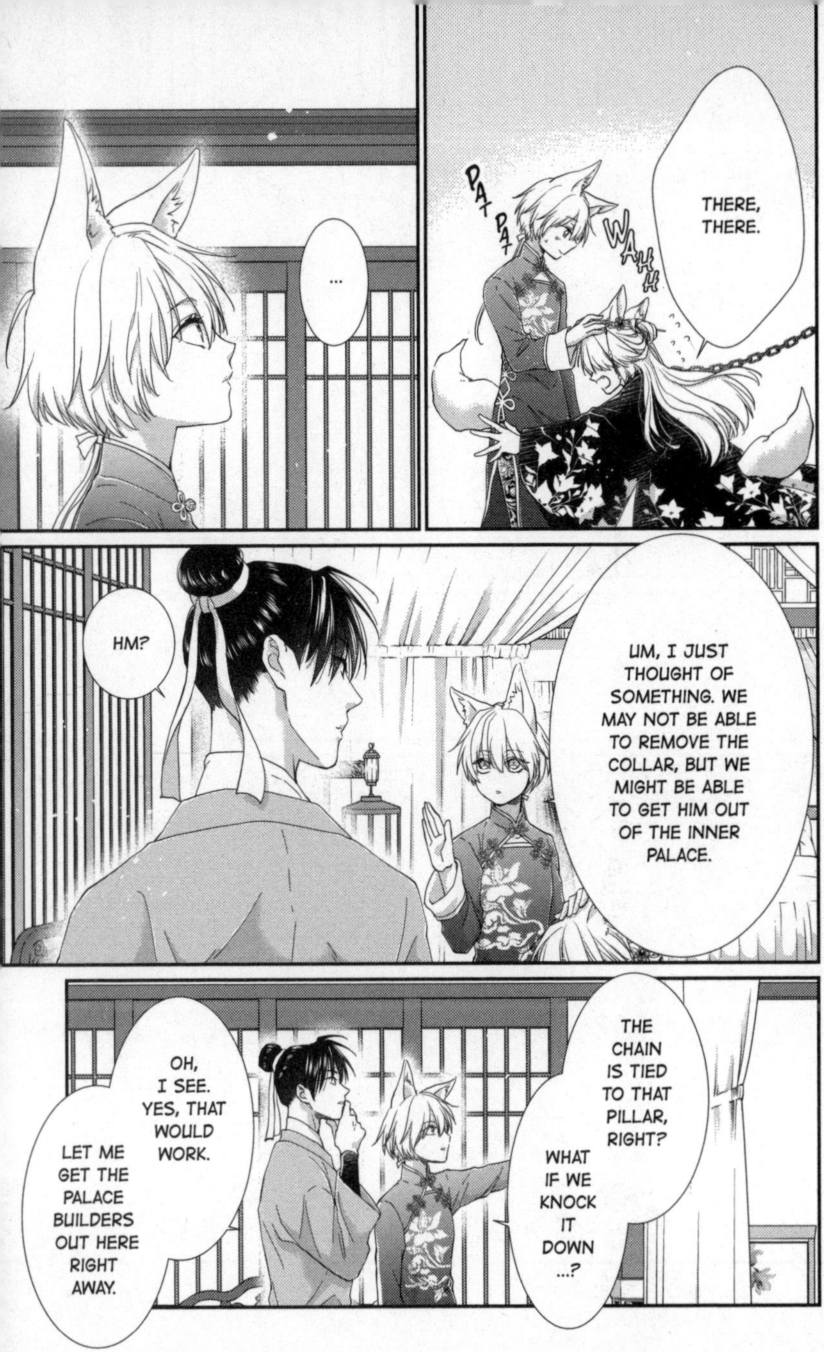
PAT PAT
WAHH
THERE, THERE.
...
UM, I JUST THOUGHT OF SOMETHING. WE MAY NOT BE ABLE TO REMOVE THE COLLAR, BUT WE MIGHT BE ABLE TO GET HIM OUT OF THE INNER PALACE.
HM?
THE CHAIN IS TIED TO THAT PILLAR, RIGHT?
WHAT IF WE KNOCK IT DOWN ...?
OH, I SEE. YES, THAT WOULD WORK.
LET ME GET THE PALACE BUILDERS OUT HERE RIGHT AWAY.

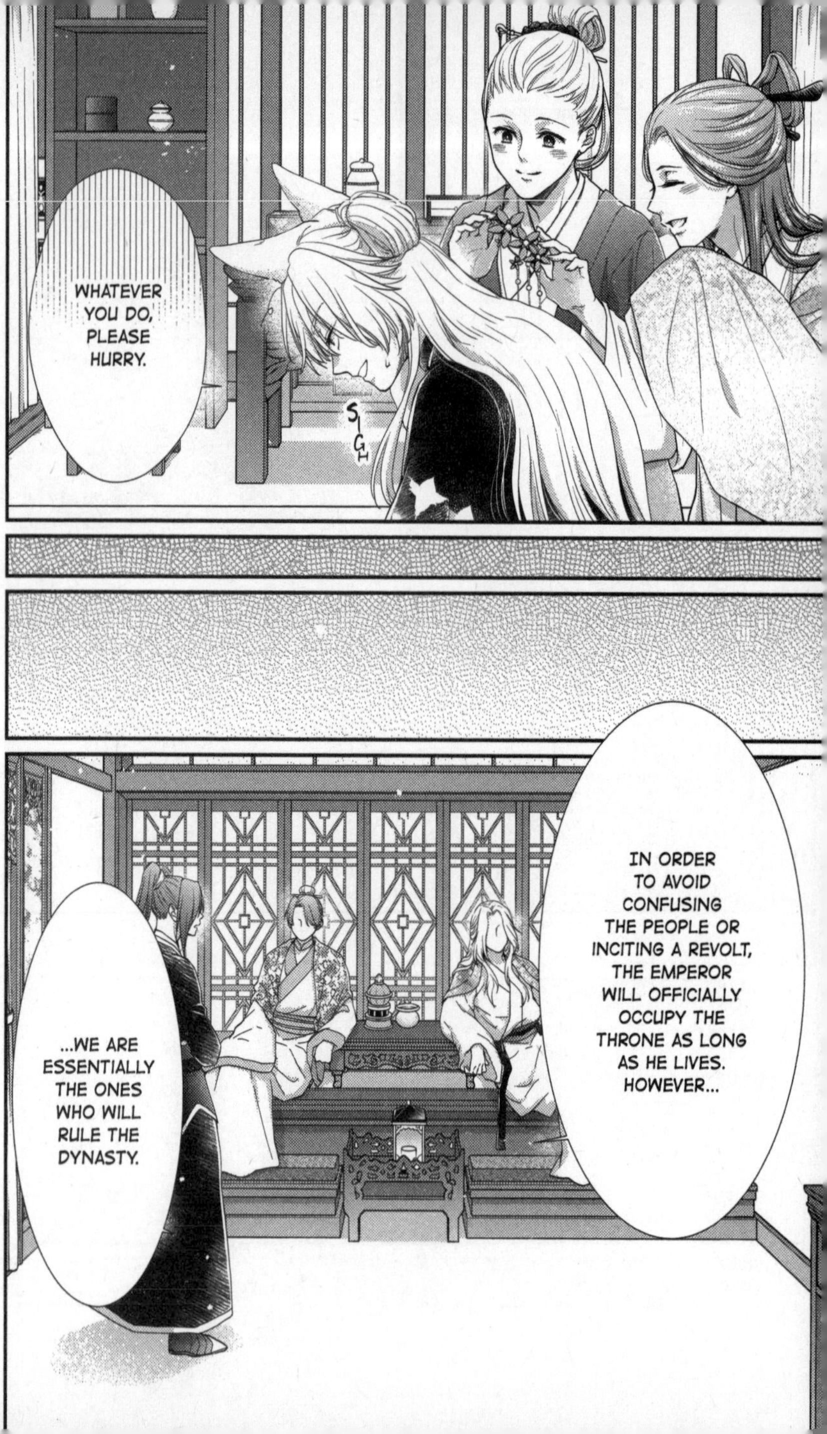
WHATEVER YOU DO, PLEASE HURRY.
SIGH
IN ORDER TO AVOID CONFUSING THE PEOPLE OR INCITING A REVOLT, THE EMPEROR WILL OFFICIALLY OCCUPY THE THRONE AS LONG AS HE LIVES. HOWEVER...
...WE ARE ESSENTIALLY THE ONES WHO WILL RULE THE DYNASTY.

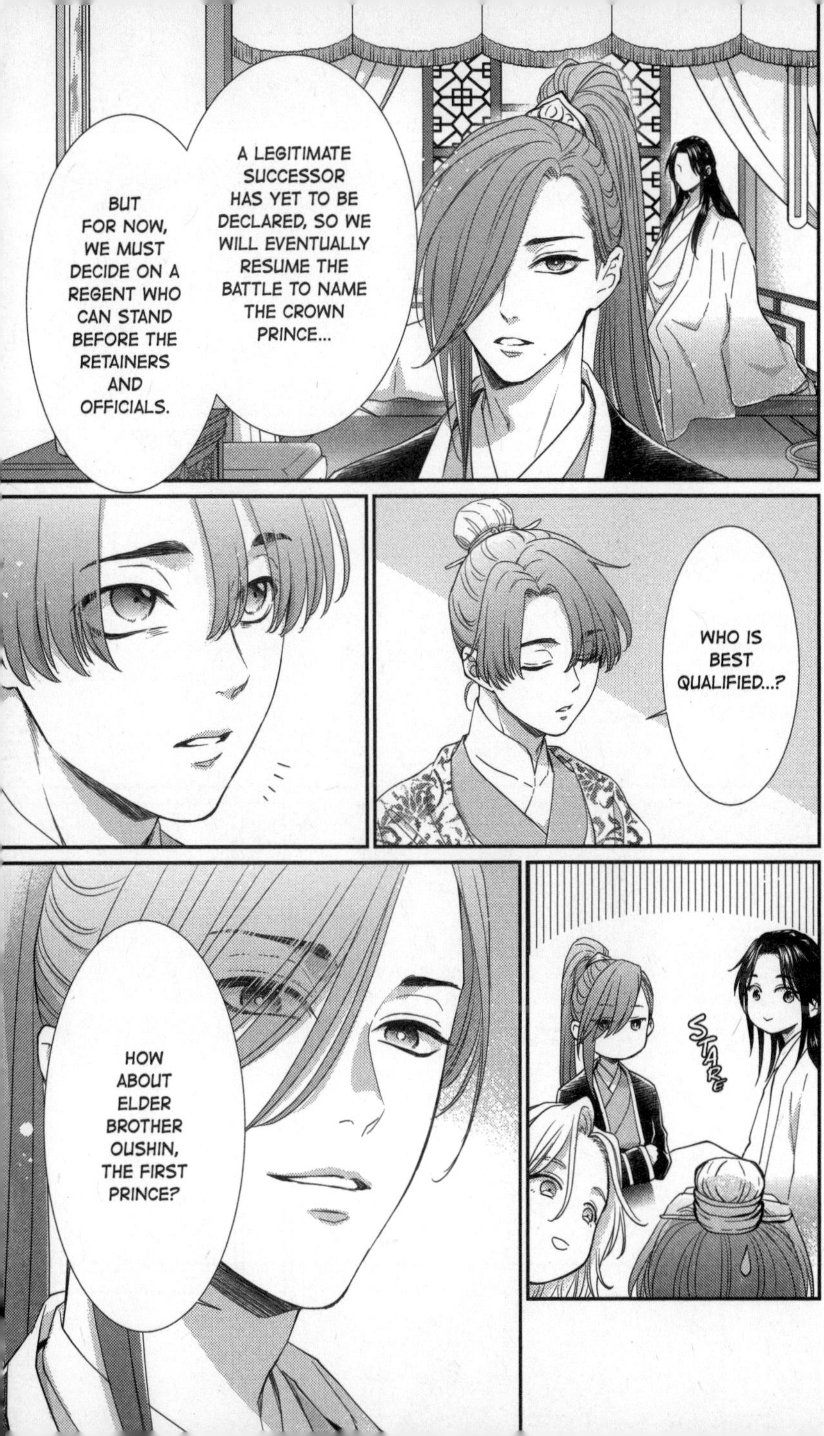
A LEGITIMATE SUCCESSOR HAS YET TO BE DECLARED, SO WE WILL EVENTUALLY RESUME THE BATTLE TO NAME THE CROWN PRINCE...
BUT FOR NOW, WE MUST DECIDE ON A REGENT WHO CAN STAND BEFORE THE RETAINERS AND OFFICIALS.
WHO IS BEST QUALIFIED...?
STARE
HOW ABOUT ELDER BROTHER OUSHIN, THE FIRST PRINCE?

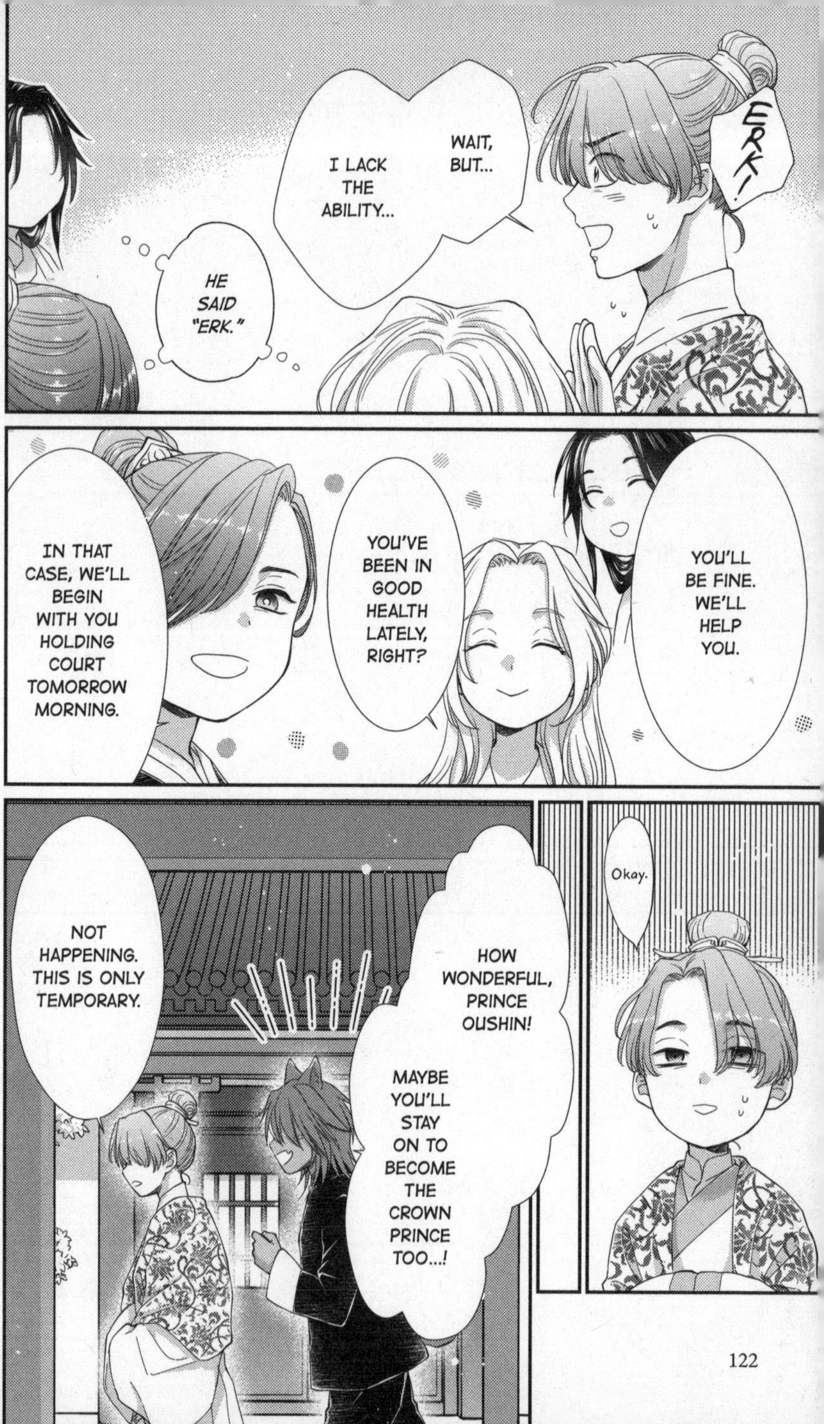
ERK!
WAIT, BUT...
I LACK THE ABILITY...
HE SAID "ERK."
YOU'LL BE FINE. WE'LL HELP YOU.
YOU'VE BEEN IN GOOD HEALTH LATELY, RIGHT?
IN THAT CASE, WE'LL BEGIN WITH YOU HOLDING COURT TOMORROW MORNING.
Okay.
HOW WONDERFUL, PRINCE OUSHIN!
MAYBE YOU'LL STAY ON TO BECOME THE CROWN PRINCE TOO...!
NOT HAPPENING. THIS IS ONLY TEMPORARY.

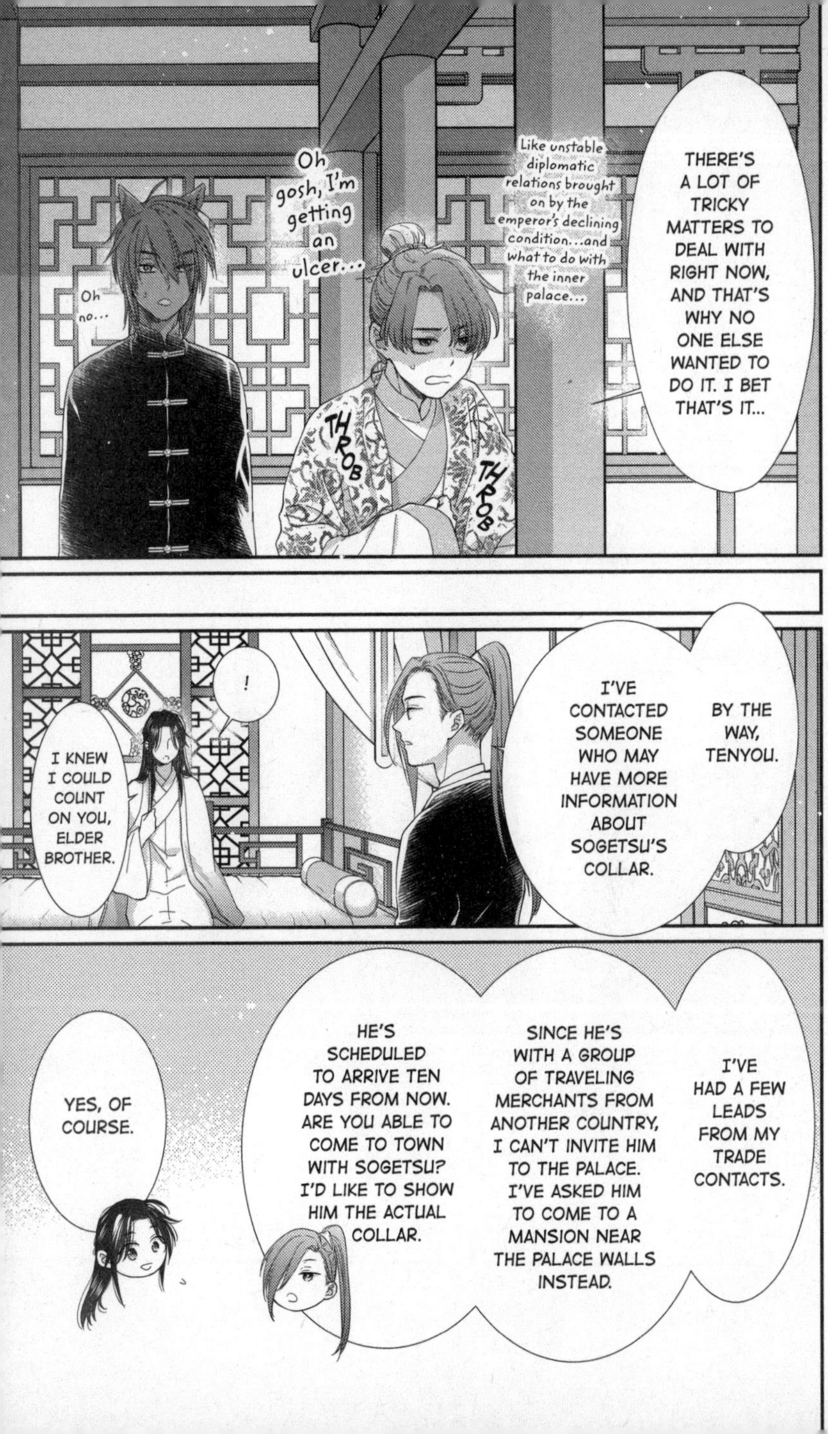
THERE'S A LOT OF TRICKY MATTERS TO DEAL WITH RIGHT NOW, AND THAT'S WHY NO ONE ELSE WANTED TO DO IT. I BET THAT'S IT...
Like unstable diplomatic relations brought on by the emperor's declining condition...and what to do with the inner palace...
Oh gosh, I'm getting an ulcer...
Oh no...
THROB
THROB
BY THE WAY, TENYOU.
I'VE CONTACTED SOMEONE WHO MAY HAVE MORE INFORMATION ABOUT SOGETSU'S COLLAR.
!
I KNEW I COULD COUNT ON YOU, ELDER BROTHER.
I'VE HAD A FEW LEADS FROM MY TRADE CONTACTS.
SINCE HE'S WITH A GROUP OF TRAVELING MERCHANTS FROM ANOTHER COUNTRY, I CAN'T INVITE HIM TO THE PALACE. I'VE ASKED HIM TO COME TO A MANSION NEAR THE PALACE WALLS INSTEAD.
HE'S SCHEDULED TO ARRIVE TEN DAYS FROM NOW. ARE YOU ABLE TO COME TO TOWN WITH SOGETSU? I'D LIKE TO SHOW HIM THE ACTUAL COLLAR.
YES, OF COURSE.

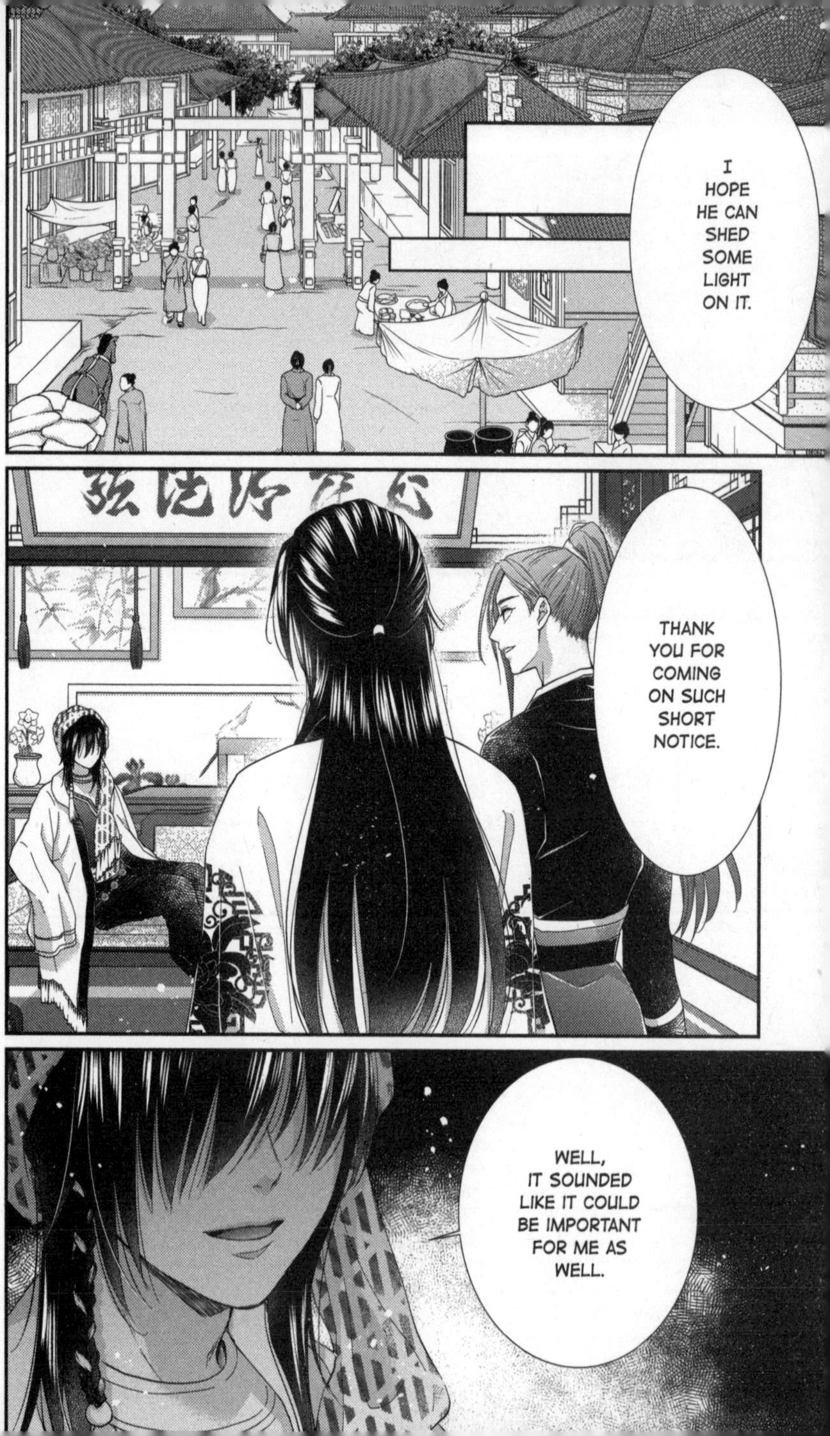
I HOPE HE CAN SHED SOME LIGHT ON IT.
THANK YOU FOR COMING ON SUCH SHORT NOTICE.
WELL, IT SOUNDED LIKE IT COULD BE IMPORTANT FOR ME AS WELL.

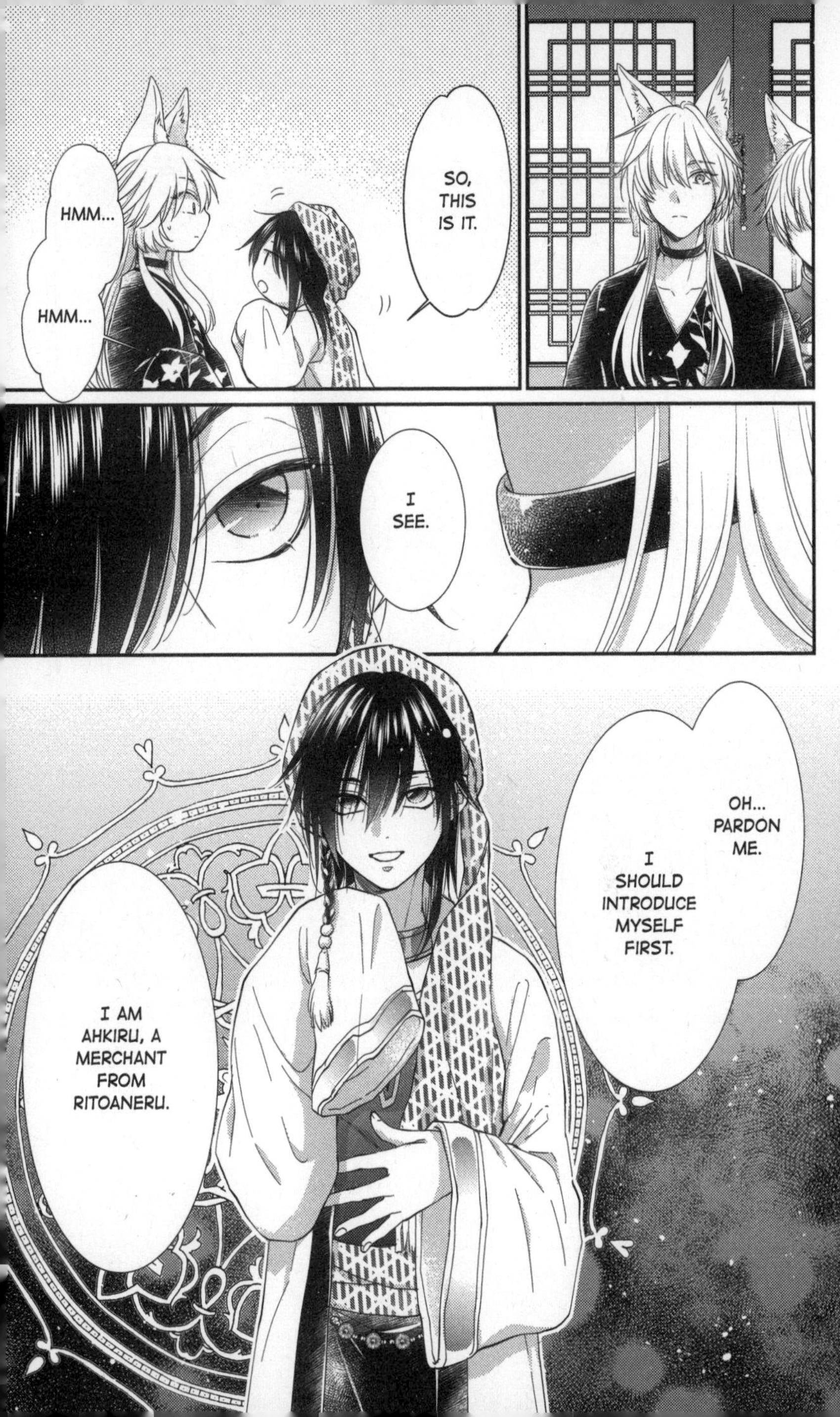
SO, THIS IS IT.
HMM...
HMM...
I SEE.
OH... PARDON ME.
I SHOULD INTRODUCE MYSELF FIRST.
I AM AHKIRU, A MERCHANT FROM RITOANERU.

THE
KING'S
Beast

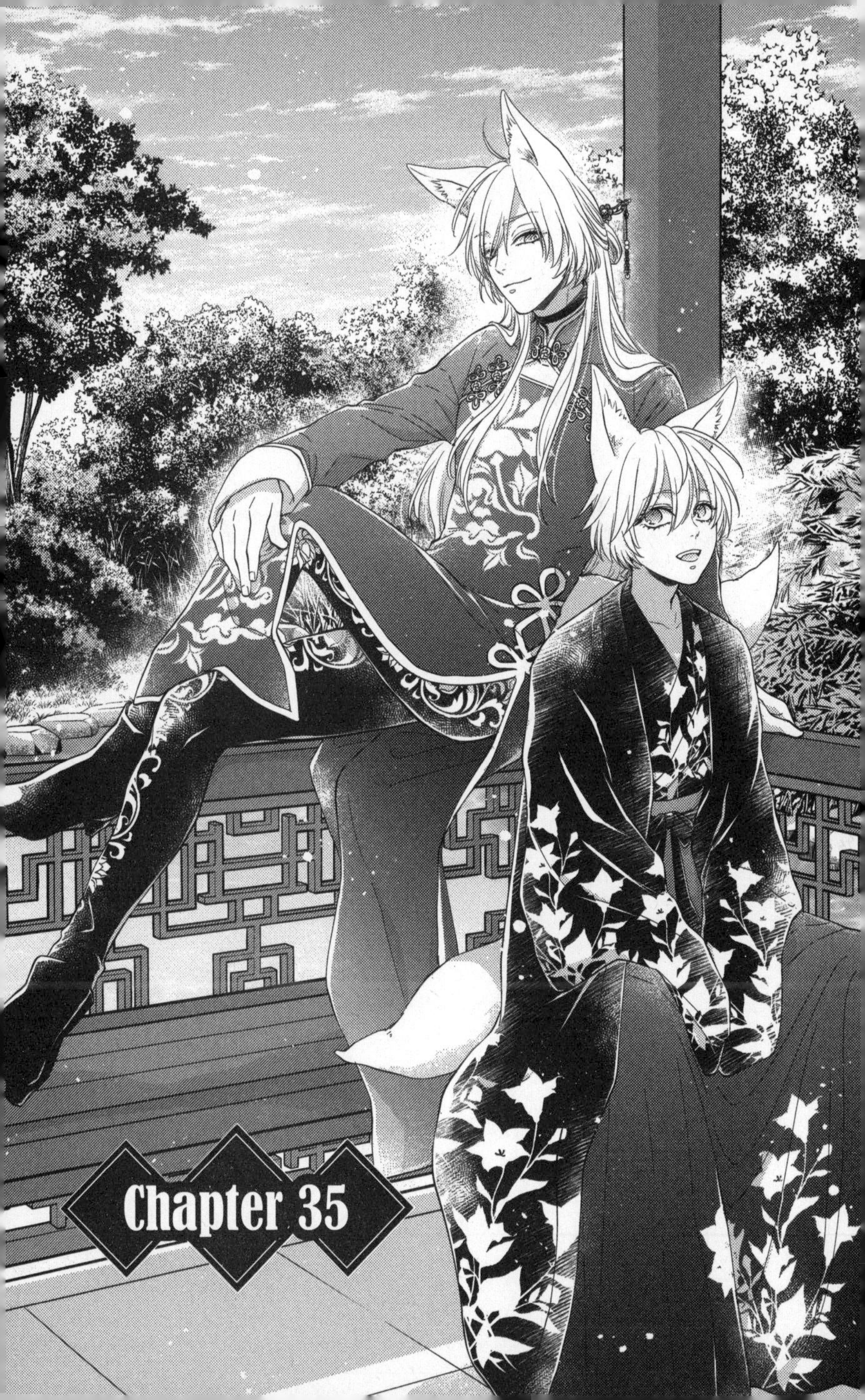
Chapter 35

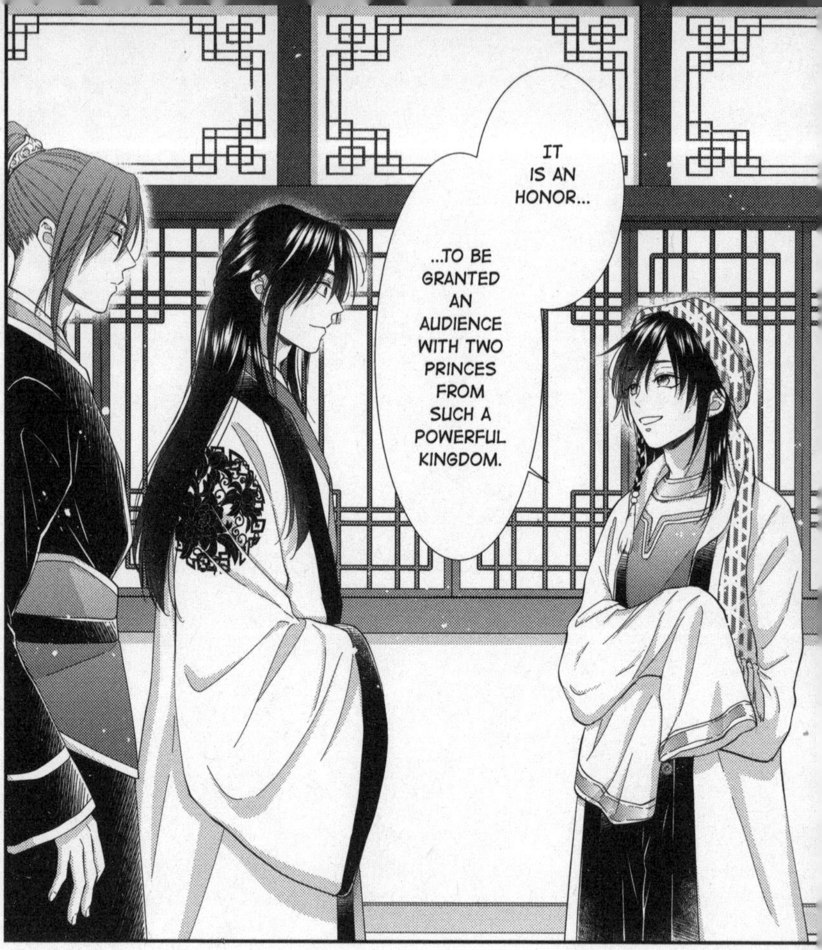
IT IS AN HONOR...
...TO BE GRANTED AN AUDIENCE WITH TWO PRINCES FROM SUCH A POWERFUL KINGDOM.

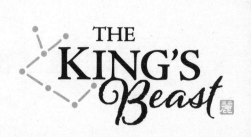

THE KING'S Beast

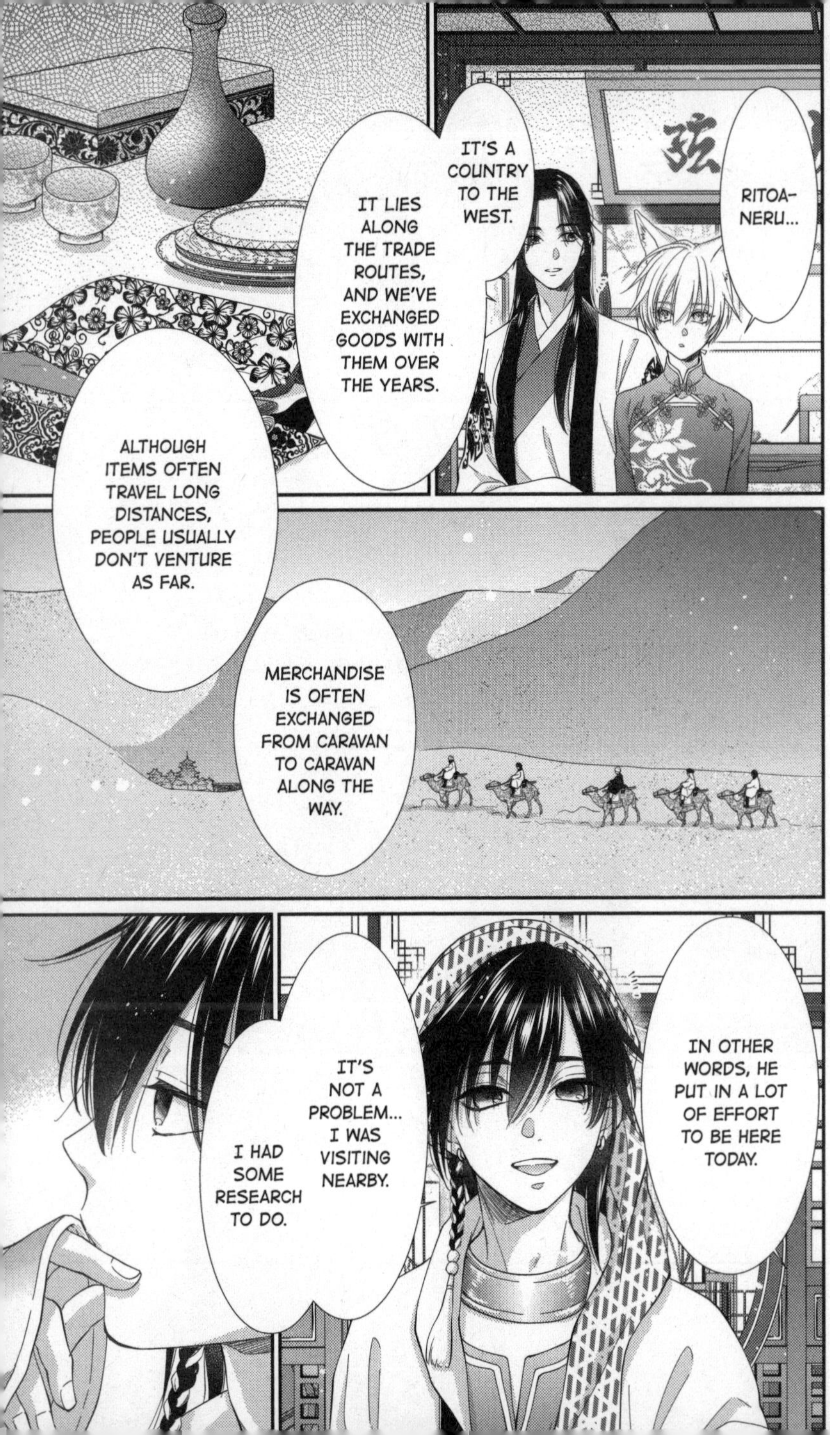
RITOA-NERU...
IT'S A COUNTRY TO THE WEST.
IT LIES ALONG THE TRADE ROUTES, AND WE'VE EXCHANGED GOODS WITH THEM OVER THE YEARS.
ALTHOUGH ITEMS OFTEN TRAVEL LONG DISTANCES, PEOPLE USUALLY DON'T VENTURE AS FAR.
MERCHANDISE IS OFTEN EXCHANGED FROM CARAVAN TO CARAVAN ALONG THE WAY.
IN OTHER WORDS, HE PUT IN A LOT OF EFFORT TO BE HERE TODAY.
IT'S NOT A PROBLEM... I WAS VISITING NEARBY.
I HAD SOME RESEARCH TO DO.

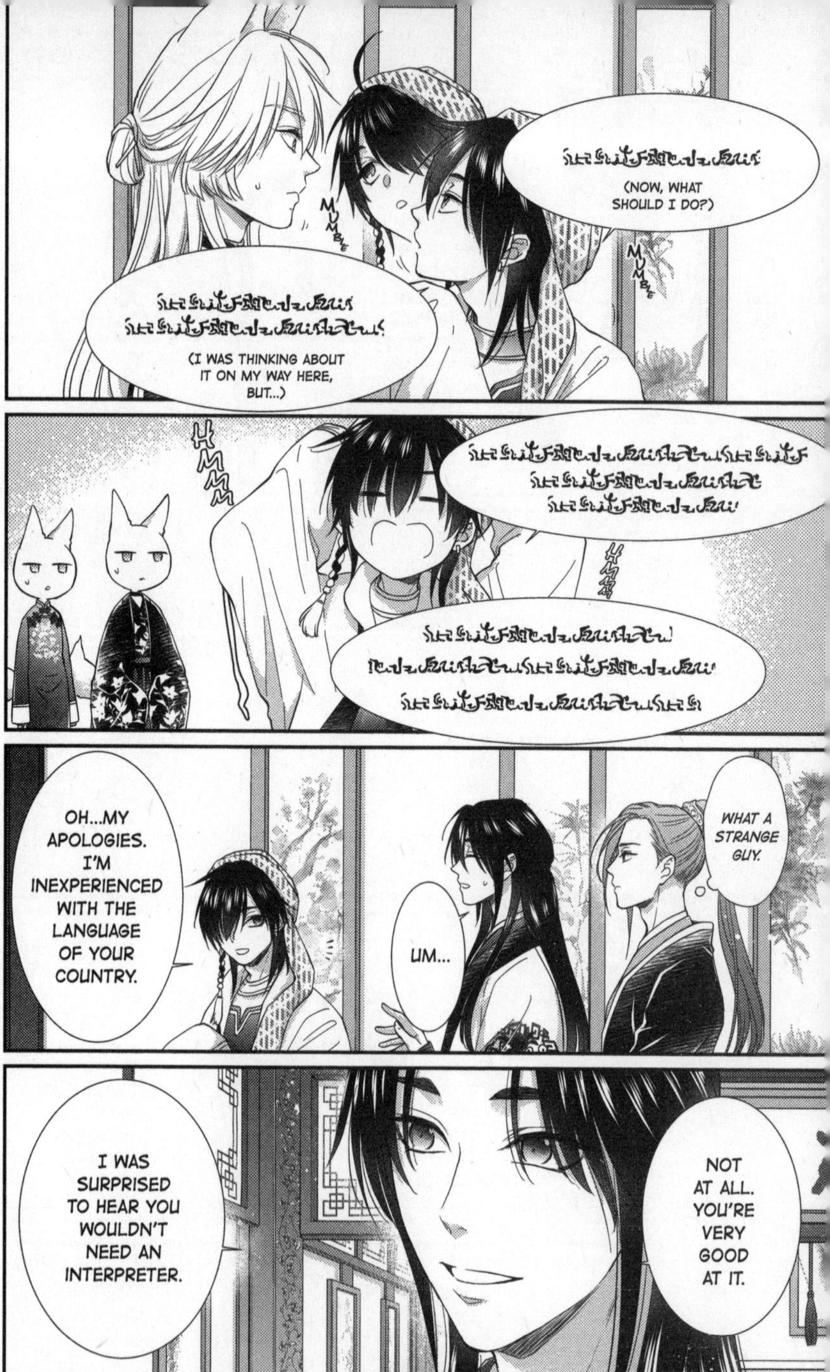
(NOW, WHAT SHOULD I DO?)
MUMBLE
MUMBLE
(I WAS THINKING ABOUT IT ON MY WAY HERE, BUT...)
HMMM
HMMM
WHAT A STRANGE GUY.
UM...
OH...MY APOLOGIES. I'M INEXPERIENCED WITH THE LANGUAGE OF YOUR COUNTRY.
NOT AT ALL. YOU'RE VERY GOOD AT IT.
I WAS SURPRISED TO HEAR YOU WOULDN'T NEED AN INTERPRETER.

ᔑᓕᐟ ᐃᔑᑲᓕᐟᑕᔑᓕᑕ ᔑᓕᐟᑲᓕᐟ
ᐃᔑᑕᑲᓕᐟᑕᔑᓕᑕᔑᑲᓕᑕᔑ

(I TAKE IT IT'S NOT THE
LANGUAGE THAT'S KEEPING
YOU FROM TALKING.)

?

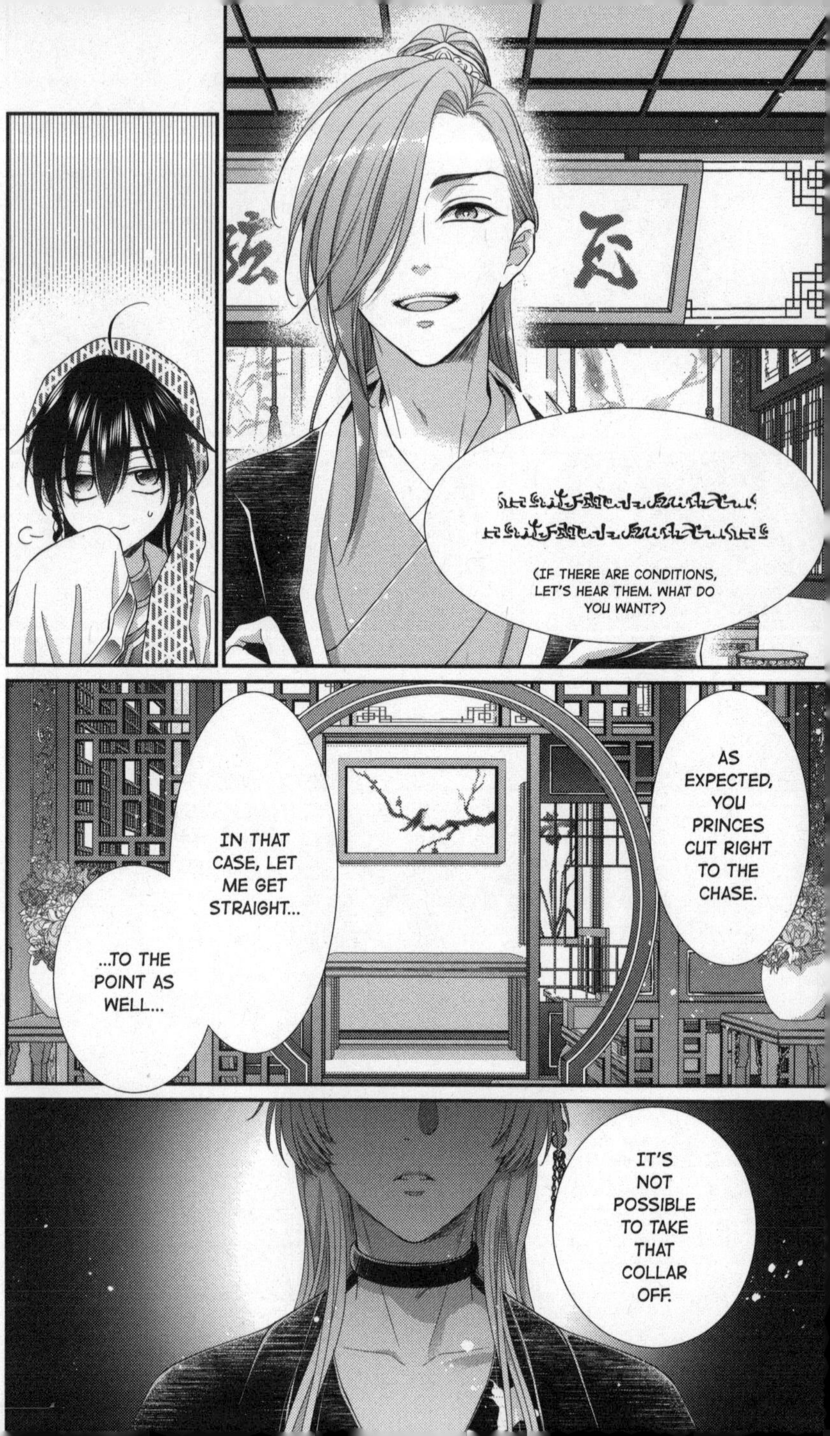
(IF THERE ARE CONDITIONS, LET'S HEAR THEM. WHAT DO YOU WANT?)
AS EXPECTED, YOU PRINCES CUT RIGHT TO THE CHASE.
IN THAT CASE, LET ME GET STRAIGHT...
...TO THE POINT AS WELL...
IT'S NOT POSSIBLE TO TAKE THAT COLLAR OFF.

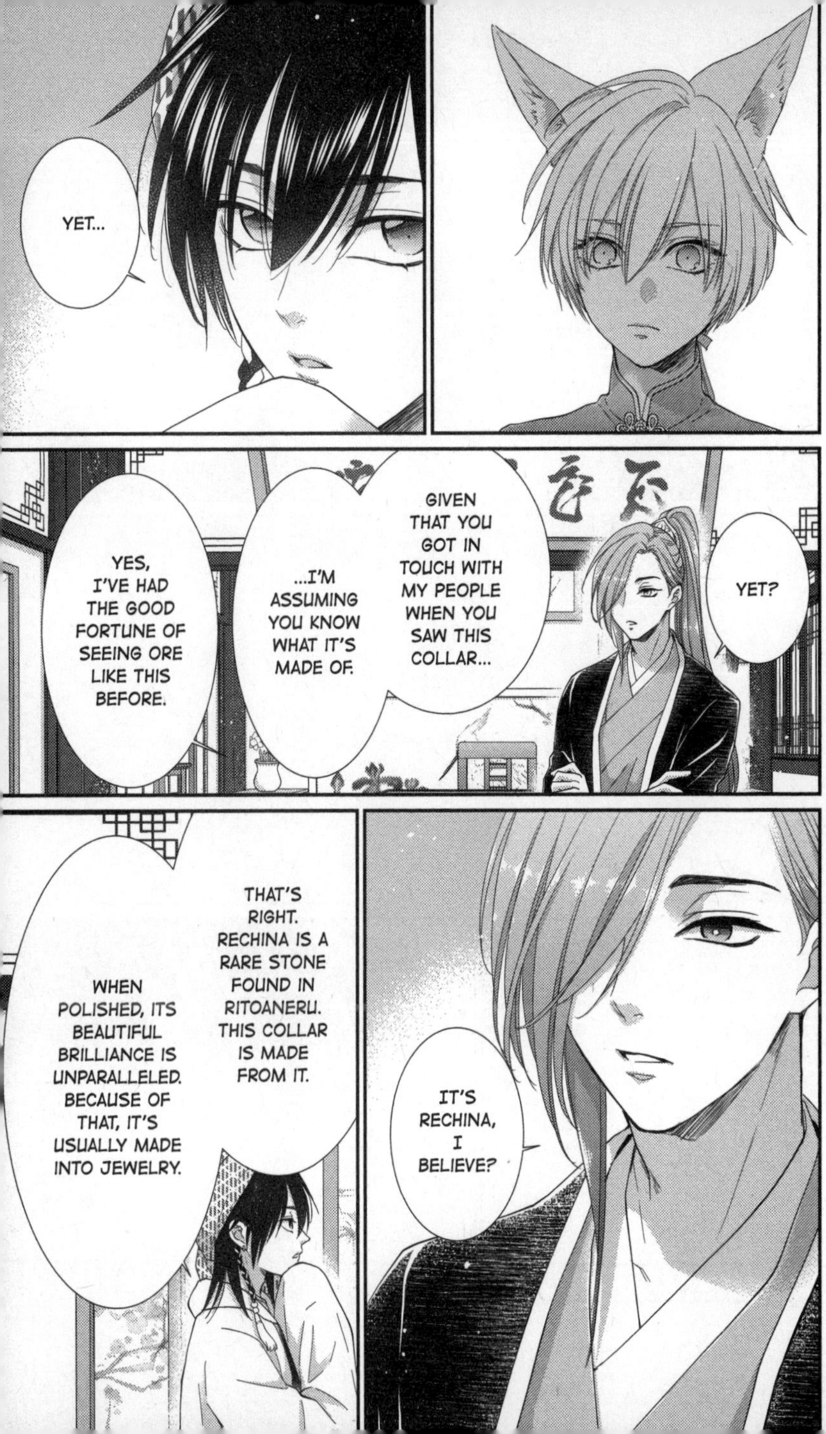
YET...
YET?
GIVEN THAT YOU GOT IN TOUCH WITH MY PEOPLE WHEN YOU SAW THIS COLLAR...
...I'M ASSUMING YOU KNOW WHAT IT'S MADE OF.
YES, I'VE HAD THE GOOD FORTUNE OF SEEING ORE LIKE THIS BEFORE.
IT'S RECHINA, I BELIEVE?
THAT'S RIGHT. RECHINA IS A RARE STONE FOUND IN RITOANERU. THIS COLLAR IS MADE FROM IT.
WHEN POLISHED, ITS BEAUTIFUL BRILLIANCE IS UNPARALLELED. BECAUSE OF THAT, IT'S USUALLY MADE INTO JEWELRY.

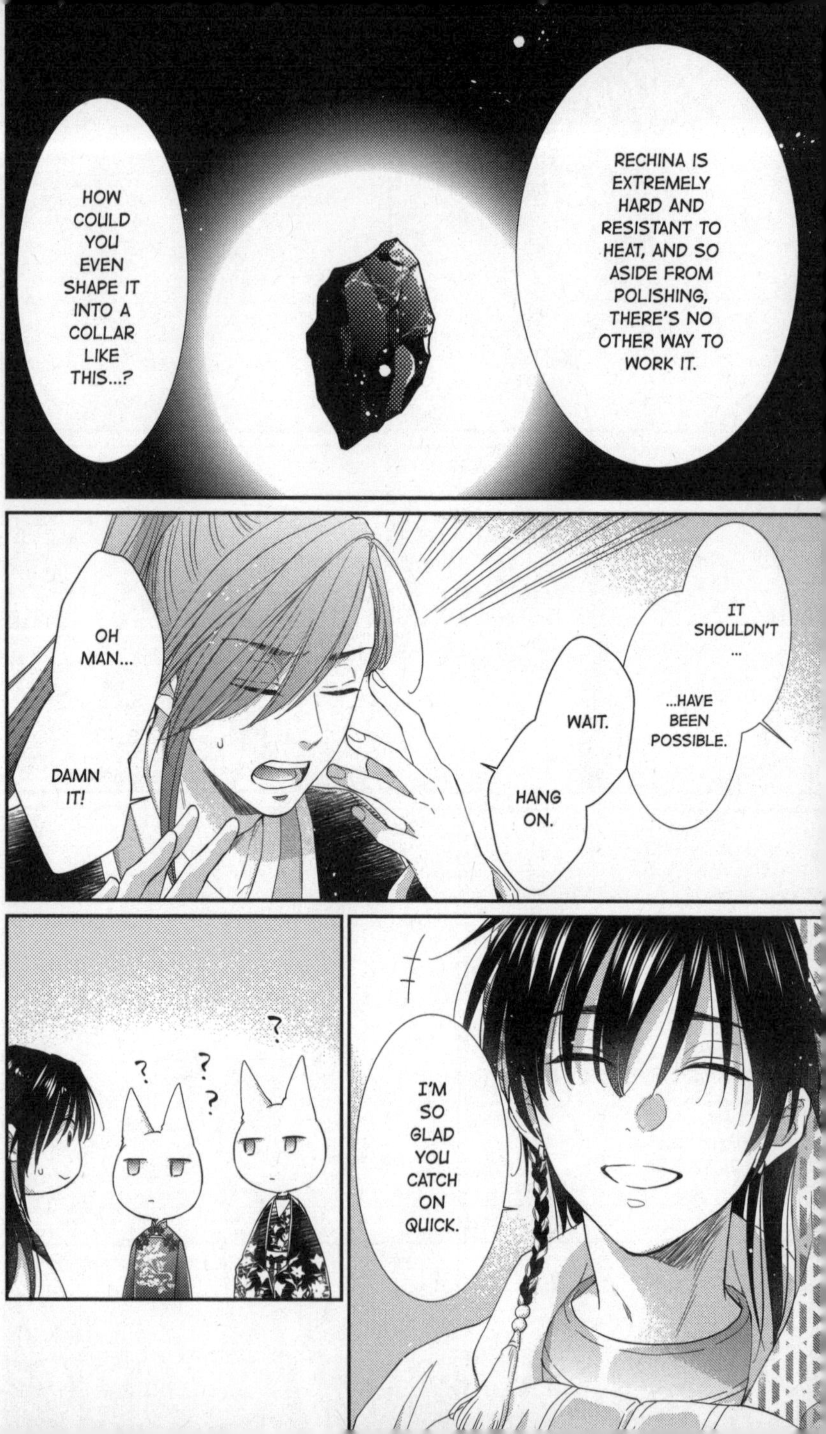
RECHINA IS EXTREMELY HARD AND RESISTANT TO HEAT, AND SO ASIDE FROM POLISHING, THERE'S NO OTHER WAY TO WORK IT.
HOW COULD YOU EVEN SHAPE IT INTO A COLLAR LIKE THIS...?
IT SHOULDN'T ...
...HAVE BEEN POSSIBLE.
WAIT.
HANG ON.
OH MAN...
DAMN IT!
I'M SO GLAD YOU CATCH ON QUICK.

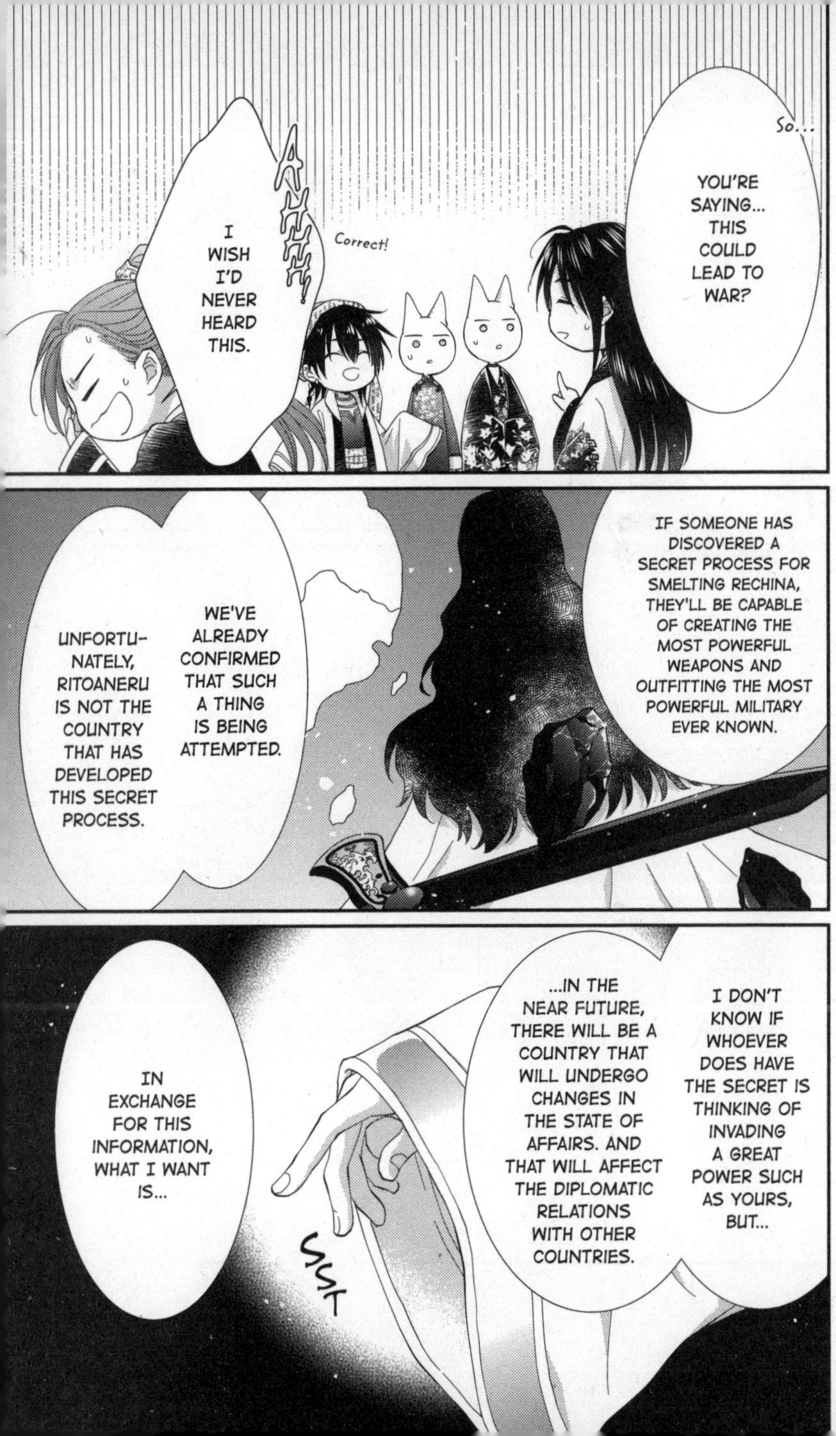
So...
YOU'RE SAYING... THIS COULD LEAD TO WAR?
Correct!
AHHH!
I WISH I'D NEVER HEARD THIS.
IF SOMEONE HAS DISCOVERED A SECRET PROCESS FOR SMELTING RECHINA, THEY'LL BE CAPABLE OF CREATING THE MOST POWERFUL WEAPONS AND OUTFITTING THE MOST POWERFUL MILITARY EVER KNOWN.
WE'VE ALREADY CONFIRMED THAT SUCH A THING IS BEING ATTEMPTED.
UNFORTU-NATELY, RITOANERU IS NOT THE COUNTRY THAT HAS DEVELOPED THIS SECRET PROCESS.
I DON'T KNOW IF WHOEVER DOES HAVE THE SECRET IS THINKING OF INVADING A GREAT POWER SUCH AS YOURS, BUT...
...IN THE NEAR FUTURE, THERE WILL BE A COUNTRY THAT WILL UNDERGO CHANGES IN THE STATE OF AFFAIRS. AND THAT WILL AFFECT THE DIPLOMATIC RELATIONS WITH OTHER COUNTRIES.
SSK
IN EXCHANGE FOR THIS INFORMATION, WHAT I WANT IS...

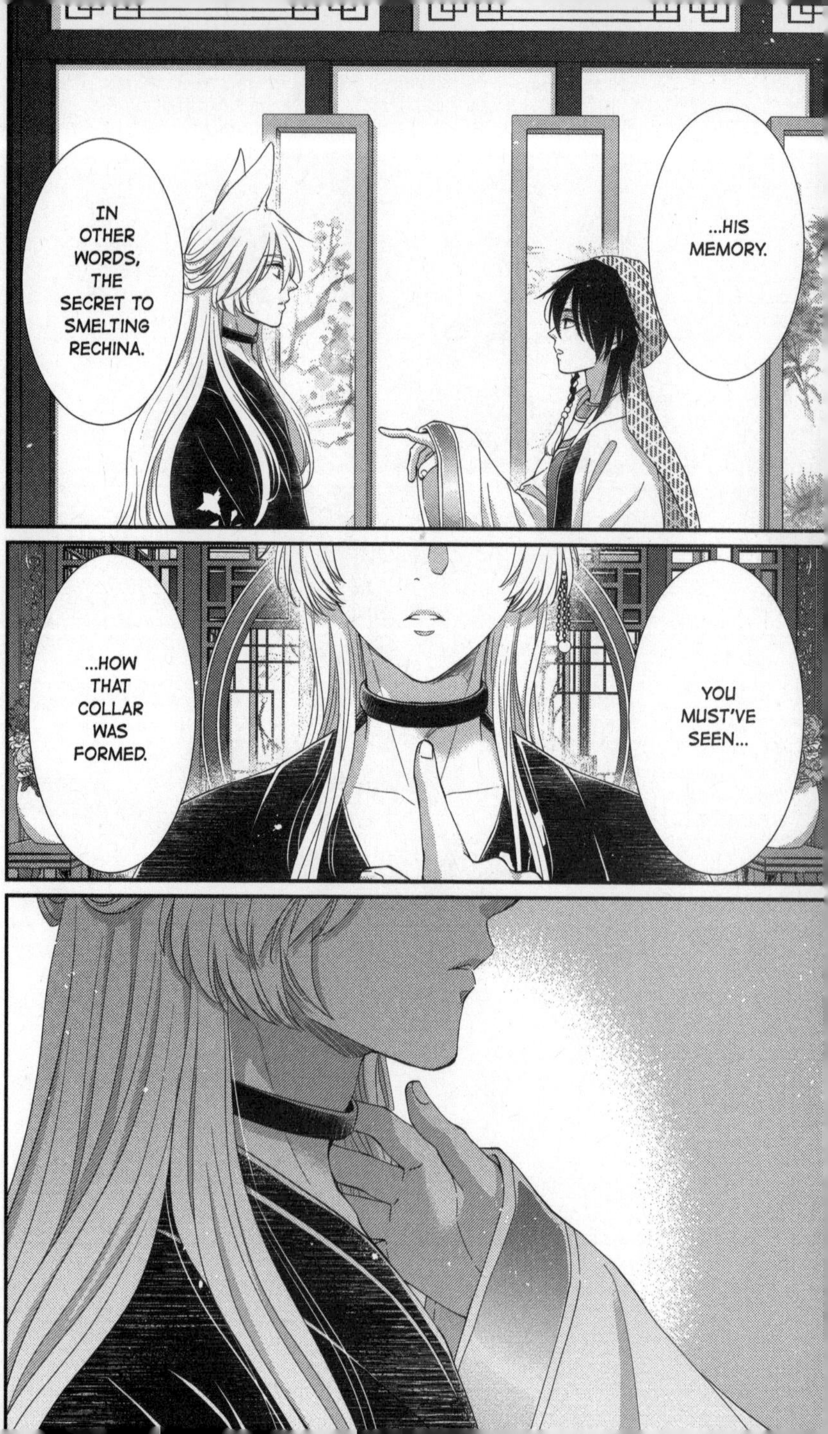
...HIS MEMORY.
IN OTHER WORDS, THE SECRET TO SMELTING RECHINA.
YOU MUST'VE SEEN...
...HOW THAT COLLAR WAS FORMED.

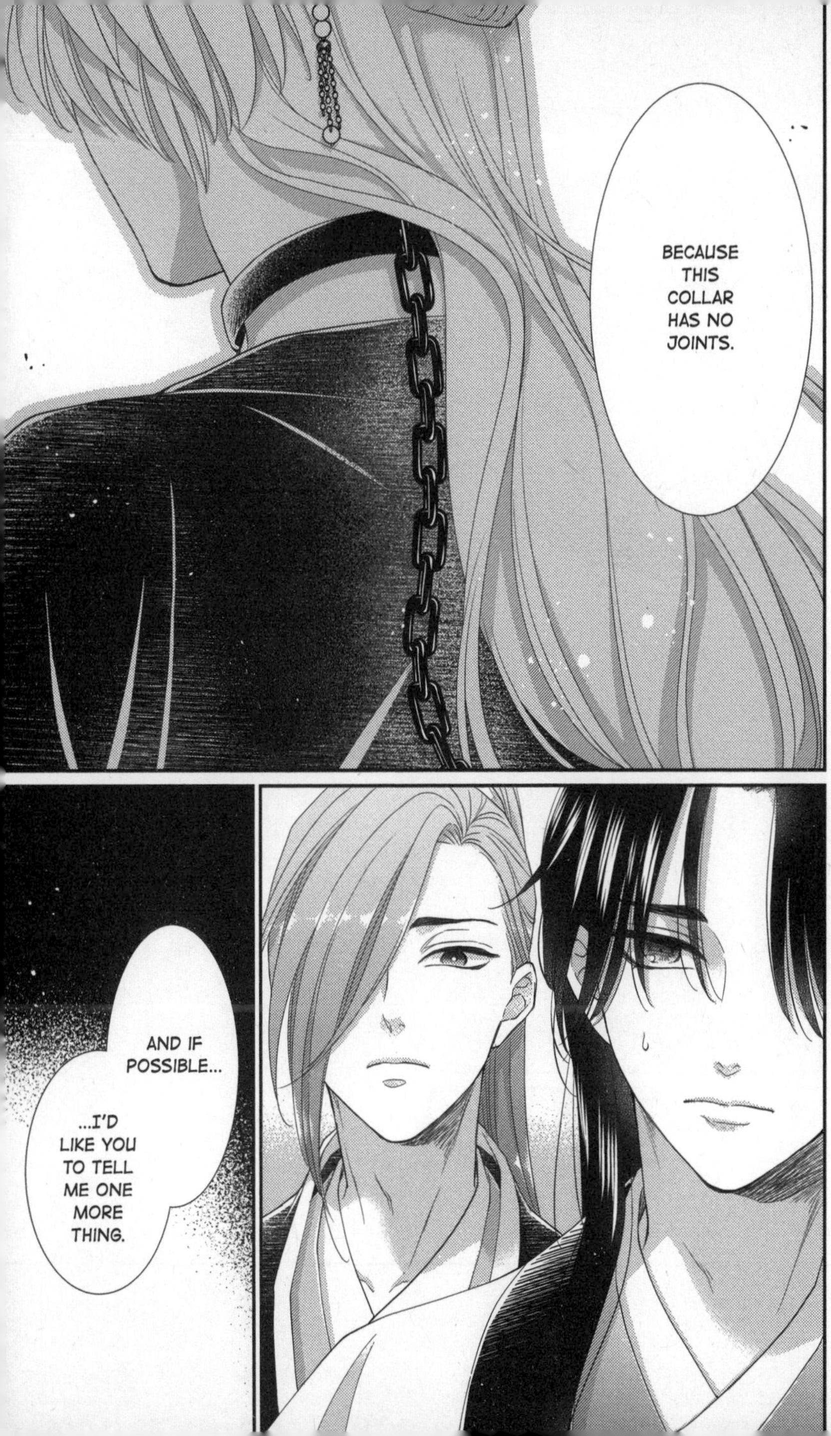
BECAUSE THIS COLLAR HAS NO JOINTS.
AND IF POSSIBLE...
...I'D LIKE YOU TO TELL ME ONE MORE THING.

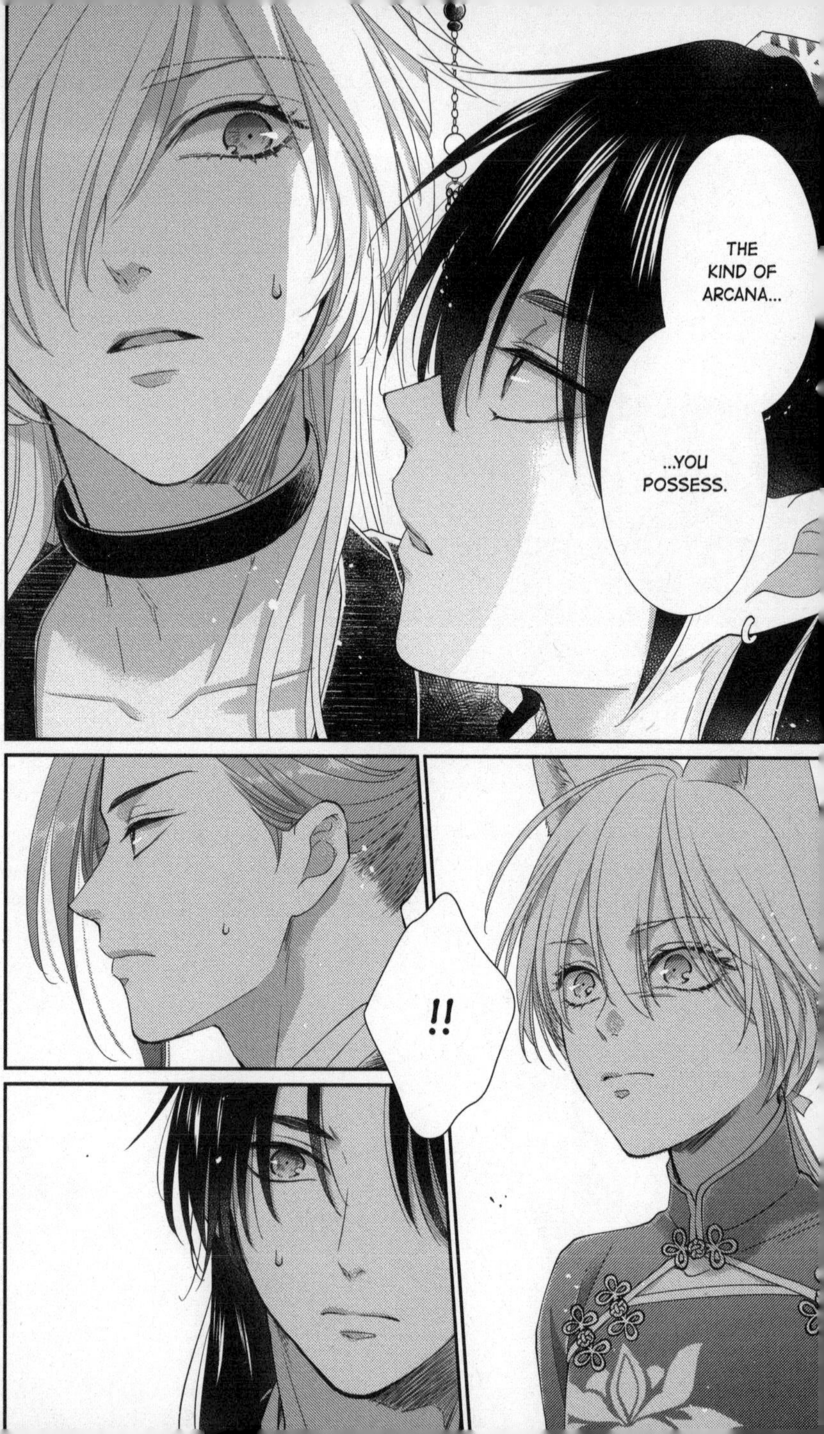
THE KIND OF ARCANA...
...YOU POSSESS.
!!

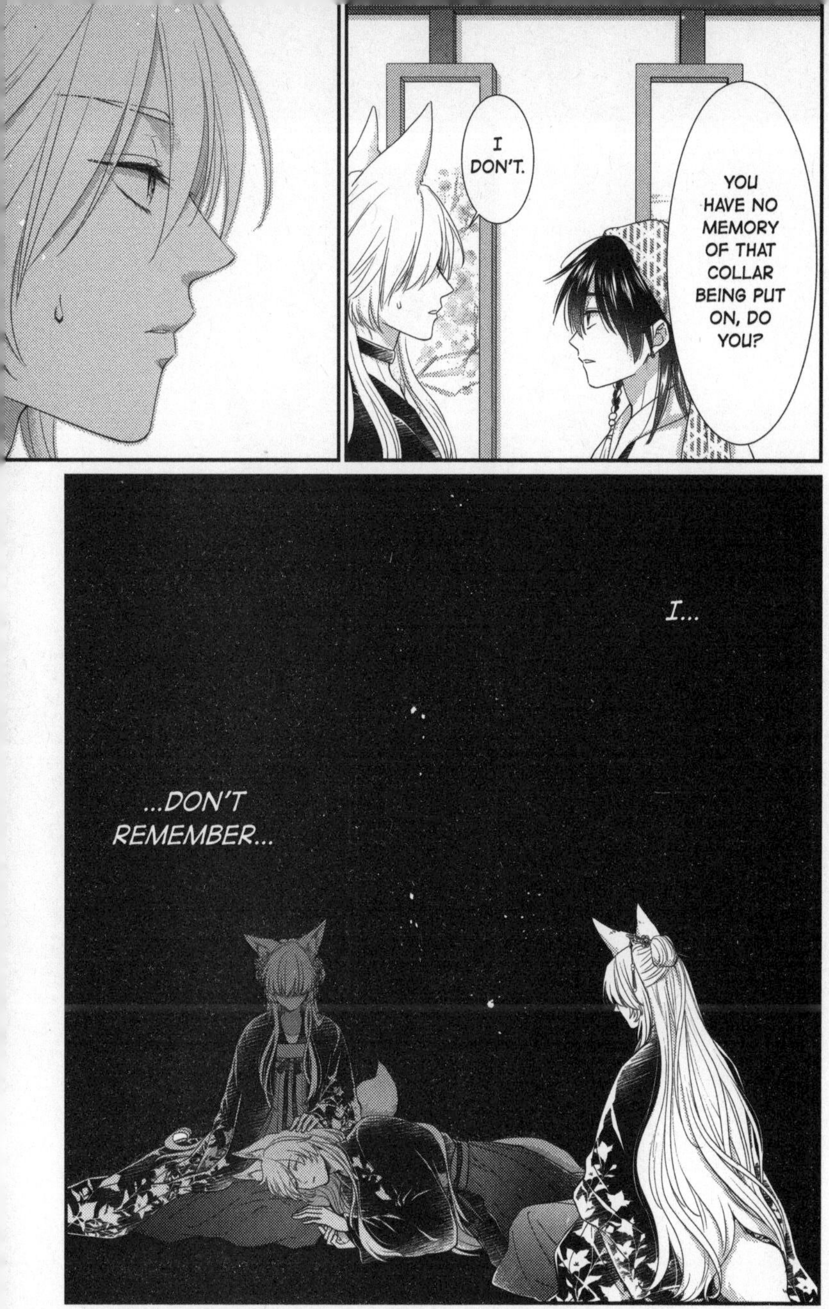
YOU HAVE NO MEMORY OF THAT COLLAR BEING PUT ON, DO YOU?
I DON'T.
I...
...DON'T REMEMBER...

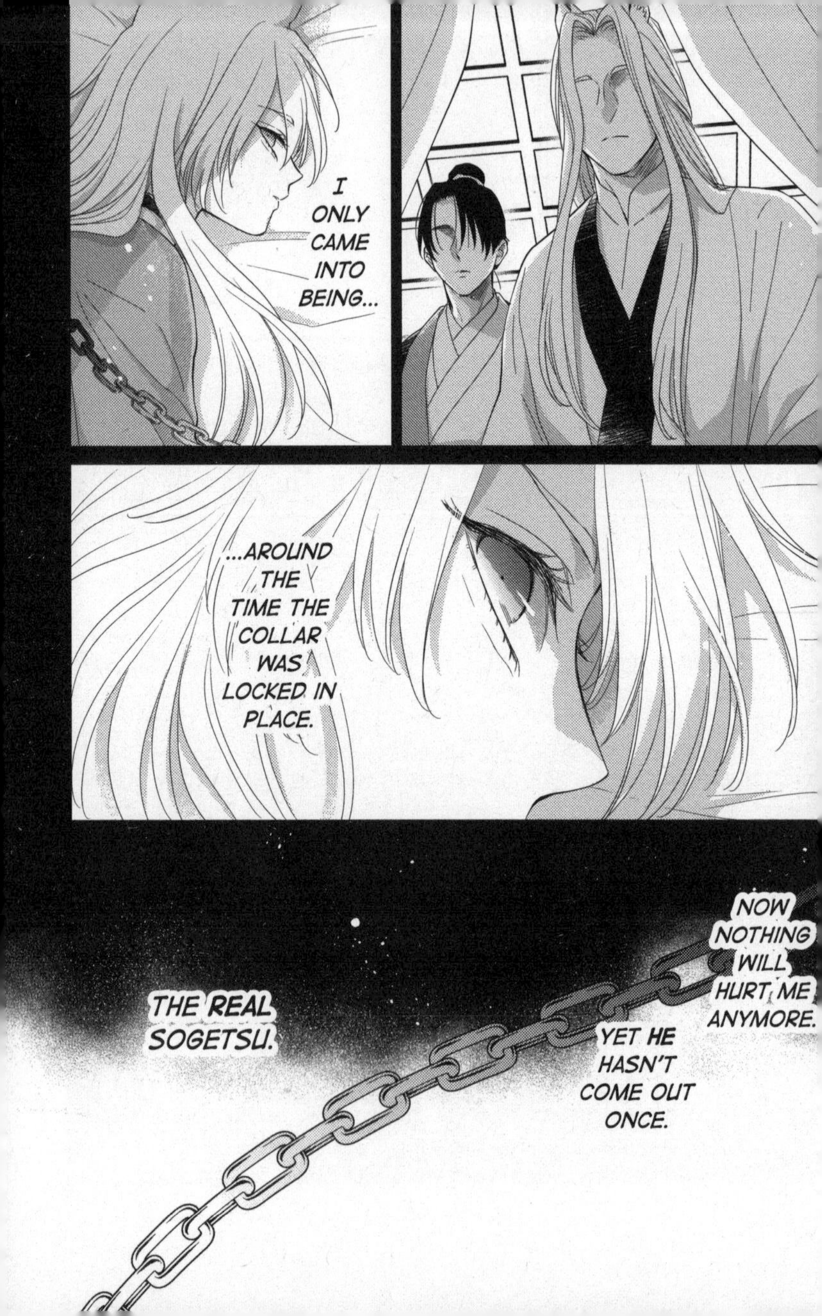
I ONLY CAME INTO BEING...
...AROUND THE TIME THE COLLAR WAS LOCKED IN PLACE.
NOW NOTHING WILL HURT ME ANYMORE.
YET HE HASN'T COME OUT ONCE.
THE REAL SOGETSU.

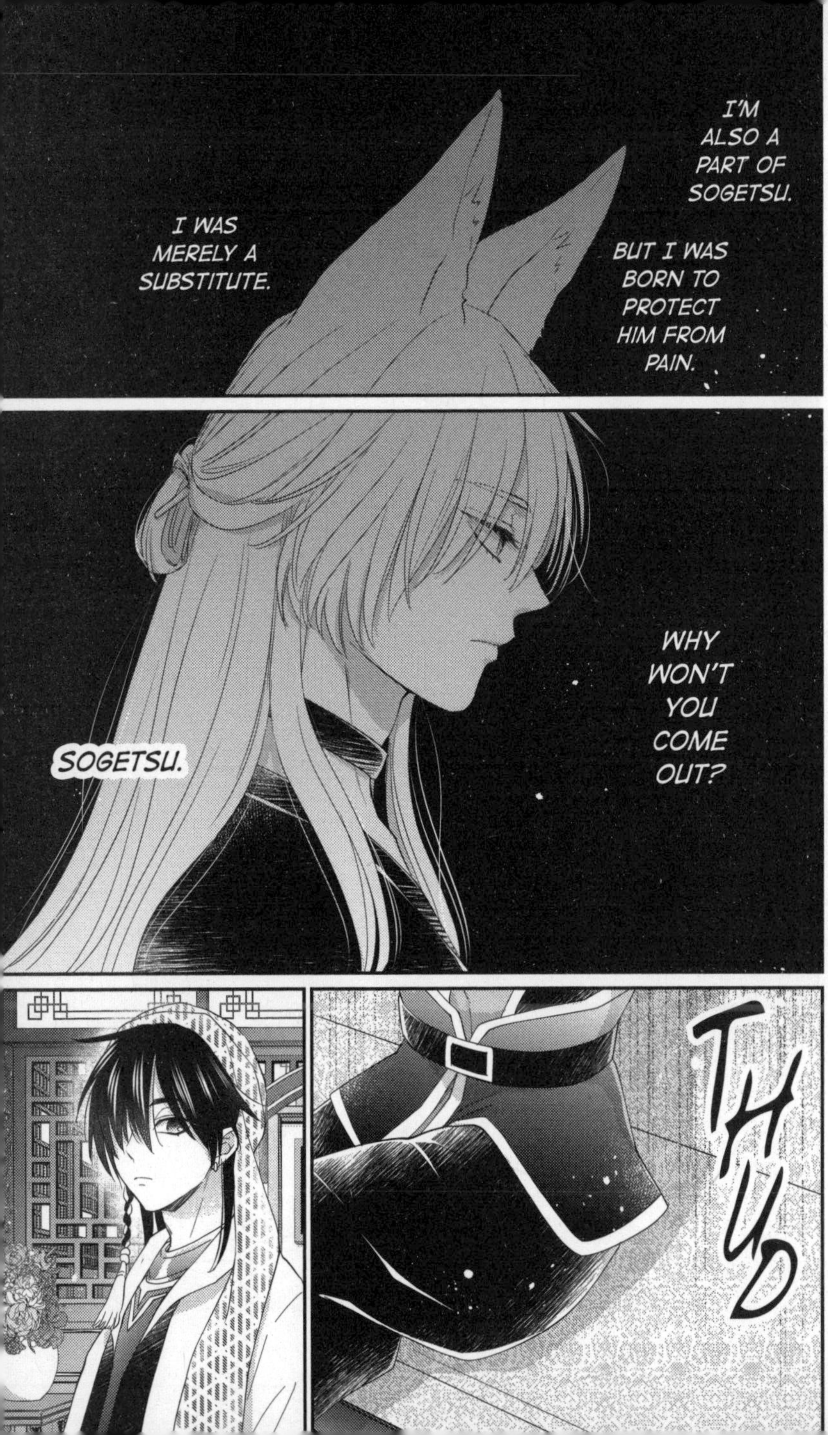
I'M ALSO A PART OF SOGETSU.
BUT I WAS BORN TO PROTECT HIM FROM PAIN.
I WAS MERELY A SUBSTITUTE.
WHY WON'T YOU COME OUT?
SOGETSU.
THUD

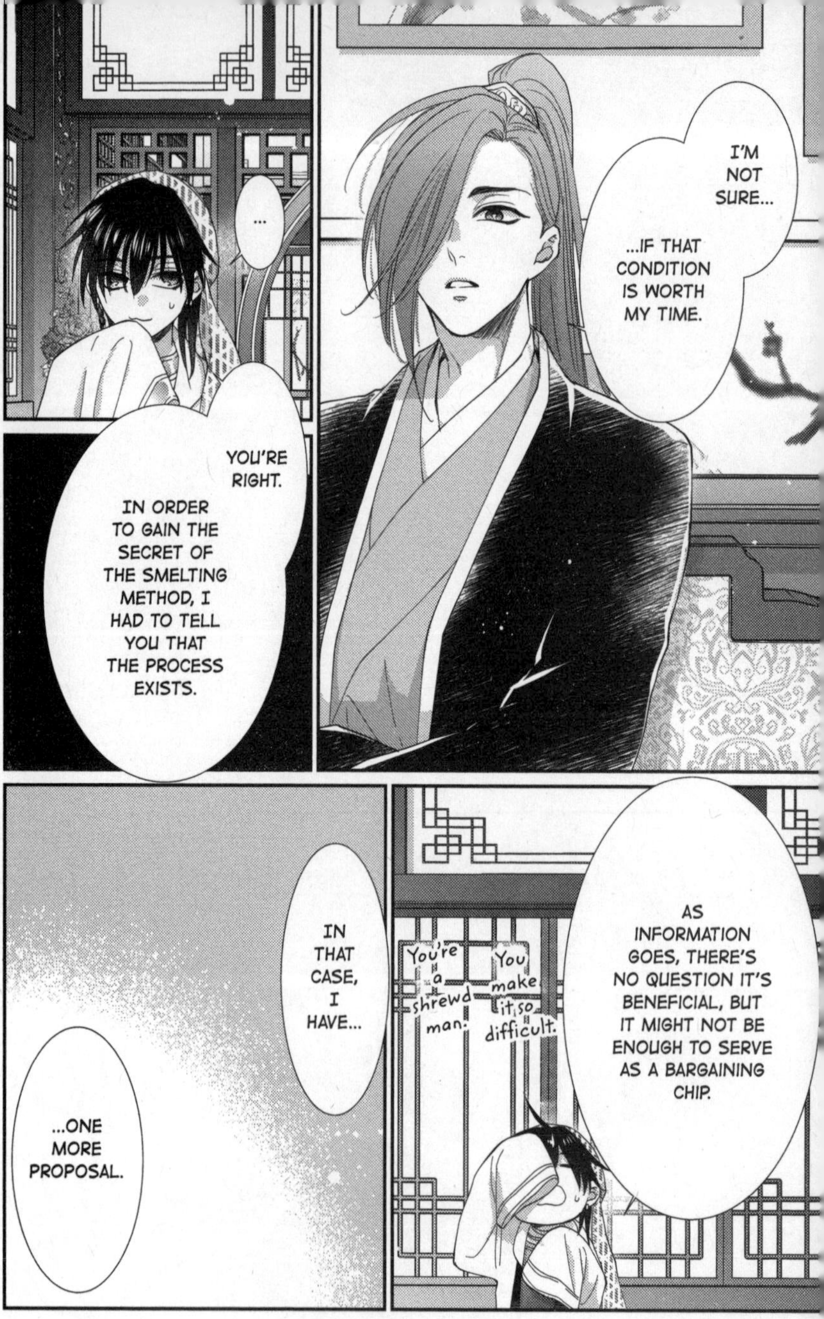
I'M NOT SURE...
...IF THAT CONDITION IS WORTH MY TIME.
...
YOU'RE RIGHT.
IN ORDER TO GAIN THE SECRET OF THE SMELTING METHOD, I HAD TO TELL YOU THAT THE PROCESS EXISTS.
AS INFORMATION GOES, THERE'S NO QUESTION IT'S BENEFICIAL, BUT IT MIGHT NOT BE ENOUGH TO SERVE AS A BARGAINING CHIP.
You make it so difficult.
You're a shrewd man.
IN THAT CASE, I HAVE...
...ONE MORE PROPOSAL.

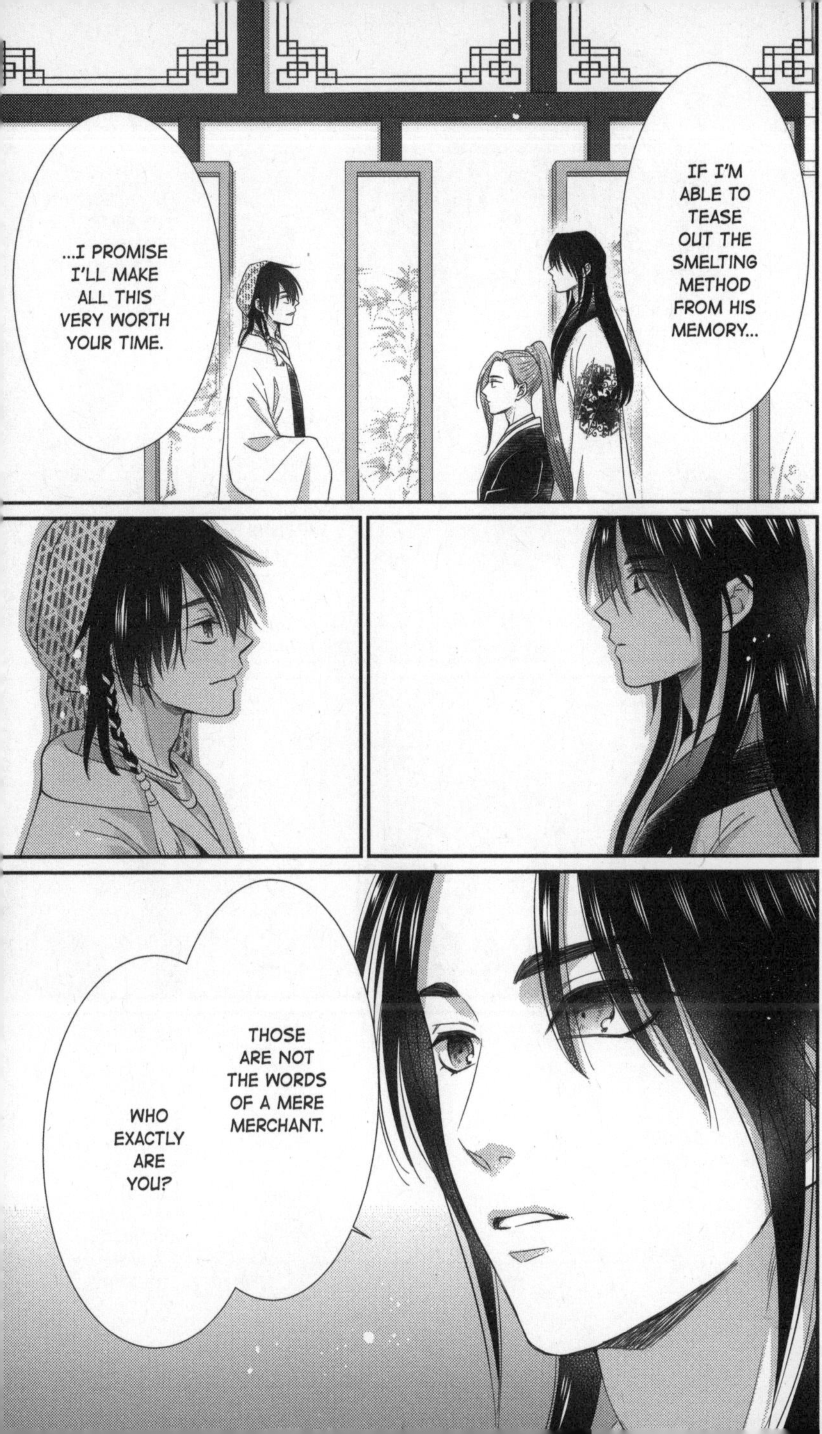
IF I'M ABLE TO TEASE OUT THE SMELTING METHOD FROM HIS MEMORY...
...I PROMISE I'LL MAKE ALL THIS VERY WORTH YOUR TIME.
THOSE ARE NOT THE WORDS OF A MERE MERCHANT.
WHO EXACTLY ARE YOU?

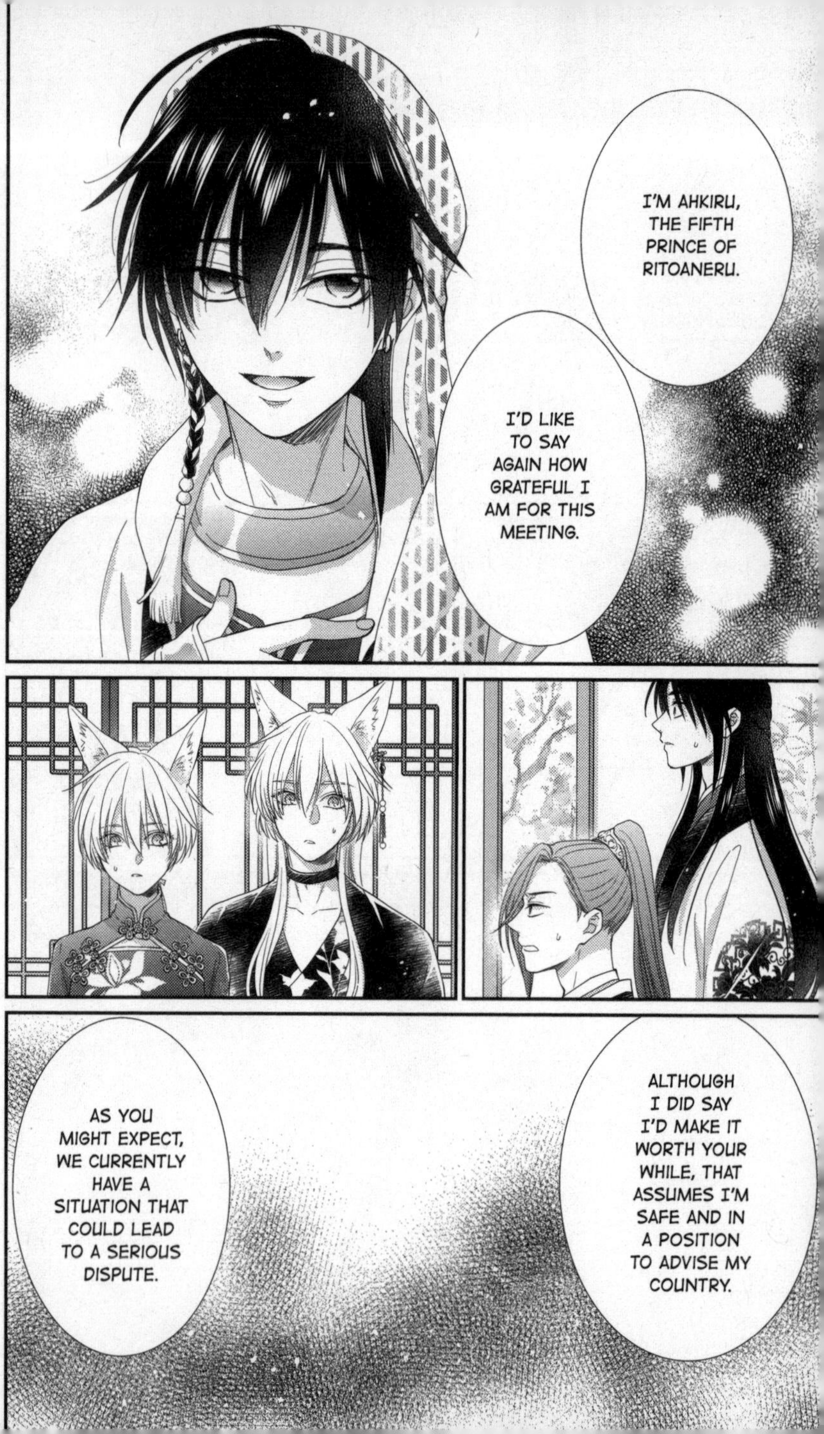
I'M AHKIRU, THE FIFTH PRINCE OF RITOANERU.
I'D LIKE TO SAY AGAIN HOW GRATEFUL I AM FOR THIS MEETING.
ALTHOUGH I DID SAY I'D MAKE IT WORTH YOUR WHILE, THAT ASSUMES I'M SAFE AND IN A POSITION TO ADVISE MY COUNTRY.
AS YOU MIGHT EXPECT, WE CURRENTLY HAVE A SITUATION THAT COULD LEAD TO A SERIOUS DISPUTE.

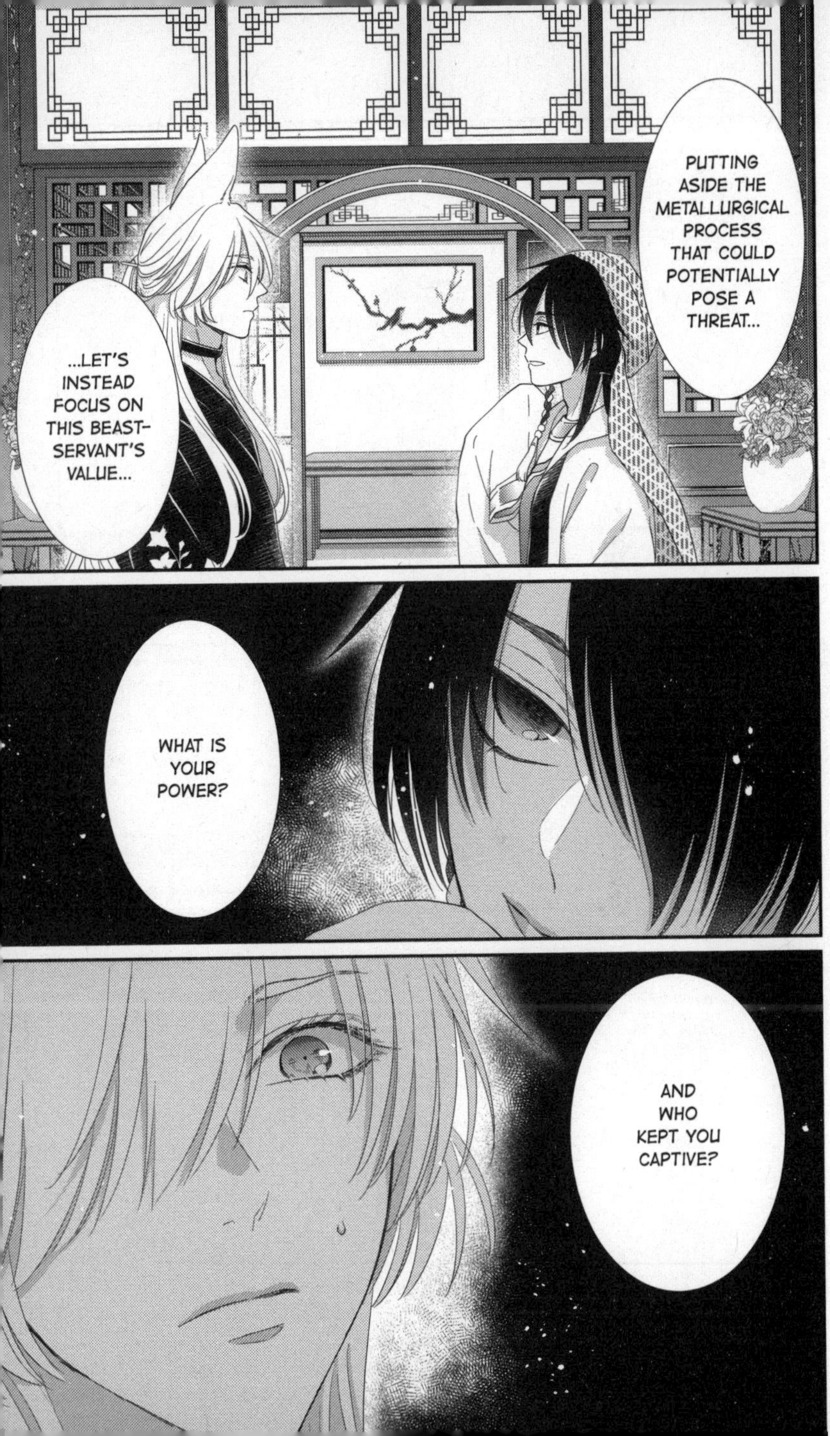
PUTTING ASIDE THE METALLURGICAL PROCESS THAT COULD POTENTIALLY POSE A THREAT...
...LET'S INSTEAD FOCUS ON THIS BEAST-SERVANT'S VALUE...
WHAT IS YOUR POWER?
AND WHO KEPT YOU CAPTIVE?

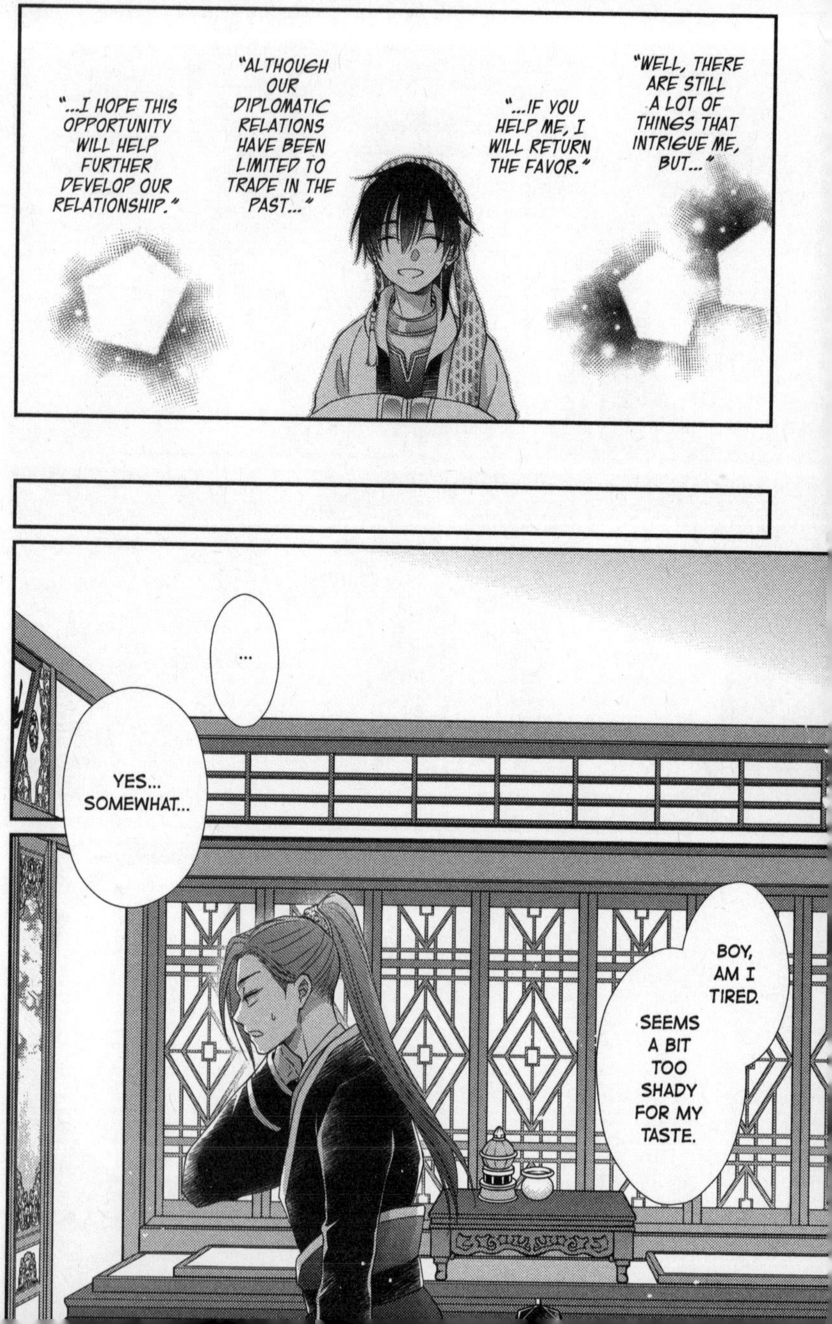
"WELL, THERE ARE STILL A LOT OF THINGS THAT INTRIGUE ME, BUT..."
"...IF YOU HELP ME, I WILL RETURN THE FAVOR."
"ALTHOUGH OUR DIPLOMATIC RELATIONS HAVE BEEN LIMITED TO TRADE IN THE PAST..."
"...I HOPE THIS OPPORTUNITY WILL HELP FURTHER DEVELOP OUR RELATIONSHIP."
...
YES... SOMEWHAT...
BOY, AM I TIRED.
SEEMS A BIT TOO SHADY FOR MY TASTE.

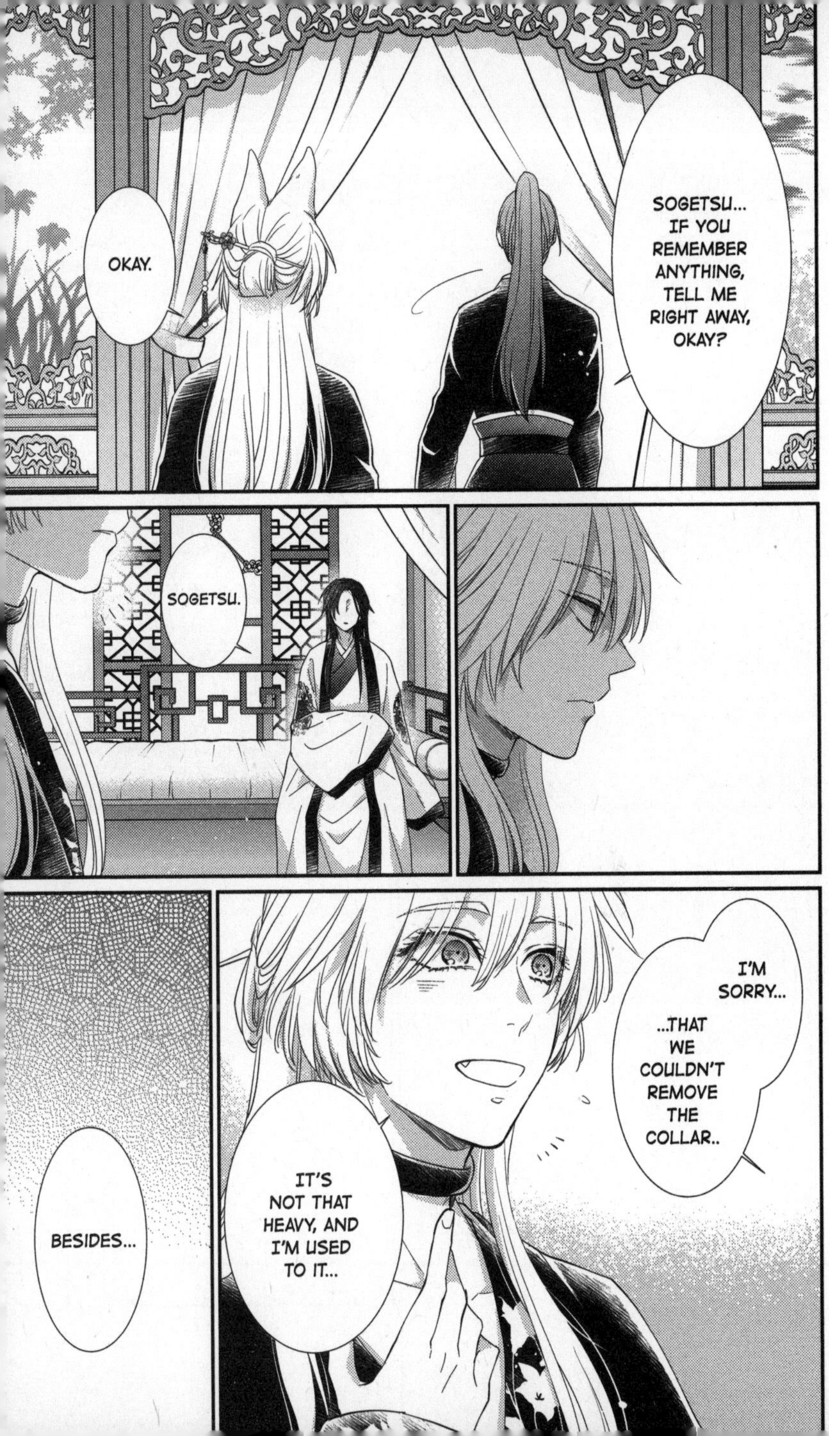
SOGETSU... IF YOU REMEMBER ANYTHING, TELL ME RIGHT AWAY, OKAY?
OKAY.
SOGETSU.
I'M SORRY...
...THAT WE COULDN'T REMOVE THE COLLAR..
IT'S NOT THAT HEAVY, AND I'M USED TO IT...
BESIDES...

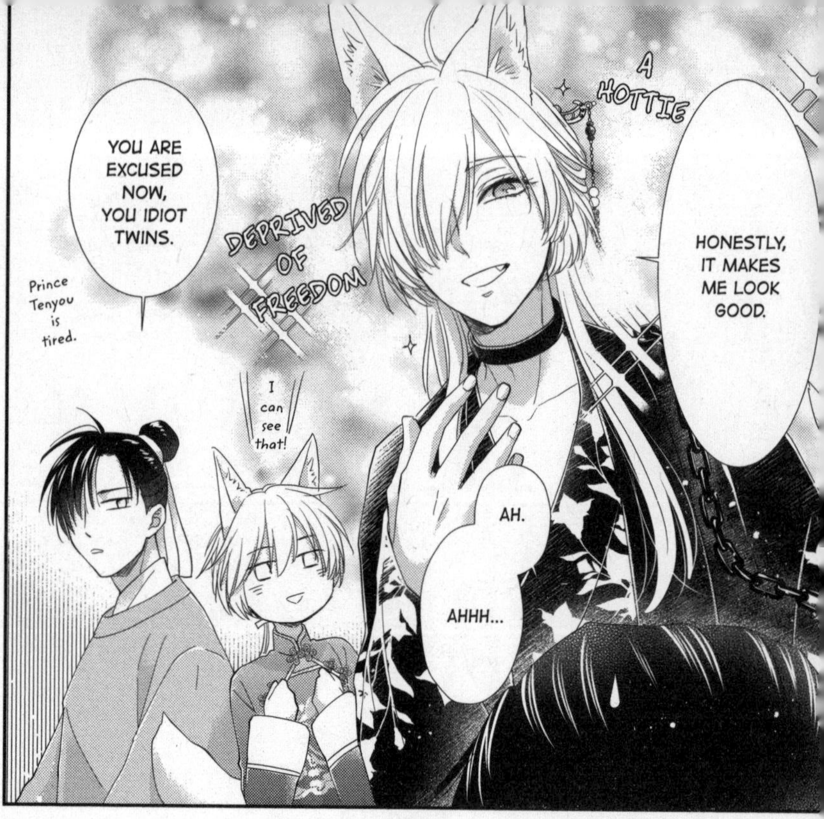
A HOTTIE
HONESTLY, IT MAKES ME LOOK GOOD.
DEPRIVED OF FREEDOM
YOU ARE EXCUSED NOW, YOU IDIOT TWINS.
AH.
AHHH...
I can see that!
Prince Tenyou is tired.
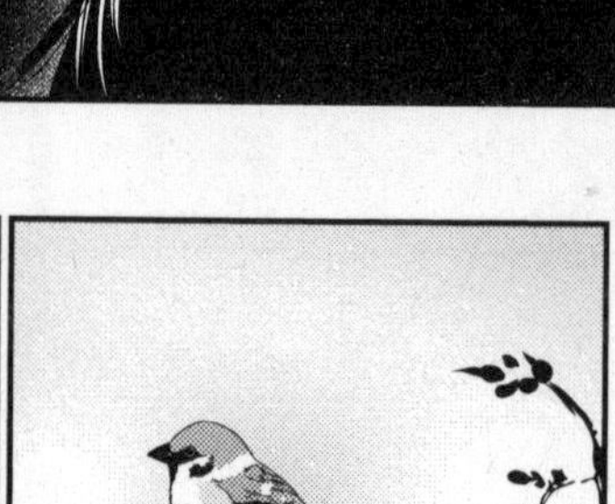
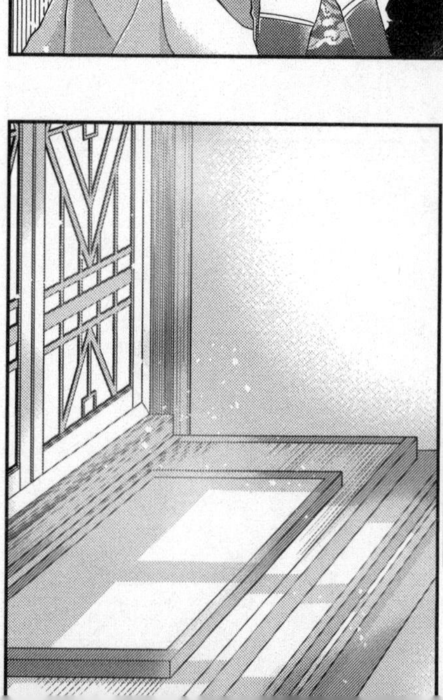

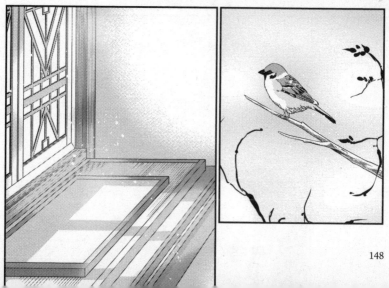

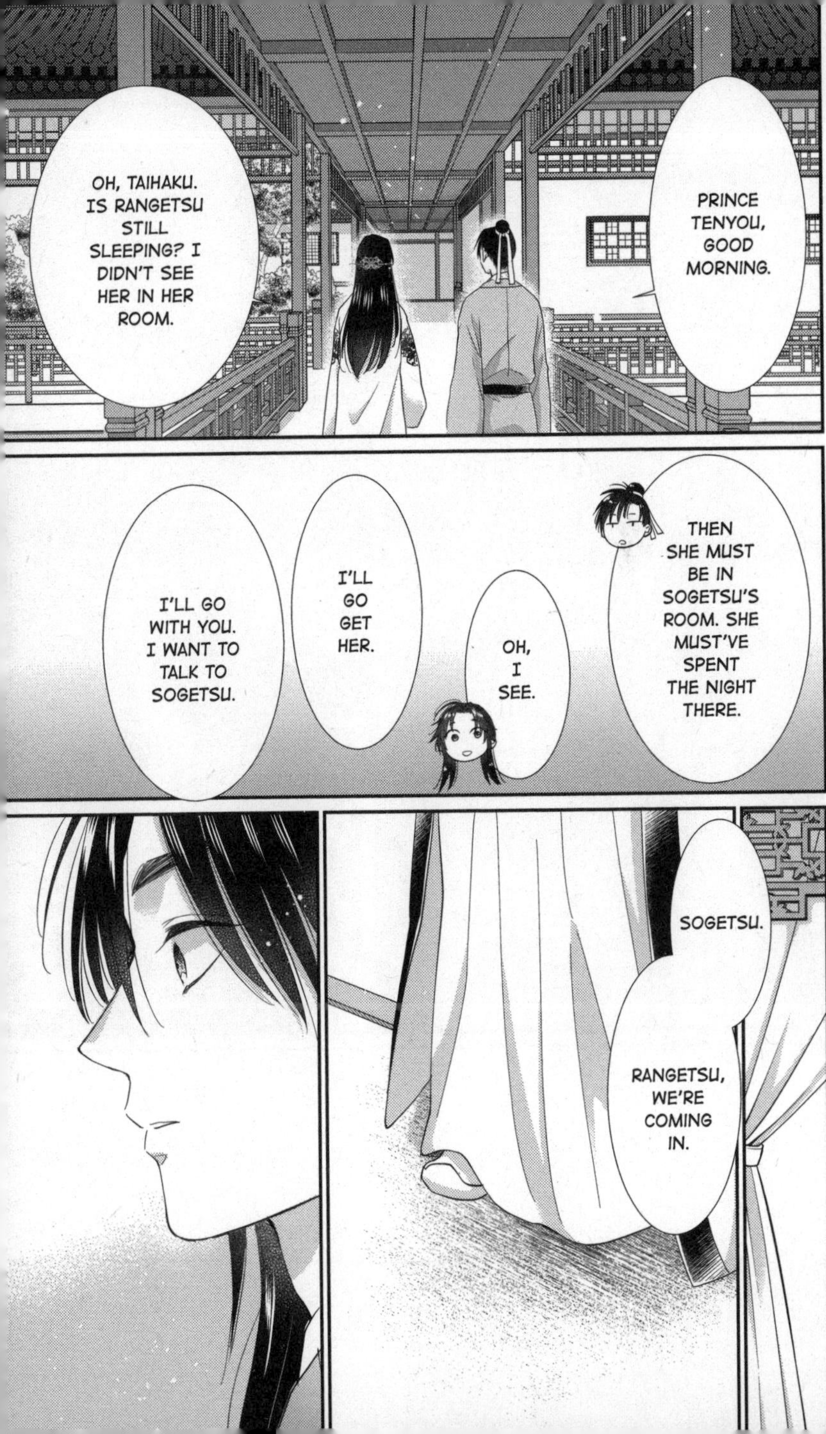
PRINCE TENYOU, GOOD MORNING.
OH, TAIHAKU. IS RANGETSU STILL SLEEPING? I DIDN'T SEE HER IN HER ROOM.
THEN SHE MUST BE IN SOGETSU'S ROOM. SHE MUST'VE SPENT THE NIGHT THERE.
OH, I SEE.
I'LL GO GET HER.
I'LL GO WITH YOU. I WANT TO TALK TO SOGETSU.
SOGETSU.
RANGETSU, WE'RE COMING IN.

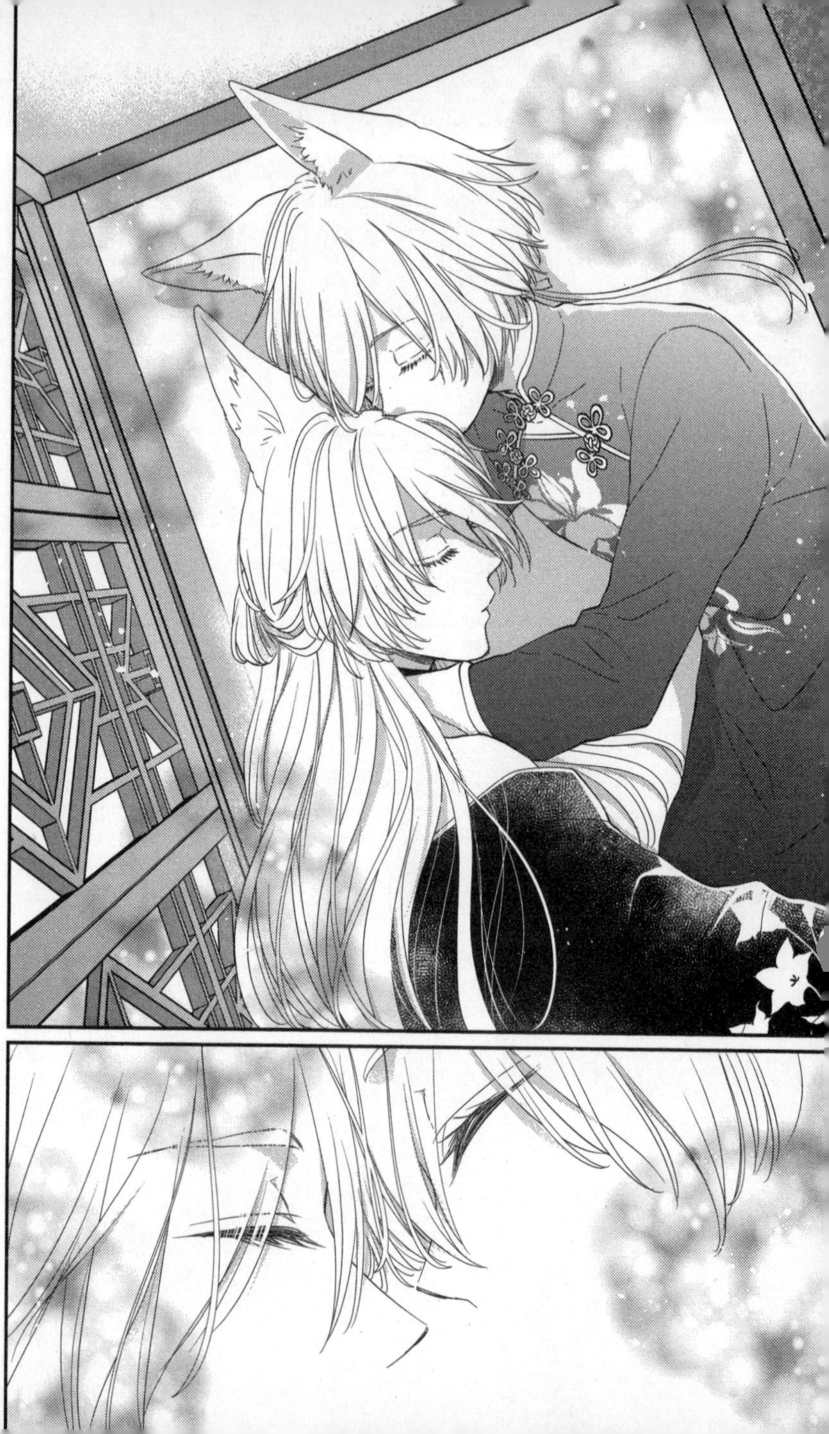

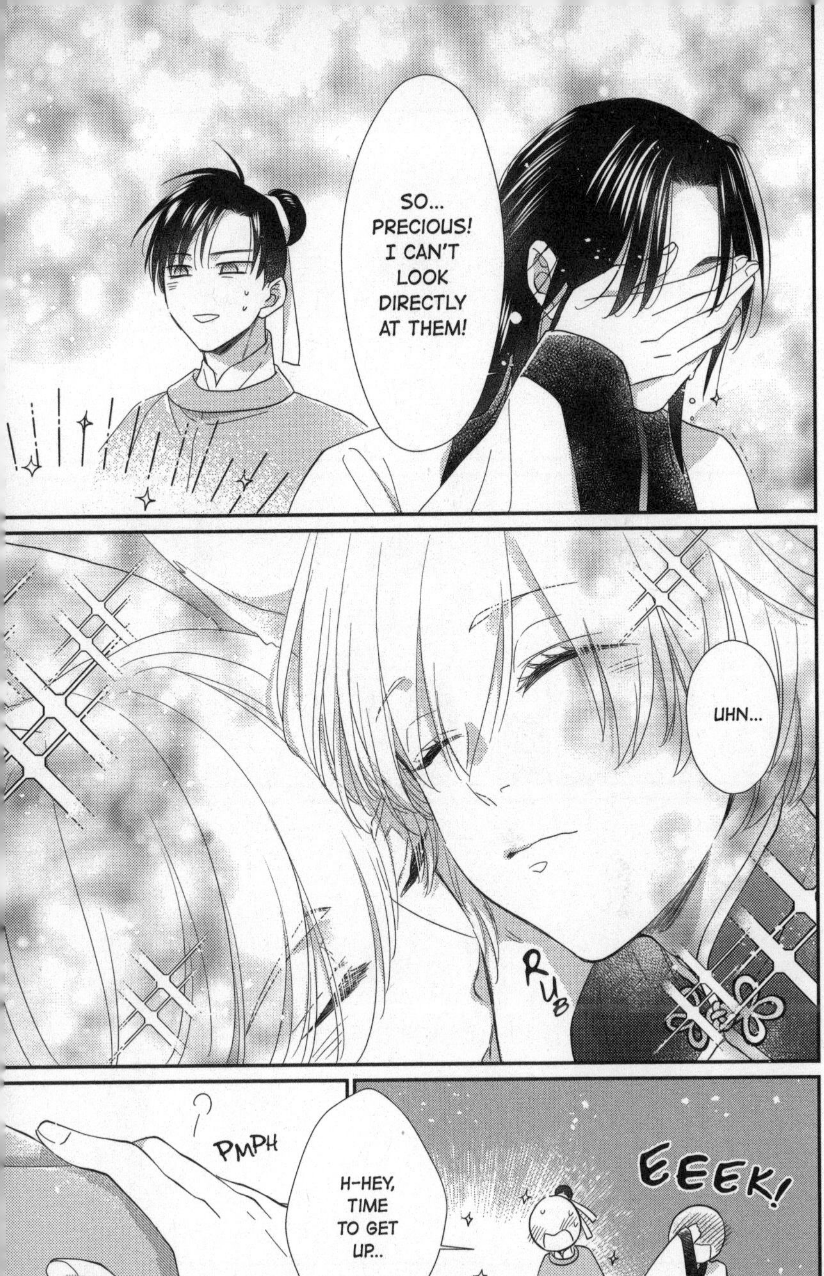
SO... PRECIOUS! I CAN'T LOOK DIRECTLY AT THEM!
UHN...
RUB
EEEK!
H-HEY, TIME TO GET UP...
PMPH

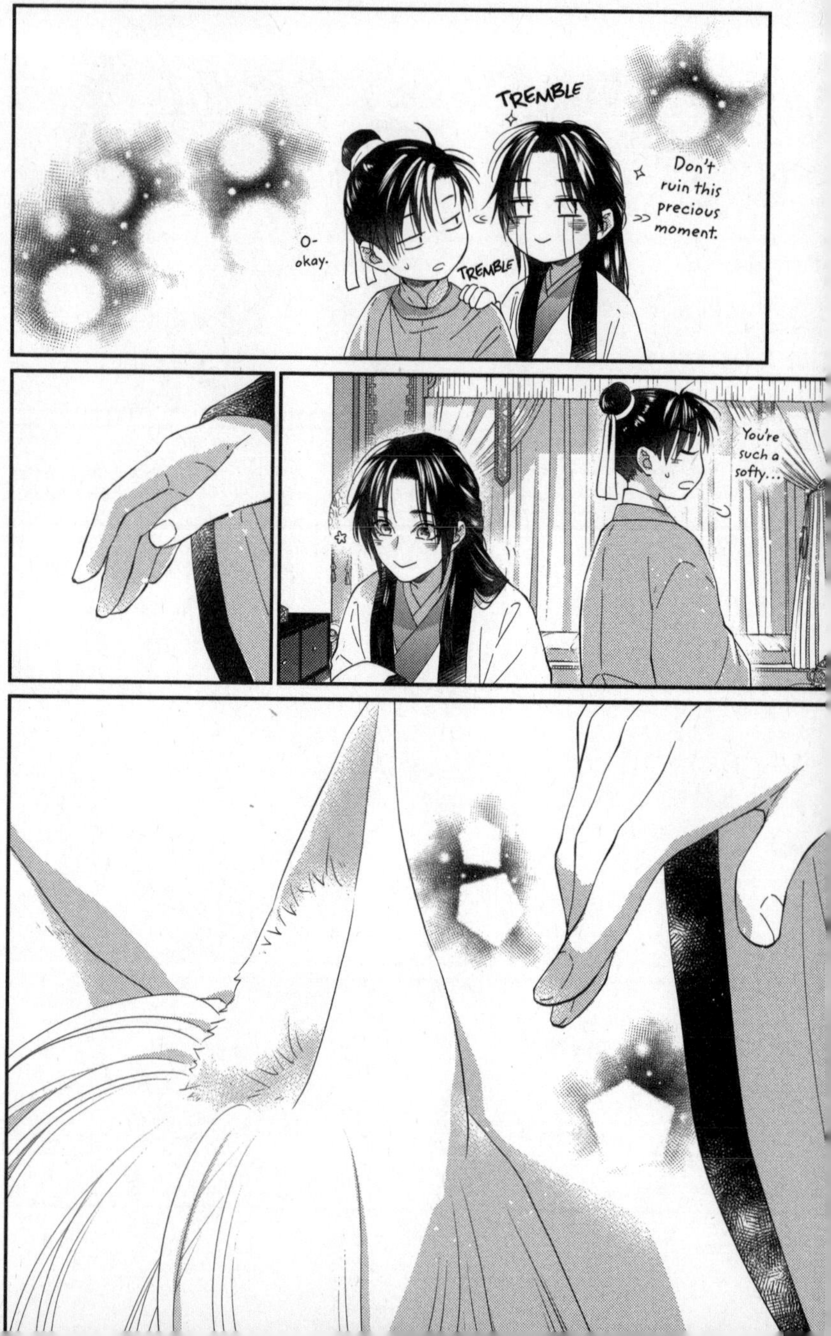
TREMBLE
Don't ruin this precious moment.
TREMBLE
O- okay.
You're such a softy...

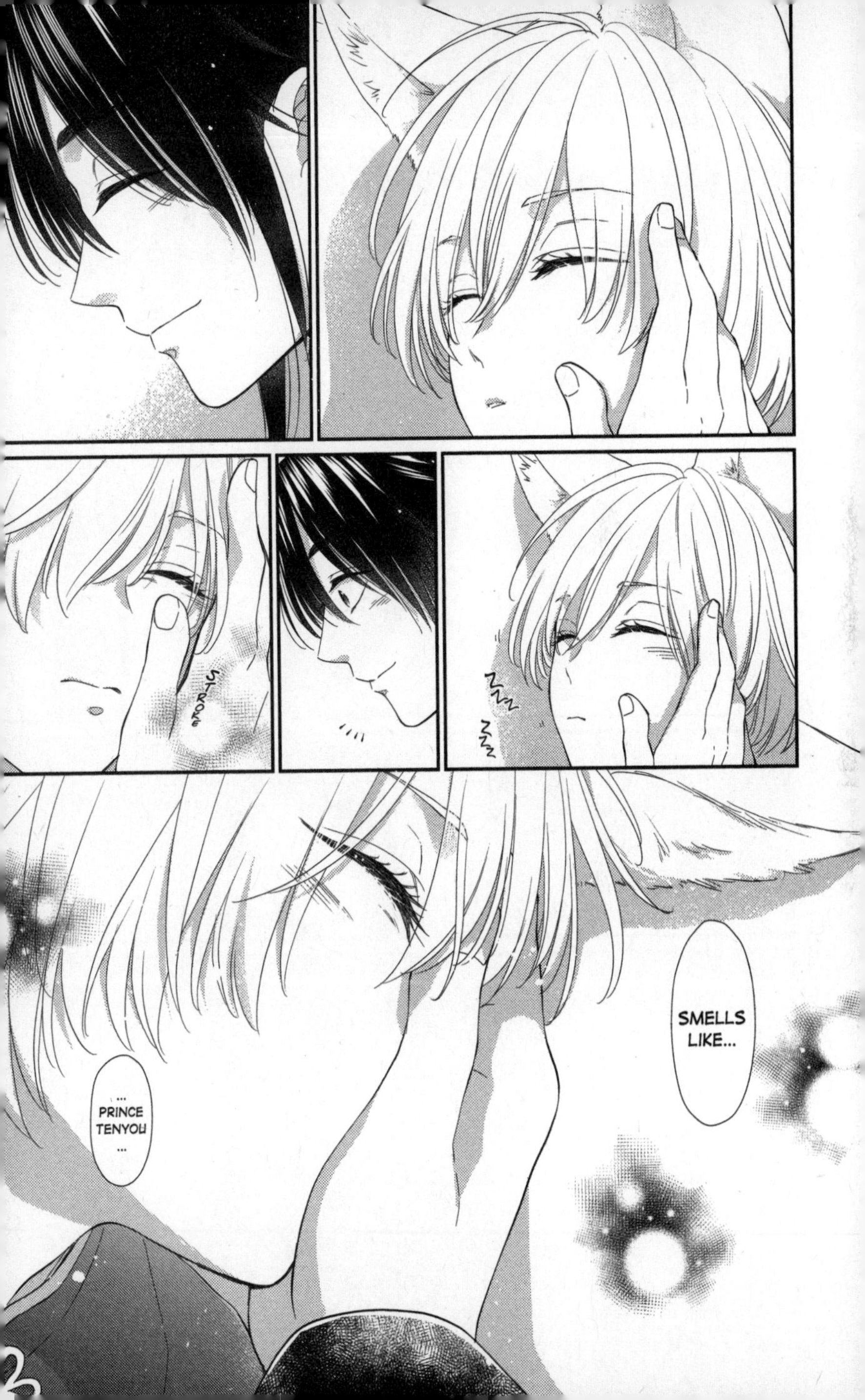
STROKE
ZZZ
ZZZ
SMELLS LIKE...
...PRINCE TENYOU...

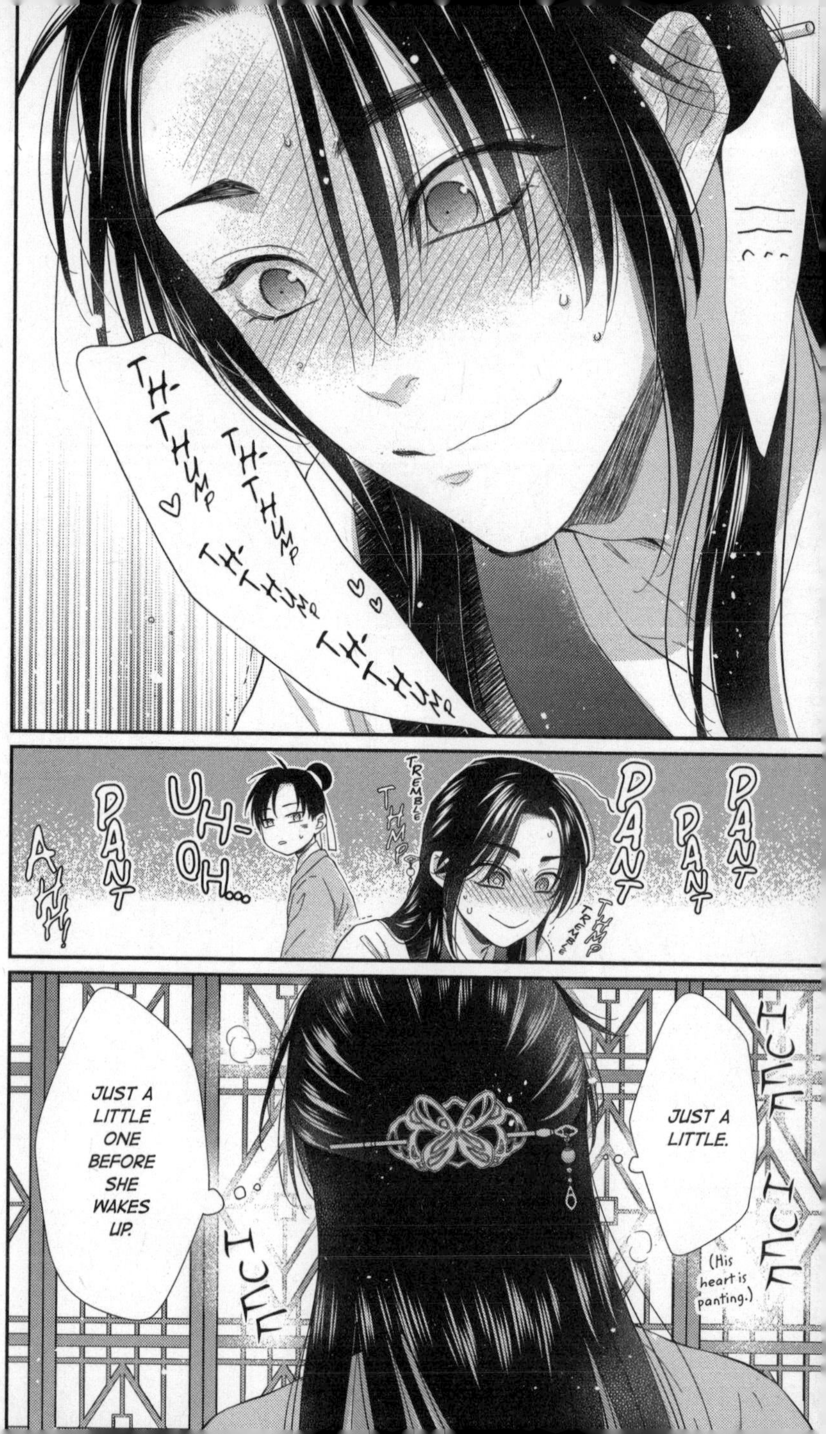

TH-THUMP ♥ TH-THUMP
PANT PANT PANT
TREMBLE THUMP
TREMBLE THUMP
UH-OH...
PANT
AHH!
HUFF HUFF
JUST A LITTLE.
(His heart is panting.)
JUST A LITTLE ONE BEFORE SHE WAKES UP.
HUFF

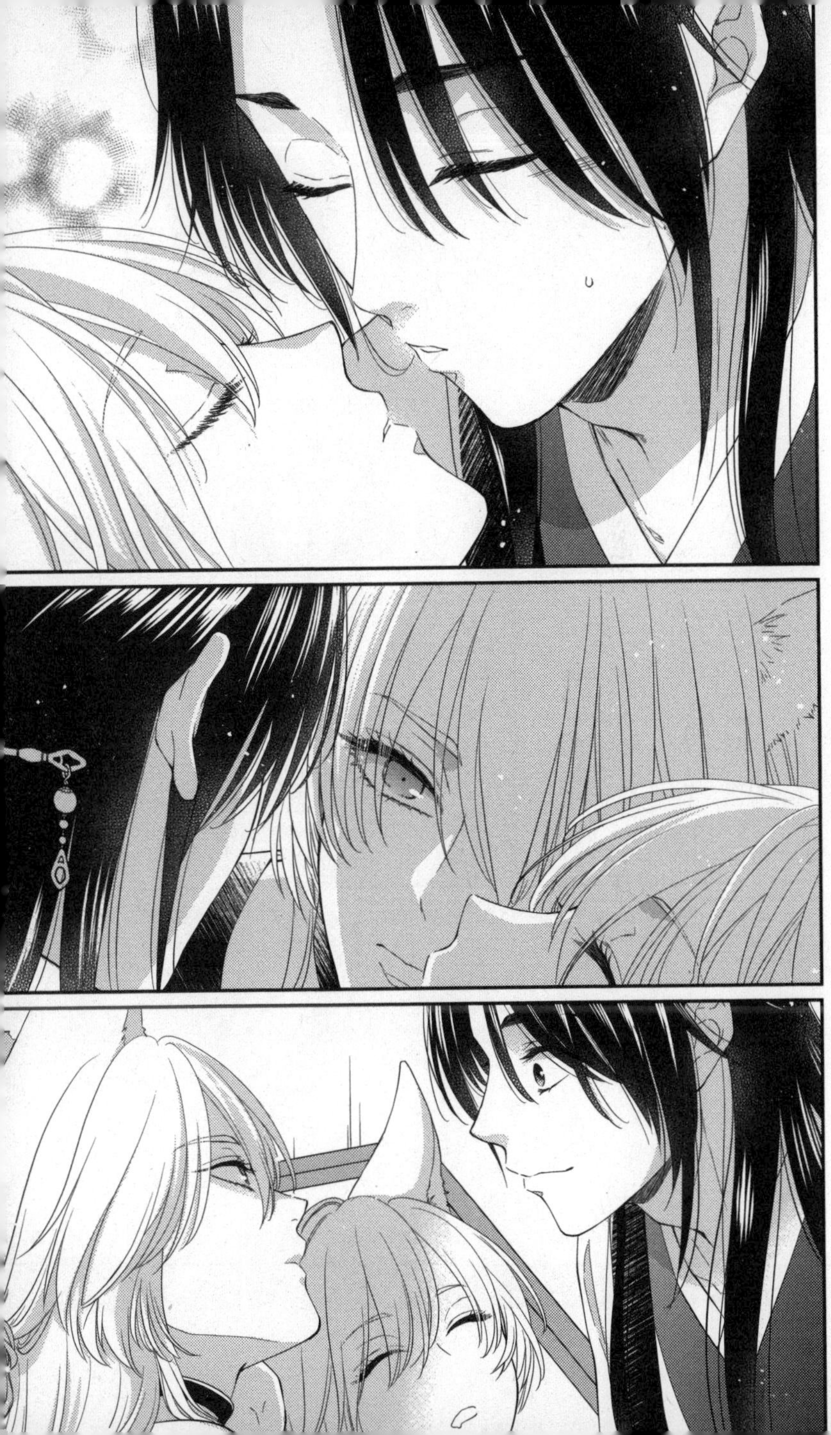

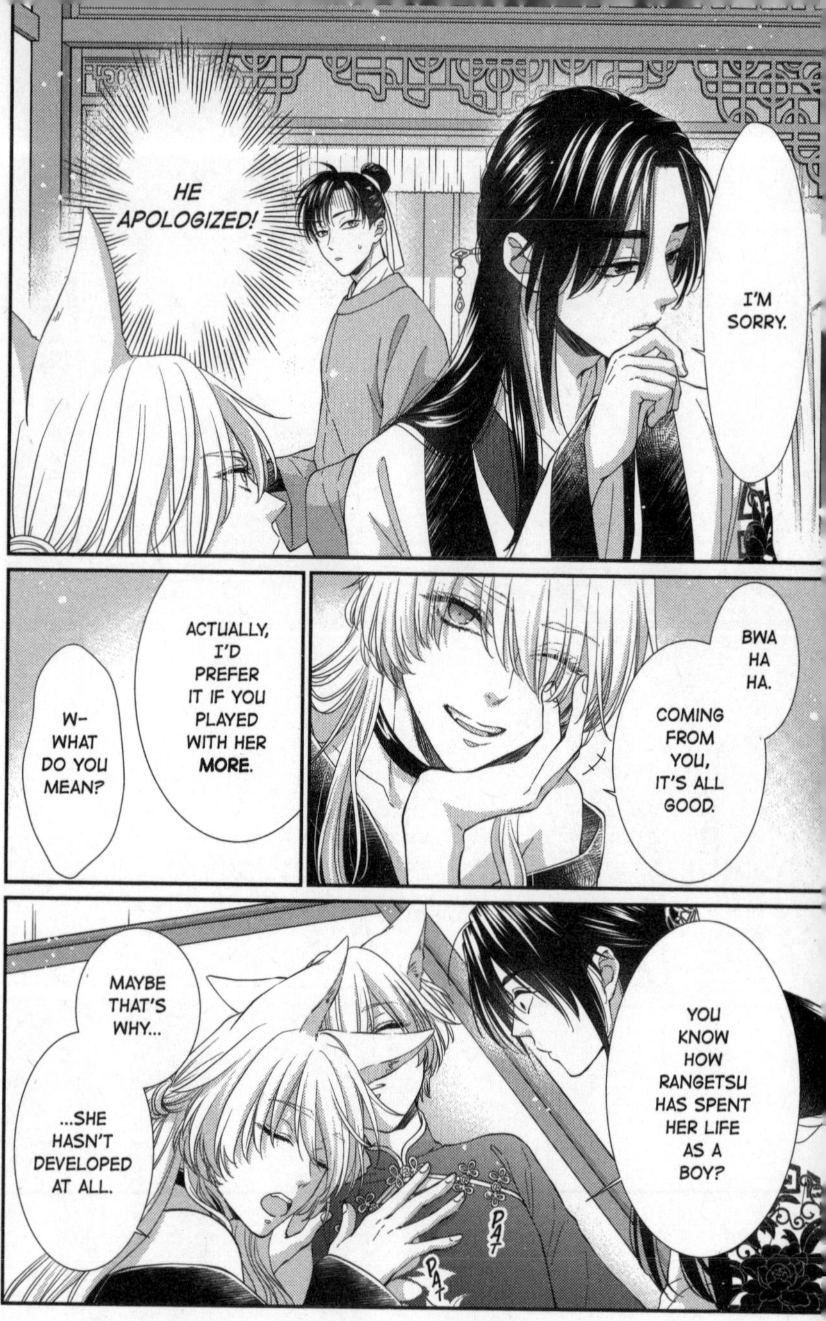
I'M SORRY.
HE APOLOGIZED!
BWA HA HA.
COMING FROM YOU, IT'S ALL GOOD.
ACTUALLY, I'D PREFER IT IF YOU PLAYED WITH HER **MORE**.
W-WHAT DO YOU MEAN?
YOU KNOW HOW RANGETSU HAS SPENT HER LIFE AS A BOY?
MAYBE THAT'S WHY...
...SHE HASN'T DEVELOPED AT ALL.
PAT
PAT

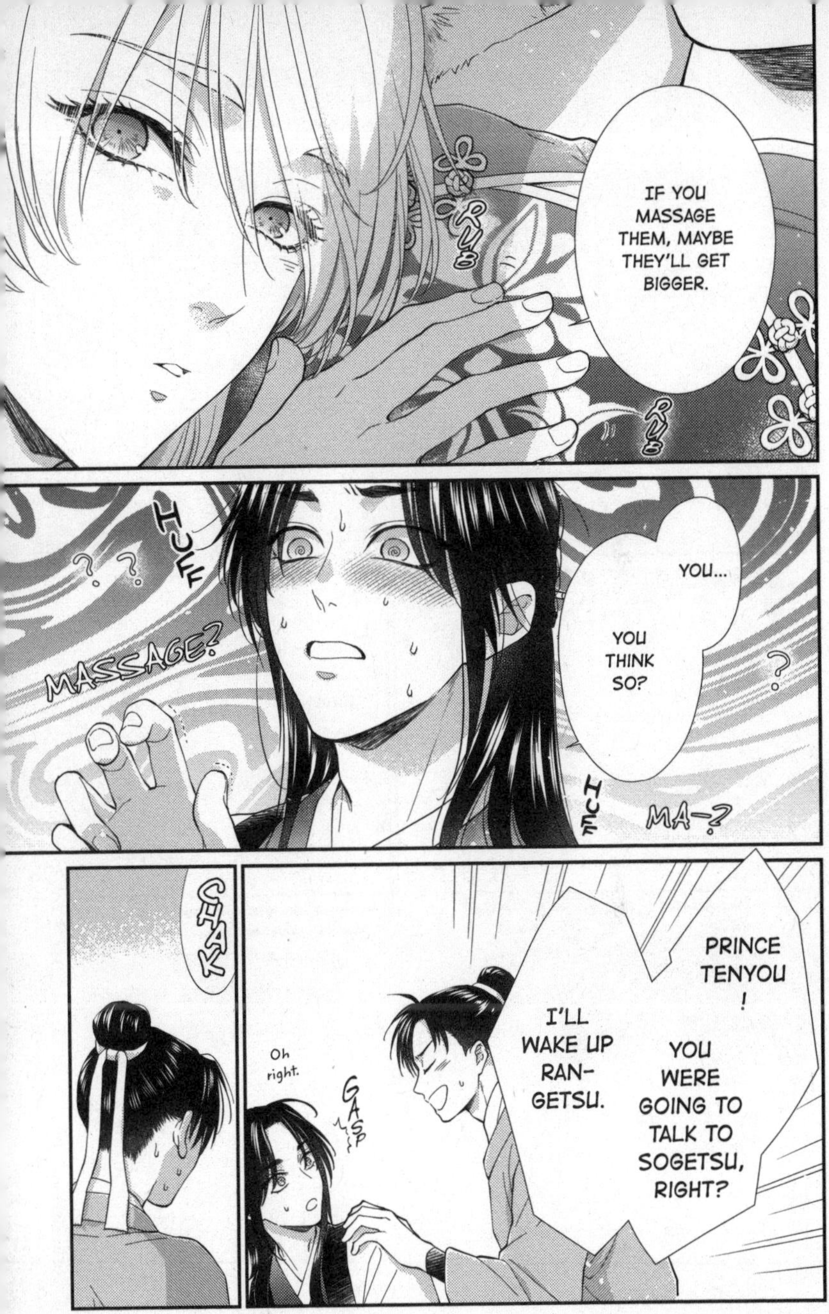
IF YOU MASSAGE THEM, MAYBE THEY'LL GET BIGGER.
RUB
RUB
YOU...
YOU THINK SO?
?
HUFF
MA-?
HUFF
? ?
MASSAGE?
PRINCE TENYOU!
YOU WERE GOING TO TALK TO SOGETSU, RIGHT?
I'LL WAKE UP RAN-GETSU.
GASP
Oh right.
CHAK

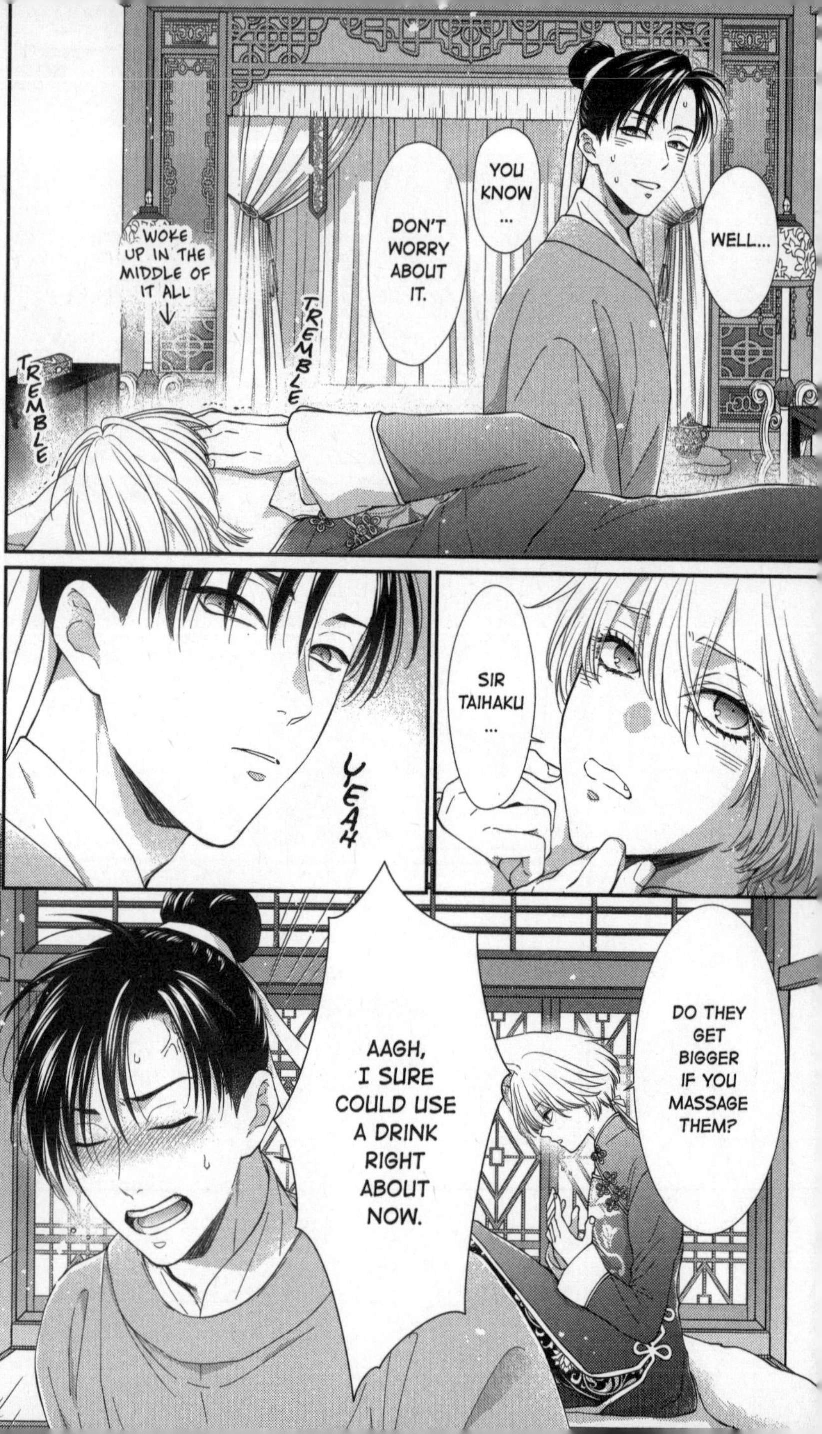
WELL...
YOU KNOW ...
DON'T WORRY ABOUT IT.
TREMBLE
WOKE UP IN THE MIDDLE OF IT ALL
TREMBLE
SIR TAIHAKU ...
YEAH
DO THEY GET BIGGER IF YOU MASSAGE THEM?
AAGH, I SURE COULD USE A DRINK RIGHT ABOUT NOW.

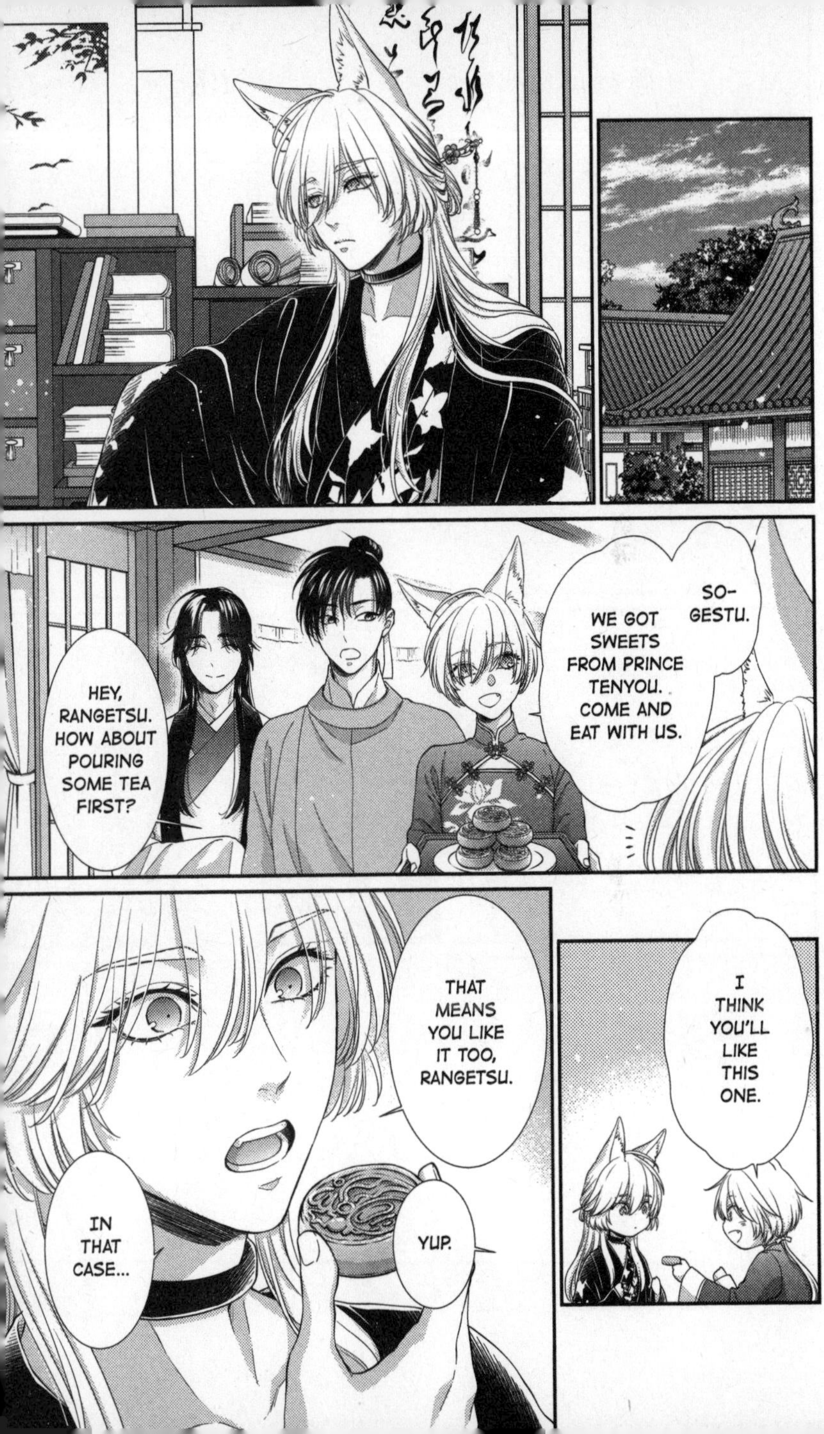
SO-GESTU.
WE GOT SWEETS FROM PRINCE TENYOU. COME AND EAT WITH US.
HEY, RANGETSU. HOW ABOUT POURING SOME TEA FIRST?
I THINK YOU'LL LIKE THIS ONE.
THAT MEANS YOU LIKE IT TOO, RANGETSU.
YUP.
IN THAT CASE...

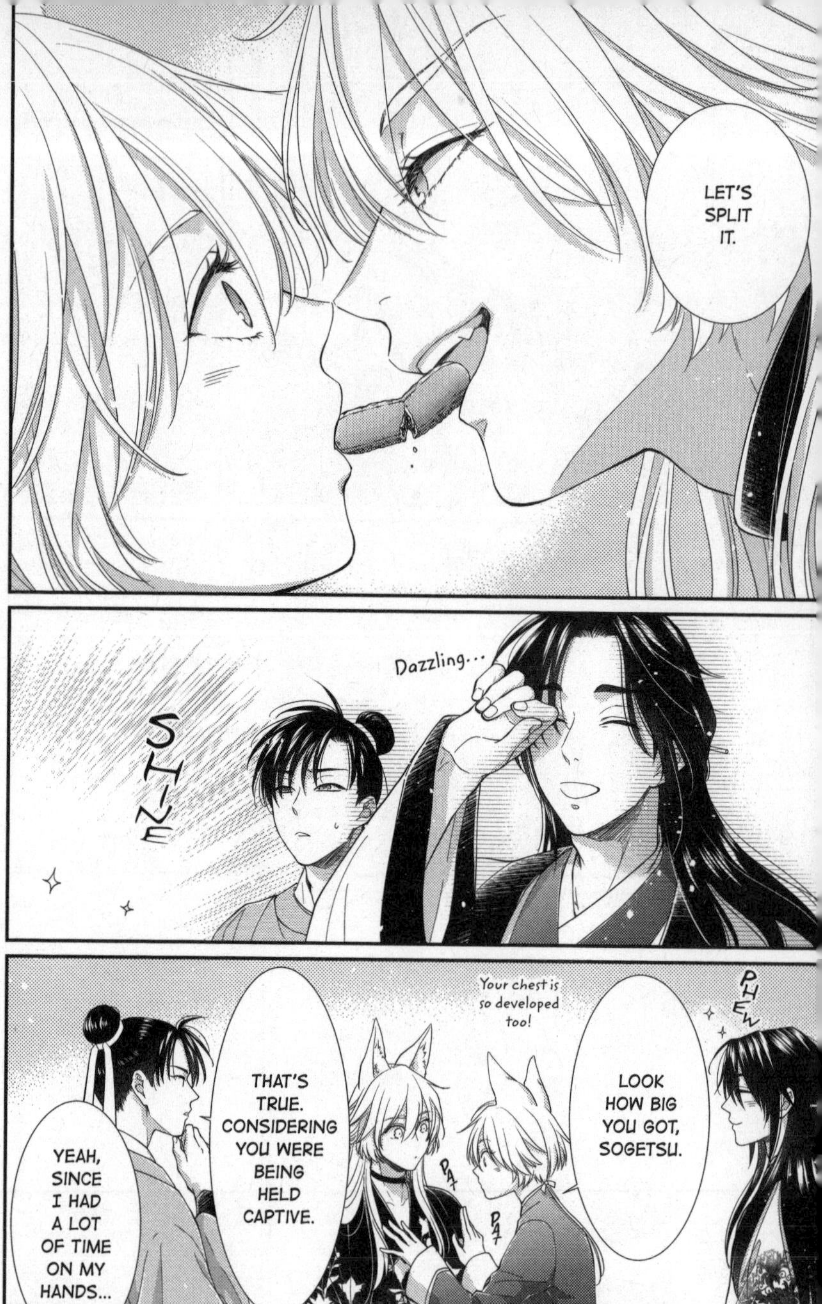
LET'S SPLIT IT.
Dazzling...
SHINE
PHEW
Your chest is so developed too!
LOOK HOW BIG YOU GOT, SOGETSU.
PAT
PAT
THAT'S TRUE. CONSIDERING YOU WERE BEING HELD CAPTIVE.
YEAH, SINCE I HAD A LOT OF TIME ON MY HANDS...

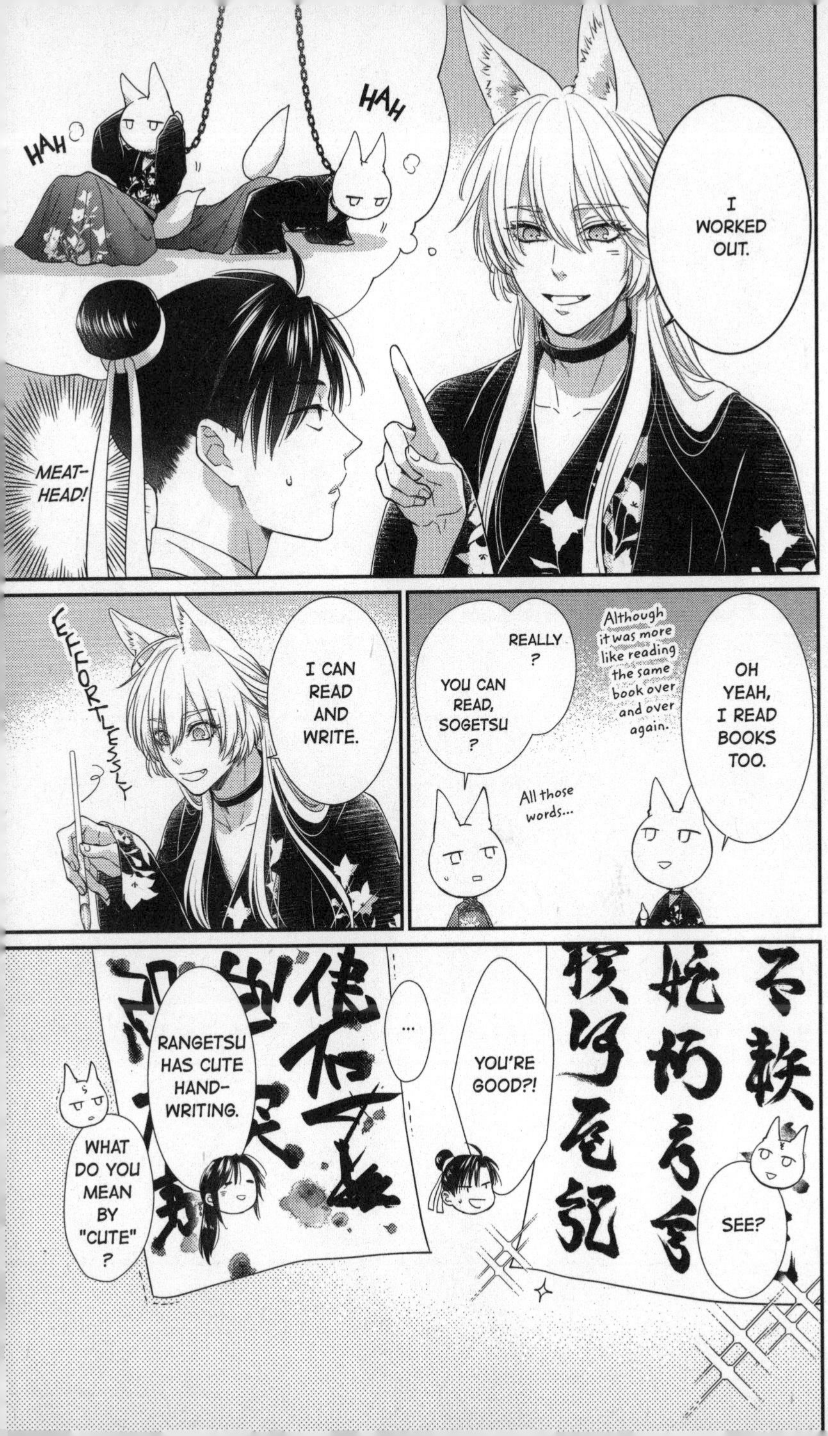
I WORKED OUT.
HAH
HAH
MEAT-HEAD!
OH YEAH, I READ BOOKS TOO.
Although it was more like reading the same book over and over again.
REALLY?
YOU CAN READ, SOGETSU?
All those words...
I CAN READ AND WRITE.
EFFORTLESSLY
SEE?
YOU'RE GOOD?!
...
RANGETSU HAS CUTE HAND-WRITING.
WHAT DO YOU MEAN BY "CUTE"?

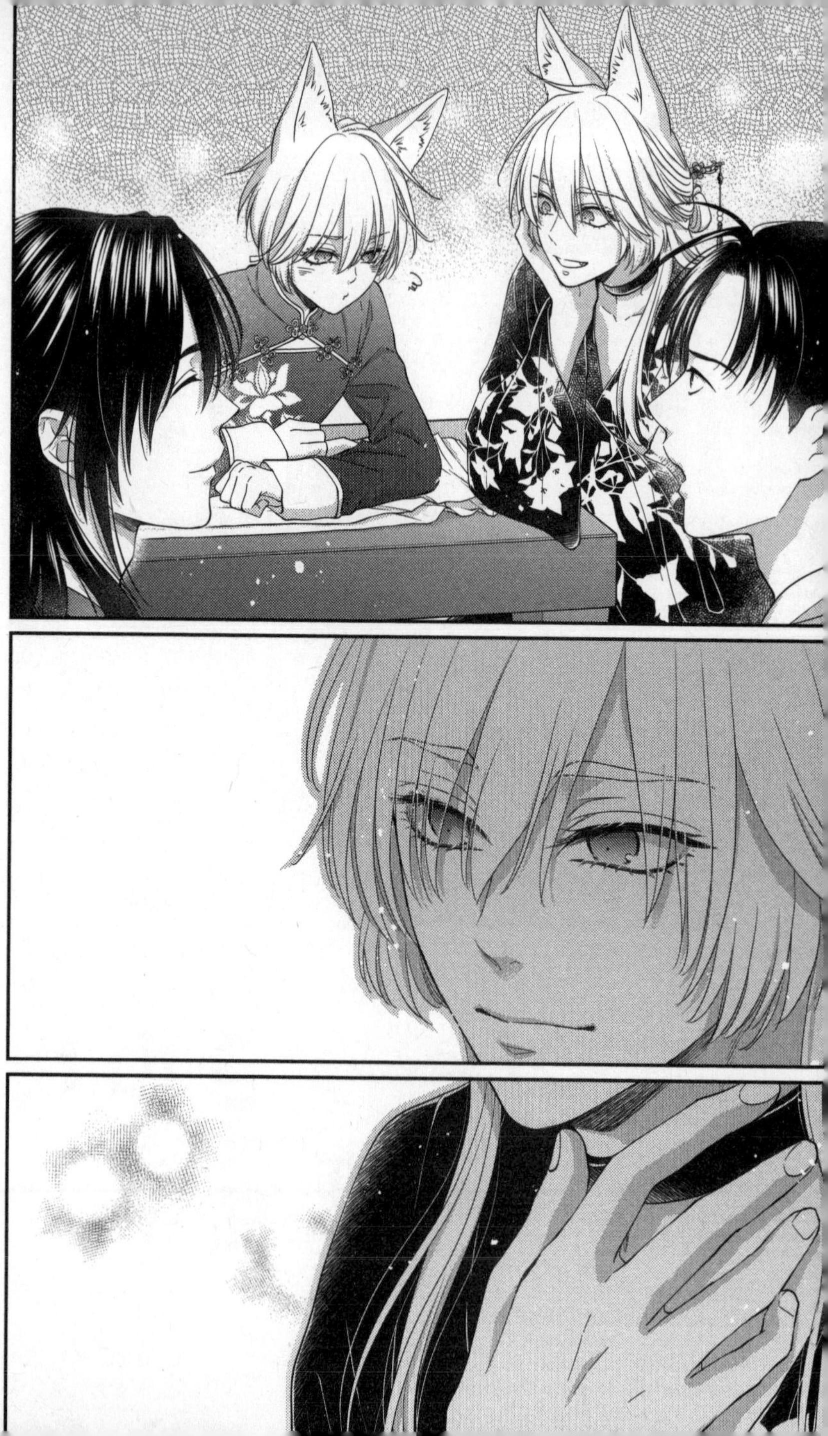

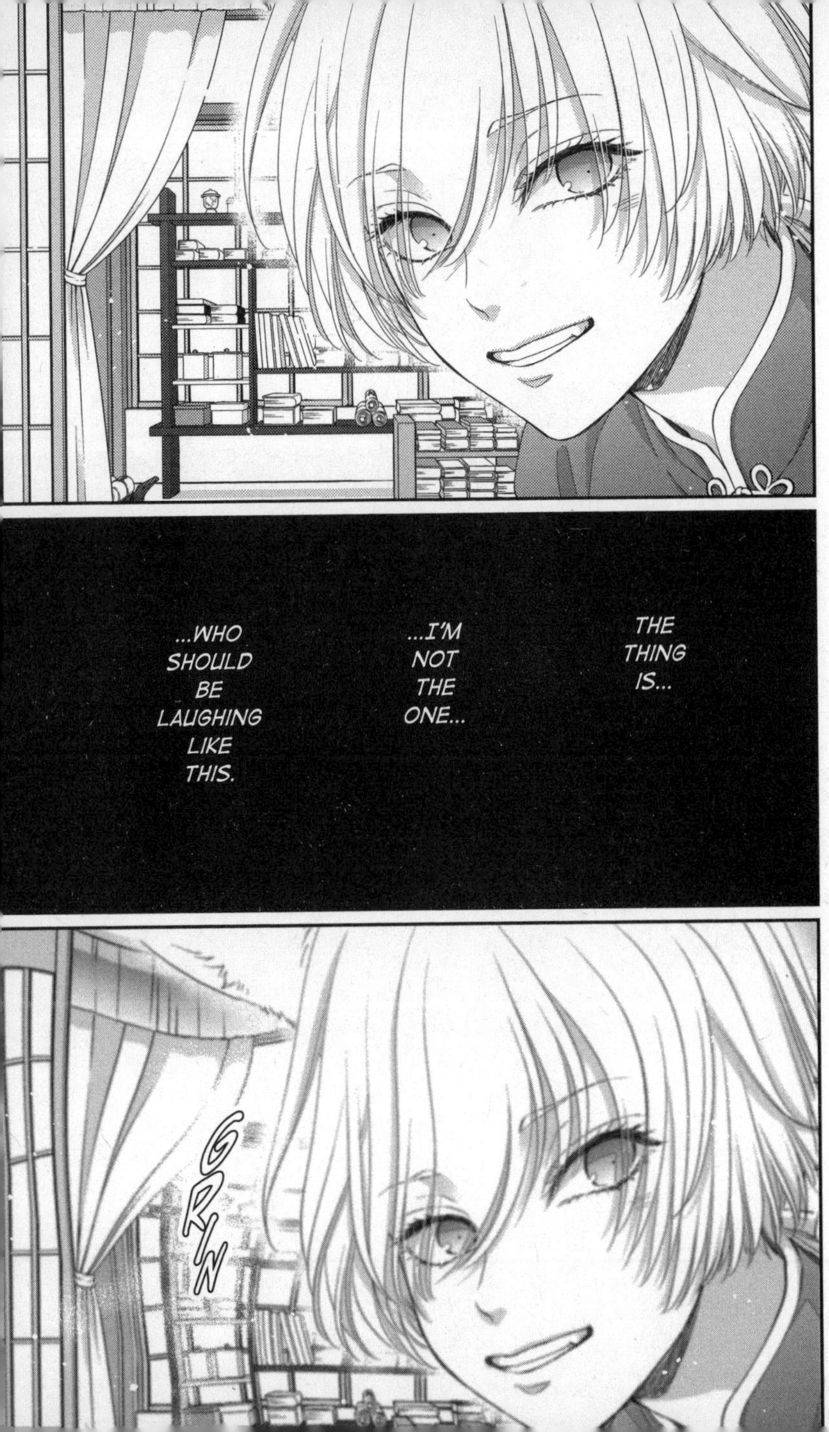
THE THING IS...
...I'M NOT THE ONE...
...WHO SHOULD BE LAUGHING LIKE THIS.
GRIN

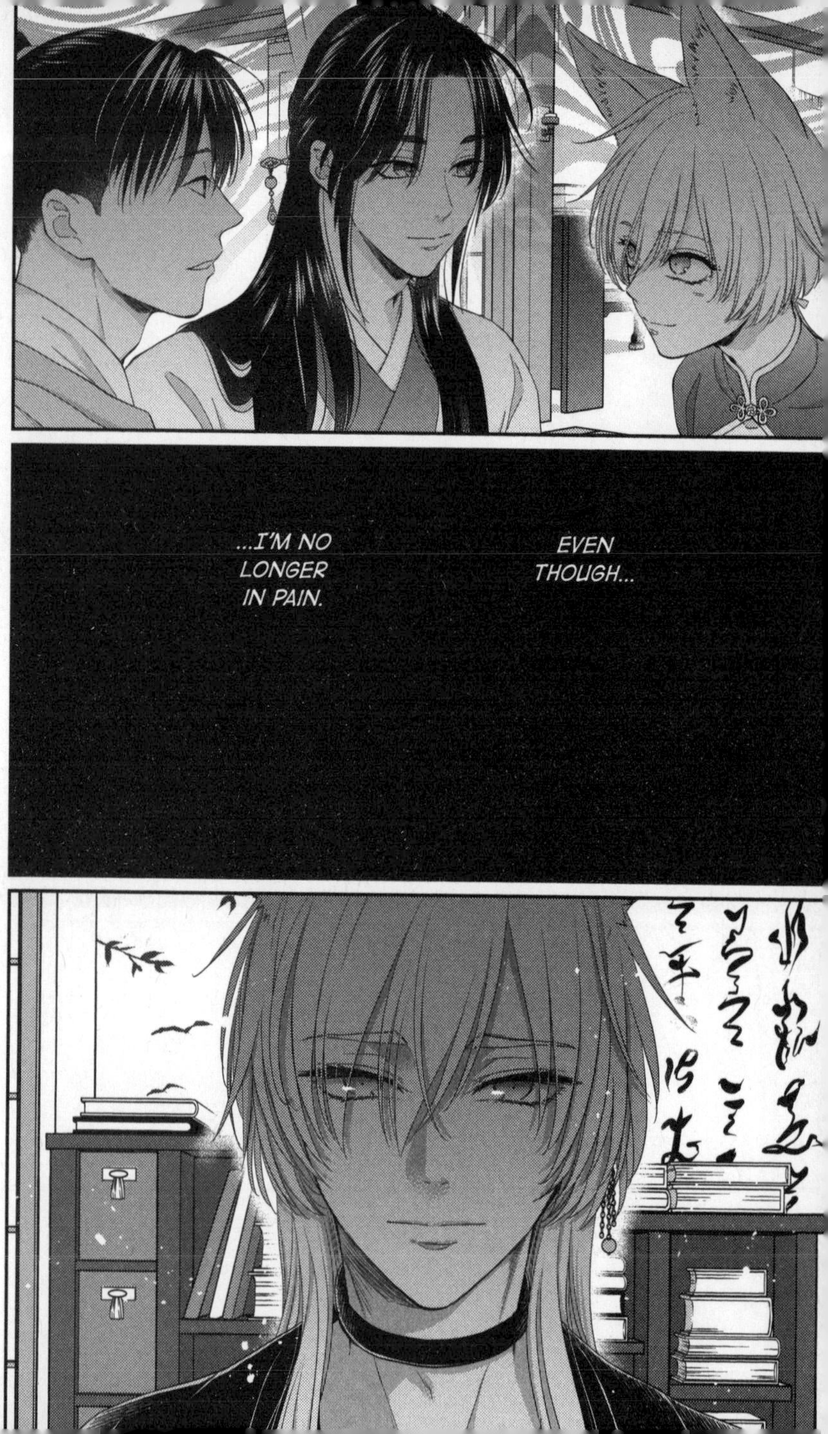

EVEN THOUGH...
...I'M NO LONGER IN PAIN.

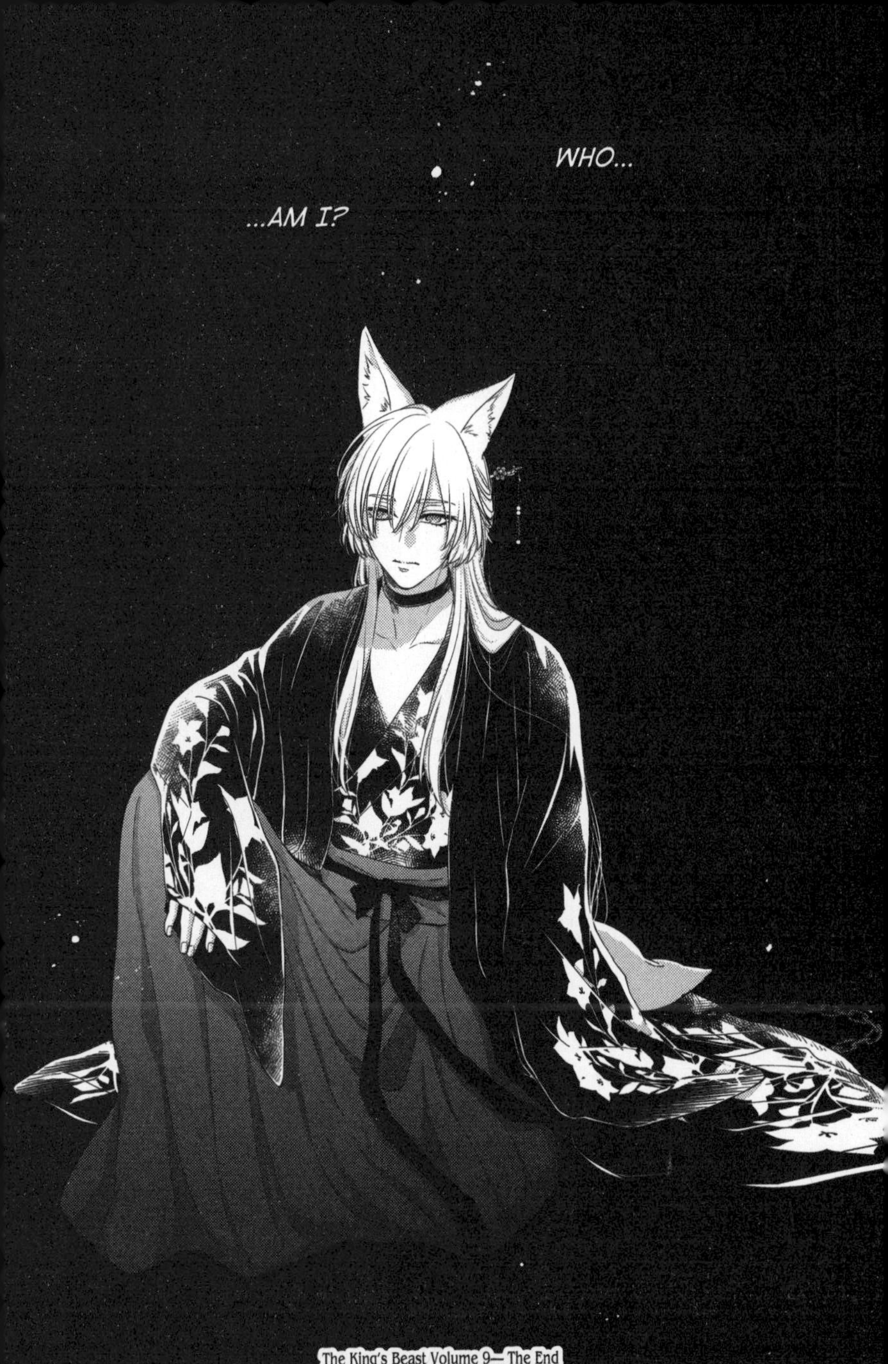
WHO...
...AM I?

The King's Beast Volume 9— The End

I'd love to go to a theme park.

—Rei Toma

麗

Rei Toma has been drawing since childhood, and she
created her first complete manga for a graduation project
in design school. When she drew the short story manga
"Help Me, Dentist," it attracted a publisher's attention
and she made her debut right away. After she found
success as a manga artist, acclaim in other art fields
started to follow as she did illustrations for novels and
video game character designs. She is also the creator of
Dawn of the Arcana and *The Water Dragon's Bride*,
both available in English from VIZ Media.

THE KING'S Beast 麗 9

SHOJO BEAT EDITION

STORY AND ART BY **Rei Toma**

ENGLISH TRANSLATION & ADAPTATION **JN Productions**
TOUCH-UP ART & LETTERING **Monaliza De Asis**
DESIGN **J. Shikuma**
EDITOR **Pancha Diaz**

OU NO KEMONO Vol. 9
by Rei TOMA
© 2019 Rei TOMA
All rights reserved.
Original Japanese edition published by SHOGAKUKAN.
English translation rights in the United States of America,
Canada, the United Kingdom, Ireland, Australia and
New Zealand arranged with SHOGAKUKAN.

Original Cover Design: Hibiki CHIKADA (fireworks. vc)

Fox Mask Design Inspired by W. Mushoku (WALTZ)
Kitsune Kuchi Men Ajisai Komendou
https://www.komendou.com/SHOP/Kom-Kt-03.html

The stories, characters, and incidents mentioned in this
publication are entirely fictional.

Printed in the U.S.A.

Published by VIZ Media, LLC
P.O. Box 77010
San Francisco, CA 94107

10 9 8 7 6 5 4 3 2 1
First printing, February 2023

viz.com

shojobeat.com

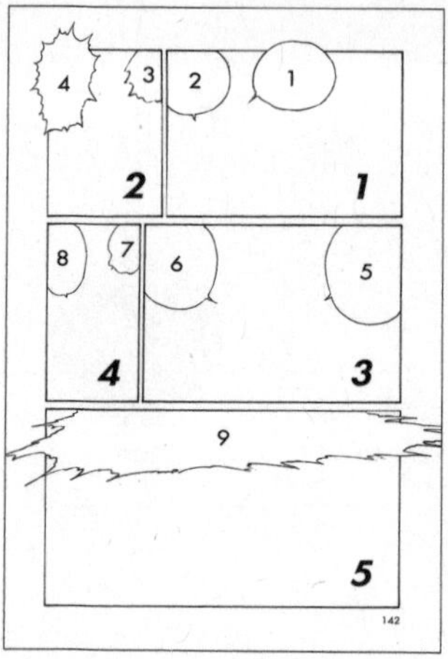
1
2
3
4
5
6
7
8
9
142

THIS IS THE LAST PAGE.

THE KING'S BEAST has been printed in the original Japanese format to preserve the orientation of the artwork.

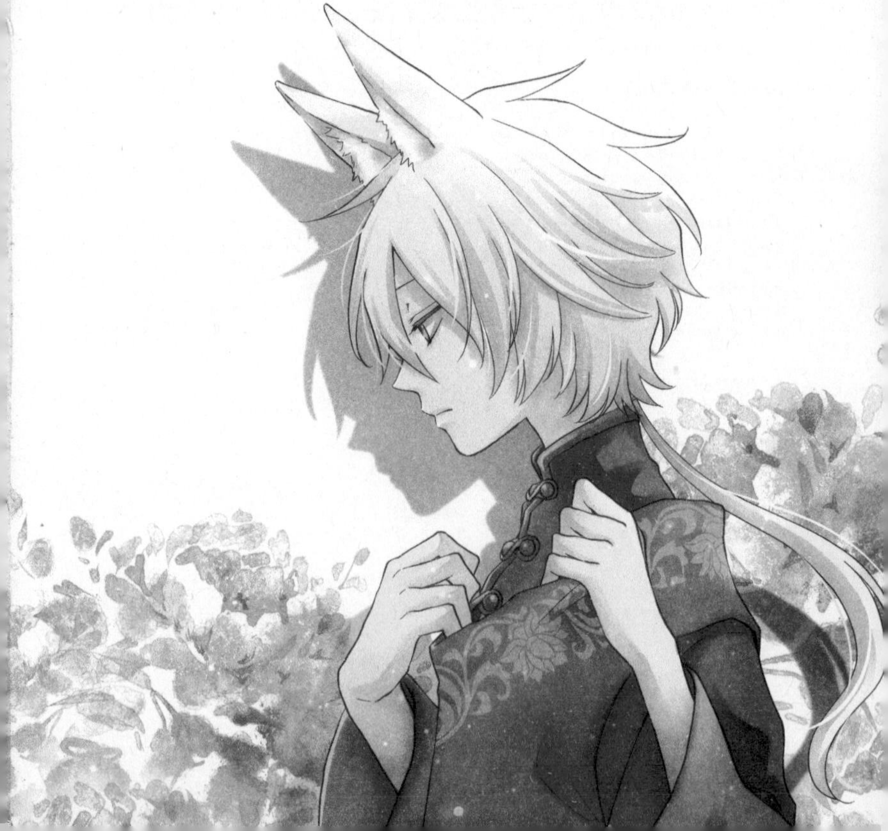